Pliny the Younger

Pliny the Younger:
A Life in Roman Letters

Rex Winsbury

Bloomsbury Academic
An imprint of Bloomsbury Publishing Plc

BLOOMSBURY

LONDON • NEW DELHI • NEW YORK • SYDNEY

Bloomsbury Academic

An imprint of Bloomsbury Publishing Plc

50 Bedford Square
London
WC1B 3DP
UK

1385 Broadway
New York
NY 10018
USA

www.bloomsbury.com

BLOOMSBURY and the Diana logo are trademarks of Bloomsbury Publishing Plc

First published 2014
Paperback edition first published 2015

British Library Cataloguing-in-Publication Data
A catalogue record for this book is available from the British Library.

ISBN: HB: 978-1-4725-1458-5
PB: 978-1-4742-3712-3
ePDF: 978-1-4725-1404-2
ePUB: 978-1-4725-1028-0

Library of Congress Cataloging-in-Publication Data
A catalog record for this book is available from the Library of Congress.

Typeset by Fakenham Prepress Solutions, Fakenham, Norfolk NR21 8NN

For Luke and Jessie

Contents

Notes on conventions ix

Pliny: the case for the prosecution
1 Your witness, your defendant 1
2 Reading the evidence: Are Pliny's letters what they seem? 15

Eye-witnessing Vesuvius
3 Youth, class and that Plinian eruption 23

Pliny the rising lawyer
4 Starring in the noisy Court of One Hundred Men 37
5 Sparring with Regulus and 'the most immoral fraud' 57
6 Pliny the prosecutor: Corruption and the limits of Roman justice 73

In the service of emperors
7 Surviving Domitian: Among the flames of thunderbolts? 91
8 Tactically praising Trajan: 'You tell us to be free: We will be' 109

Marriages and money
9 Love letters to Calpurnia: Marriages but no children 125
10 How rich was Pliny? Assets, income and expenses 135
11 His posh country villas: A literary house and garden tour 147

Pliny as man of letters
12 A fine crop of poets: Pantomime in the salon 159
13 His literary circle – who's in, who's out, where's Juvenal? 173

Pliny as imperial trouble-shooter
14 Nervous in Bithynia: Those quarrelsome little Greeks 185
15 Christians – what is the crime and what is the punishment? 203

Your verdict?
16   Meeting Pliny   217

Notes   229
Bibliography   237
Index of Names   239
Index of Place Names   241
Index of Latin Terms   242
Index of Subject Matter   243

Notes on conventions

Where Pliny's letters are quoted, the letter number is given alongside in brackets and in bold type, rather than in the footnotes. The convention CE (Common Era) is used rather than AD (*Anno Domini*, Year of our Lord), especially in light of Pliny's hostility to Christianity. Years given are CE (or if you will, AD) unless stated otherwise. The generally excellent and widely available translation of the letters by Betty Radice is used throughout, with very few exceptions. Modern authors are cited in the notes and in the Bibliography. Where sparingly used, Latin words are in italics, with a translation (usually but not necessarily literal) added.

I stood among the flames of thunderbolts dropping all around me

Pliny, Letter 3.11

1

Your witness, your defendant

As a successful lawyer, the man we are (cross)examining starred as chief prosecutor in some of the great political show-trials of his day, at the height of the Roman Empire. He was by the standards of his time a fine public orator, in the law courts and in the Roman Senate. As an administrator and friend of emperors he rose to the pinnacle of Roman society as consul. He pondered deeply about the ethics and restraints on absolute political power. He wrote movingly about his love for his much younger second wife, and mourned his lack of children. He tells most of what we know about how in his day Roman writers and authors went about their literary business. He gives us unique evidence about the early days of Christianity. And he witnessed and survived the great eruption of Mount Vesuvius in 79 CE.

But many moderns have accused him of being a hypocrite and a turncoat, a fraud and a liar who knowingly falsified the evidence about his career; or perhaps worse, a bore with an inflated opinion of his own mediocre literary and political talents. He has suffered both neglect and contempt, especially by odious comparison with his contemporary and friend, the great historian Tacitus. Even his qualifications as a lawyer have been challenged. Christians have condemned him as an evil persecutor of their burgeoning new religion. His conduct during his successive appointments to the highest offices in the empire has been dismissed as feeble and weak-willed. About the only appointment he received for which he was really qualified, sneer his extreme critics, was to be in charge of the sewers of Rome.

He usually gave his full name as Gaius Plinius Secundus. But by modern convention he is called 'Pliny' by English-speakers and 'Pline' by French-speakers. To distinguish him from his uncle and adoptive father with a similar name, he is conventionally called Pliny the Younger. But his friends – and at least one if not two of the emperors he served were also his friends – called him simply 'Secundus', and this is his biography. It explores the many aspects of life at Rome in which Pliny took part and which are illuminated in Pliny's writings and which in turn illuminate Pliny – the legal system, the literary scene, Rome at leisure, family life, the perils of politics – so as to reach a rounded assessment of Pliny the man, both the public man and the private man. For the first time it pulls together in one place all the various aspects of Pliny's life to show what sort of person Gaius Plinius Secundus was, what his life tells us about contemporary Rome at the turn of the second century, and why his eventful career has given rise to such a wide spectrum of hostile accusations and defensive justifications. If Pliny were on trial, what would our verdict be?

Pliny was not a Roman made famous on stage and screen like Julius Caesar or Marc Antony. He did not become a Shakespearean tragic hero nor the star of a Hollywood toga epic. Nor is his career dramatised in modern best-selling novels like the life and death of the doomed republican orator and politician Cicero. Even Romans sometimes got him mixed up with his uncle and namesake. His career was both less dramatic and less romantic than the lives of Julius Caesar or Cleopatra, less overlaid by myth, but more revealing about the nitty-gritty of how imperial Rome, the Rome of the Caesars, actually worked, both in good times and in bad – especially in bad. And he did give his name to a particular type of volcanic eruption.

> To the modern historian, Pliny is a very important person. Not because he did something special, but on the contrary, because he is typical of the senatorial class of the high empire.[1]

Cicero's public struggle to preserve some semblance of open politics at Rome had taken place a century and a half before Pliny's time. Rome was now an absolute autocracy or monarchy in which the Senate, once the heart of Roman government, was but a shadow of its former self. The travails of the old Roman republic in which Julius Caesar, Marc Antony and Cicero starred were long in the past – but not forgotten. As a prominent orator, lawyer and writer of his time, Gaius Plinius Secundus knew his history but had to take the world as he found it, adapt to it and survive in it – but at what cost? The mere fact that he chose to leave such a detailed record of his hopes and fears, his weaknesses and pretensions, all of it evidence that could both condemn and justify him, means that he was something more than a typical man of his time.

Pliny was certainly no hero, no leader of an opposition, not a risk taker or champion of lost causes such as those untrammelled freedoms of expression enjoyed by the old Roman republic that had so acrimoniously and bloodily destroyed itself in internecine civil war well over a century before his time. But in a career that straddled both a 'bad' emperor, Domitian, and a 'good' emperor, Trajan, Pliny grappled with this dangerous but recurring problem of how an apparently decent man could live out a public career under the rule and whim of an absolute monarch. How far should he compromise, even collude, with the exercise of supreme power? How far could he personally be implicated and still retain his pride, honour and reputation in the eyes of posterity? What was the price, the reward and the penalty of compromise? How could a man be, and claim to be, free under an autocracy? If autocracy was the established order of the day, as at Rome, what sort of freedom might be possible, and for whom? What sort of political deal could be struck between autocrat and subjects, between the emperor and the senators who, like Pliny, were the chief instruments of his rule?

His letters as evidence

We know about Gaius Plinius Secundus because over the period 100–110 CE he published a carefully constructed collection of his letters to his friends and contemporaries, and this collection has survived, if only just, for us to read. His letters offer insight into an astonishing range of activities and institutions that underpinned and defined Roman society in his time. Pliny's life was lived as a member of the tiny and wealthy upper class of Rome. He tells us little about the life of the man in the Roman street. But he is an invaluable witness to the cultivated leisure habits of the Roman upper class, to their immense wealth and spending power, their numerous houses and slaves, their reading habits and literary pretensions, their mutual social obligations and their professional codes of conduct or misconduct, their infighting and greed, their often deadly competitive games of political power and survival. He shows us the inner machinations and rivalries of that small elite group of men who between them, despite the autocratic post-republican political dispensation, still managed that huge empire of Rome.

With that qualification, the letters bring us – or appear to bring us – personally closer to Pliny than to any other Roman except Cicero, and give us an insight into the life and times of Rome second only to Cicero's much larger letter collection. In theory it ought perhaps to be obvious from a large collection of personal letters, even ones written two millennia ago, what sort of man Pliny was. Letters are after all revealing of the person who wrote them, and epistolography – the art of writing letters intended or destined for later publication – is a deliberate act of self-advertisement that has been fashionable in many ages since Pliny, though not in our own. But such letters are inevitably coloured by the intent to publish, both in their selection and in their subsequent editing. There is also a certain smugness about his letters that has brought down on his head charges of glossing over the faults and excesses of the Roman regime and Roman society. Tacitus, it is fairly said, shows us the dark side of Rome, Pliny the light side. But Pliny was far from being the benevolent writer of chatty letters about relaxed dinner parties and poetry readings that a casual read might suggest. Genial Pliny may be in the general tone of his letters – often irritatingly so. But when he lashes out at contemporaries he can be vicious in his animosity.

The questions about Pliny

Pliny's autobiography in letter form also bristles with unfinished questions, both about Pliny personally and about the history of his time. Some of the questions about Pliny are the obvious ones. How and where did he get his start in life? Why was it the Inheritance Court – the oddly named Court of One Hundred Men – in which he made his legal career? Why was this court so important to Roman society, why was it a forum in which Pliny could shine, and how did it work? How do we assess Pliny's perhaps tortuous relationship with the 'bad' Emperor Domitian? Was his life really in danger, as he claims? How do we assess Pliny's famous but often despised speech in praise of the 'good' Emperor Trajan, the so-called *Panegyricus*? Was the literary circle to which Pliny belonged just a nest of dilettantes or was it capable of producing works of genuine creative value? How well did Pliny perform as a powerful state official, particularly in his time as governor-plenipotentiary of the troublesome Roman province of Bithynia-Pontus?

Some of the questions are less obvious. For example, what does Pliny tell us about Roman government attitudes towards early Christianity? For Pliny became an inadvertent expert witness to the intense and fateful debate that raged within the Roman administration of the time over what to do about the Christians and the cult of Christianity. Two centuries later, this religious movement was to turn their world upside down more surely than any transitory imperial dictator. But this was the early days, when attitudes were in flux.

More generally, as a successful lawyer, senator and rising star of the imperial civil administration, Pliny faced that fundamental question that recurs repeatedly in subsequent political history down to our own recent times: how can a man be principled and free, but at the same time be the loyal subject of an absolute autocracy such as ruled the Roman Empire? His career and writings circled around that key issue. How could some vestiges of the principles of freedom, competition of ideas and open political debate that underlay the old Roman republic be preserved and re-expressed in the new political dispensation of one-man rule? What is liberty in such a context (if it exists at all)? That is what makes Pliny – whether you like him or not – relevant to later generations, to a modern world where autocrats still flourish and still tumble, and where arguments rage about the meaning, limits and practicalities of personal and political freedom.

Some say that in those circumstances there was no freedom at all, and by definition could not be. Referring to Pliny's early career in the public office of *quaestor* on the lower rungs of the Roman civil service promotion ladder, that great historian of Rome Sir Ronald Syme wrote gloomily:

> When the *quaestor* recited the imperial dispatches to the sad submissive senators, they endured the hollow phrases of deference, the dishonest asseverations of their collective loyalty and patriotism … Pliny has not chosen to tell how he fared during his uncomfortable apprenticeship in the arts and hypocrisies of public life … indulging in solemn make-believe.[2]

Syme clearly believed that Pliny was mired beyond redemption in 'the hypocrisies of public life' and 'solemn make-believe' – a sad submissive figure himself. On the other hand, there is a more generous view of Pliny. Betty Radice, on whose excellent 1963 translation of the letters I have relied throughout (except for the *Panegyricus*), in her introduction denies that Pliny was just 'a time-server' when in public office. She writes that:

> Pliny is a witness to the fact that competence and honesty can survive a corrupt regime. Someone must keep the civil administrative machine working, and it is the Plinys of all times and places who form a civil bureaucracy to carry on while governments come and go.[3]

That version of Pliny, however, is too simple, swings too far the other way. It is modelled on the modern concept of an independent civil service and a government periodically changed by elections. Rome was not like that. Nor is it really true to say, as does Radice, that 'his interests were not really political'. With an absolute autocrat wielding highly centralised power over military, civilian and religious life, there was no clear or agreed dividing line between politics and administration, or between government and at least the upper echelon of the governed. A shifting but small upper class straddled all these functions, mainly as senators, military commanders and governors of provinces of the empire, and was the class from which the emperor himself was chosen, and from which his successor or replacement would be drawn, by heredity, by army proclamation – or by assassination. The separation of functions between parliament, the executive and the judiciary, key to a modern democracy, was unknown to Rome.

In this context, Pliny was ambitious, and that meant being involved in Rome's often dangerous version of politics. He liked the status and wealth that went with success, and enjoyed the lifestyle and prestige that went with membership of the senatorial elite of Rome. The question, rather, is how he survived the political process, what compromises he made on the way, and whether all his statements about it are to be taken at face value

Dramatis personae: Domitian, Trajan – and Regulus

What brings these political questions to life and personalises them is that three men in particular stalk the pages of Pliny's letters and speeches. For each, Pliny provides a vivid pen portrait – whether accurate or otherwise remains to be argued – built up over different items of his correspondence. One is the emperor Domitian, in effect Pliny's first boss. The question there is, how far did Pliny go in colluding with a 'bad' emperor like Domitian, only to use his published letters as a desperate cover-up to hide actions or omissions of which he was later ashamed, or which he felt would tarnish his reputation in the eyes of posterity (as has in fact happened)?

Then there was the emperor Trajan, Pliny's second boss. The question with Trajan is exactly the reverse – how far did Pliny go in colluding with a 'good' emperor like Trajan by shamelessly indulging in flattery and subservience. Did that merely confirm the autocracy in its hold on power and in its legitimacy in the eyes of its subjects?

Pliny chooses to illuminate these dilemmas by reference to a third man – not an emperor, but a fellow lawyer and rival named Regulus. Pliny had this one particular hate figure who he mocks and satirises repeatedly, and with whom he frequently sparred, both in the courts and in politics. He is the villain of the piece. Regulus, says Pliny, always did whatever he should not do. Worse, by his political denunciations he had innocent blood on his hands. Pliny's portrait of Regulus in action, face make-up, eye-patch and all, is the most vivid character sketch – or character assassination – in any collection of letters I know. Yet the career of Regulus was in many respects similar to Pliny's own. Wherein, exactly, lay the difference between the two men, rough contemporaries in the same profession?

There is a striking symmetry about Pliny's animosities, intended or otherwise, literary device or not. He had one great political hate figure, the emperor Domitian, and just as 'bad' Domitian is contrasted with the later 'good' emperor Trajan, so too 'bad' Regulus is contrasted, by thinly-veiled implication, with 'good' Pliny. Is character assassination of Regulus a means of character vindication of Pliny himself? A central theme of this biography is whether that symmetry is a literary artifice to cover up an altogether messier picture of Pliny's advancement to the top level of Roman society. Is Pliny's hostile portrait of Regulus in fact a deliberate exercise in negative self-definition? Is the conventional contrast between 'bad' Emperor Domitian and 'good' Emperor Trajan, itself reliant in part on Pliny's evidence, really justified, or was it dreamed up by Pliny and his friends in Pliny's own interest? Regulus survived Pliny's hostility, just as Pliny adroitly survived the attacks on him by Regulus. Was survival their only real common denominator?

Vesuvius – but not with his uncle

Like his letters, which only by chance escaped relegation to the dustbin of lost Roman classics, Plinius Secundus himself survived to tell us his version of his life, but only just. When was still scarcely 17 years of age there occurred the most famous and catastrophic episode of his career. Vesuvius, the long-dormant volcano across the bay from where he was staying with his uncle near Naples, blew its top. Pliny was quite lucky to escape with his life. In his letters he has left us a much-quoted description of that famous eruption, the one that by chance preserved for our admiration and the Italian tourist trade the smothered Roman towns of Pompeii and Herculaneum. But his uncle, who was also his adoptive father, died in that same volcanic eruption while trying to save lives.

The elder Pliny also wrote books – lots of them. Pliny lists them [3.5]. They include a manual on javelin throwing while on horseback, a history of Rome's wars against the Germans, and an examination of problems in grammar – a politically safe topic, says Pliny, as it was written in the time of the dangerous and suspicious Emperor Nero. Of Pliny the Elder's books, only the bulky *Natural History* has survived and been admired to this day, like the Younger's letters. The Elder, like the Younger, was also an imperial civil servant, but of a different sort and status, and that fact also illuminates our Pliny's career.

Even though a distinguished author, career civil servant and close friend of emperors, notably the emperor Titus, Pliny the Elder had ducked the most difficult political questions by remaining firmly on the lower of the two rungs of the Roman elite, the so-called equestrian class of knights (*equites*). This class usually stayed out of the more dangerous game of social and political advancement up the status ladder that took you into the Senate and into the ranks of the men from whom a successor might be found for the sitting emperor – peacefully or otherwise. So the mere fact that Pliny chose to enter into the formal procedures and promotion ladder by which a man entered the Senate, that central institution of Roman governance (he could have chosen not to) meant that he was involved, to one degree or another, in Roman politics. Our Pliny opted for the more demanding, ambitious and potentially dangerous task of, on the one hand, trying to lead the life of a civilised man of wealth, and on the other, agonising over problems of power in society, the limits of protest, and the shifting morality of being a faithful servant of a highly centralised and often capricious regime.

Wealth, assets – and slaves

As his character sketch of Regulus shows, Pliny was a good storyteller with an eye for drama and detail. His letters shed light and atmosphere onto many aspects of life at the top of Rome. He tells us about the law courts and the hubbub and bustle that turned them into open-air theatre. He tells us about the villas and estates that he owned, magnificent places even though he was not among Rome's super-rich. From his comments about money we can roughly estimate where he stood on the rich-list. He tells us about the very Roman system of patronage, in which men of influence bestowed favours and job recommendations upon men younger or of less status than themselves, in the expectation that the favour would one day be reciprocated or called in in some form or other.

Pliny also makes clear the central enabling role that slaves, highly skilled and educated slaves, played in his life and activities. He owned a lot of slaves, though how many he does not say. Up to a point, Pliny is informative on the whole subject of slaves, their place in a rich man's urban household, what their duties and skills were, and how a man of Pliny's status was supposed to look after them and even grant them freedom. Many of these men were highly literate, perhaps deliberately trained in reading, writing, grammar and language. Pliny could become fond of them, look after them when they were ill. Yet they were still slaves. Pliny tells us some details about such personal slave/secretaries and about his treatment of the other household slave members who were close to him.

But at the same time he relegates to near-invisibility the bulk of the large rural slave-holdings that worked his estates. His comments are very revealing of Roman social attitudes. About the only thing he advertises about his rural slaves is that he, the benign Pliny, does not keep his agricultural slaves in chains, without commenting on those slave-owners who evidently did. Nor does he question the morality of slavery – no Roman did. But at least Pliny shows the more humane side of Rome's otherwise obnoxious slave system, whether or not he always observed it.

Poetics and politics

The letters also shed a bright light on the literary efforts of Pliny and his contemporaries. Were these just men of relative leisure passing agreeable social evenings devoted to a fashionable hobby of imitative plagiarism? Or was it a salon society that encouraged creative skills that sometimes but not always gave birth to works of merit, though not in the case of Pliny? The roll call of authors who were rough contemporaries of Pliny, and who are still known and read today, is impressive, suggesting that talent was nurtured by the system – sometimes anyway. Most notably Tacitus and Suetonius, but also Martial, Juvenal and Statius belonged to this era, which has until recently been conventionally dubbed 'the Silver Age' of Latin literature, the last era during which creative or memorable Latin literature was created.

Pliny was actually close friends with some of these authors, notably Tacitus and Suetonius, and was a patron of Martial. But he also knew many others who have, probably deservedly, sunk into obscurity. He gives us the best description we have of how such men went about their literary business, the stages of composition of a new work, the interplay between oral and written. However forced and artificial Pliny's descriptions of literary evenings for a select few may sound, however imitative the spare-time auteurs may have been, however much plagiarism was the order of the day, it is an open question whether the publishing system he describes was any the less conducive to real achievement than the literary and publishing conventions of other eras, our own included.

What Pliny also draws to our attention is the close link between literature and politics in the Roman social system, or at least the upper-class portion of it. One commentator refers to:

> A quintessentially Plinian marriage of law and literature, of poetics and politics, the difference between past and present, and the inextricability of literature and governance in the Trajanic senatorial elite.

As an example, in just one single letter [**8.14**], says the same writer,

> We meet Pliny the littérateur and Pliny the lawyer, Pliny the poetic alluder and Pliny the politician – the ideal Trajanic senator in a nutshell … here (as elsewhere) poetics go hand in hand with politics.[4]

So Pliny in his letters describes not just a literary process but a process by which the elite of Rome defined both itself and their right and justification to rule. Pliny is himself an example of this process, and that is explored in this biography. But whether Pliny's own literary efforts were any good is another matter. That his attempts at creative literature, poetry or prose were not very good is suggested by the quality of his own infrequent quotations from his compositions. But it may be unfair to judge from such a small sample. That his speeches were long and possibly boring to anyone other than a contemporary audience is suggested by the *Panegyricus*, his long-winded if much undervalued speech in praise of the emperor Trajan. But that assumption may again be unfair, since it is the only one of Pliny's speeches to survive. We don't know what his other speeches were like.

Dates – not what, but when?

Reader, beware. Running throughout any reconstruction of Pliny's life and character is one great historical fault line – the problem of dates. The trouble for both biographer and reader is that Pliny's letters do not present a complete portrait of their author. Pliny is irritatingly vague about potentially interesting details of his life, such as dates. Much has to be reconstructed. Of course he was not writing a school textbook, even though he has become one; nor does he pretend that it is an autobiography expressed in a different form. But besides dates there are other areas of irritating vagueness, for example ambiguity about his private life, and about his marriages. Married he was – but how often? Some believe he was married twice, some believe it was three times. And why did he never have any children? It was to his great regret, so he said – or was it a tax dodge? Maybe here too he stood to gain advantage, which he later tried to cover up.

But biographical assessment of Pliny is particularly bedevilled by this infuriating ambiguity about the dates at which he reached certain critical points in his life, even the dates of his birth and his death. All in all, given how much personal evidence we have about Pliny compared to almost any other Roman except Cicero, there is a surprising amount of imprecision about almost all the main dates connected with his life. Sometimes that does not matter at all, sometimes not much, but sometimes it matters a great deal for our estimate of Pliny. The order in which he held the various great offices of state is usually clear enough. But the time at which he held them is the subject of continuing argument, and for good reason. The dates are often the key to the interpretation of Pliny's career and character.

The date of his birth (in today's dating system) is either 61 or 62 CE, a fact not very important in itself except when it contributes to more significant date problems later in his career. The date of his death is vague. In his last posting on official business, we know from internal evidence how long he was in the province of Bithynia-Pontus as governor with special powers, but we do not know exactly when he was there – estimates vary by three years. It is generally assumed that he died from illness while in office there, soon after writing the last of his letters to the emperor Trajan who had sent him there, since this letter sequence breaks off suddenly and we hear no more about Pliny after that. But that is an assumption, if a plausible one. Some argue that Pliny could just as well have returned to Rome on sick leave at that point. We know he had been ill, for he tells us so. Just maybe he lived on in retirement at one of his villas, for who knows how long.

When was he *praetor*?

But there are two particular dates that stand out as key to assessing Pliny's life and character. Both are disputed. One is the date at which he was appointed to the high office of *praetor*, a senior position in the administrative hierarchy of Rome with particular responsibility for legal questions and the law courts – a job for which Pliny was eminently suited, given his career in the courts up to then. With that job came entry into the inner circles of the Roman elite, and likely progression to the pinnacle – the most prestigious appointment of all, that of consul. But at what date did this appointment happen? Was it, as usually supposed, in 93 CE, under the 'bad' Emperor Domitian, at the very point at which Domitian's alleged 'reign of terror' was setting in? In that case, Pliny owed his most important advancement to the emperor whom he later labelled as an evil tyrant, and, if that is the case, Pliny stands accused of hypocrisy, whitewash, even collusion in imperial misdeeds. But is another interpretation possible?

When was he prefect of the military treasury?

The second date that is central to our view of Pliny follows on from the first. Between which dates did he hold the important administrative post of prefect in charge of the military treasury? This certainly followed the job of *praetor*, but was it immediately after? If so, and if he was *praetor* in 93, then his three-year term in the new treasury office would have straddled the years 94 to 96, the very years during which Domitian was hunting down the supposed opposition to his rule and right up to the point when that emperor was assassinated. In that case, the weight of evidence is doubled for Pliny's apparent role as a nominee and favourite of Domitian the 'evil monster' (Pliny's words), and Pliny is doubly convicted of (at its mildest) hypocrisy in his later letters in which he denigrates and denounces Domitian.

But could those dates be wrong? Was he not in office at all during those terrible purge years, but lying low, keeping his head down, not a hero but a prudent survivor? That is what he says he did. Are we to say he was a liar in this? If so, what other lies did he tell? Or at worst was Pliny economical with the truth? So the apparently dry and technical issue of dates goes to the heart of our assessment of Pliny. This biography sets out at least a plausible answer to this conundrum.

What this book is not

This biography does not try to replicate the fine specialist works that have been written during the resurgence of interest in Pliny over the past 20 years, although I have consulted and, I hope, fully acknowledged all of them where relevant (see Bibliography). It is not primarily a literary analysis, either of the style of the letters or of the composition and structure of the collection, although these matters are referred to in the book and may be pursued further by the interested reader. Still less does it seek to be a commentary on Pliny's letters or in any sense rival the monumental work of A. N. Sherwin-White (1966). This book is a commentary of a different kind. What is the life that lies behind and between the letters, what gives them a context, and what activity generates them? How well do we really know Pliny, as seen mainly through the (perhaps distorting) lens of his letters, and what, finally, do we think of him?

This biography follows a roughly but not strictly chronological order. It is structured around the various legal and political aspects of Pliny's life and career in approximate date order, so as to illuminate each one of them in turn. In short, it is a biography, the story of a man's life.

Reading the evidence: Are Pliny's letters what they seem?

We know a lot about the younger Pliny only because he left behind his published collection of letters, and that collection survived the collapse of the western Roman Empire, against the odds. The letters are the great and enduring achievement of the younger Pliny. In all, there are 247 letters in his main collection, written to over 100 correspondents. These letters are divided by Pliny into nine separate books, in the Roman sense of 'books' (more like instalments), and probably published, in the Roman sense of 'published', separately but then put together later to form a single volume. Publication at Rome meant putting into circulation by means of hand-copying and distributing among his immediate circle of friends and colleagues, and so into libraries.

To this total of 247 private letters are added 121 official letters exchanged between Pliny and the emperor Trajan when Pliny, late in his life, was sent out on state business to what is now a part of northern Turkey. If it is true that Pliny died in office, as most suppose, these must have been edited and distributed by some later unnamed editor, who may (or may not) have been Pliny's friend, client and fellow author Suetonius, writer of the famous and much quoted *Lives of the Caesars*. These now form Book Ten of the collected letters, but may have been physically added much later to the previous nine books, to form the present 10-book edition that is familiar to modern readers. But what sort of collection is it, and are the letters even real letters?

The collection is not in itself an autobiography. Rather, it has been called a set of disordered autobiographical fragments in which biographical information is lost between the letters. Some but not all of this missing detail can be filled in, thanks to a long and detailed inscription found at Comum, perhaps from Pliny's tomb, most of which is now lost but which is known from a fifteenth-century copy.[1] Nor does the collection purport to be history. Pliny says that he is not writing history; that is a different art form. On the other hand, his letters are a form of history.

> The epistle was an ideal flexible medium for writing about recent history in the imperial age.[2]

Why ideal? Because the letters lent themselves to vivid narrative; were segmented and fragmented, unlike a full history book, so less intrusive; and by their very nature involved the addressees, who in effect colluded and became co-owners of their contents. At a time when writing history was a dangerous, even lethal occupation because of its implications for contemporary politics, letters spread the risk. That must have appealed to the ever-cautious Pliny.

So if not as autobiography or history, how else may we picture Pliny's letter collection? Often it is likened to a mosaic, in which the artist (in this case Pliny) assembles a large number of small individual items which, if taken together, form some larger picture. But there is a snag here as well.

> What the static 'mosaic' metaphor cannot convey is the sense of constant shifting movement inherent in the process of actually reading Pliny.[3]

So instead, the collection has been compared to a kaleidoscope, with the caution:

> Shake Pliny's kaleidoscope, and no second peek will ever exactly repeat the patterning.[4]

Pliny himself adopts a much more casual attitude. In the first letter of the first book into which he arranged his letters, Pliny adopts a nonchalant tone. Here they are, he says, just as they came to hand. They are, he affirms, real letters, only they are ones written with greater care than the rest (*epistolae curatius scriptae*). Few believe that literally. Pliny's nonchalant air is surely a pose. Also, it is not a complete collection – he says so.

Rearranging the truth, or polishing it?

But some have even gone as far as doubting the basic authenticity of the letters. Did he perhaps make them up, or some of them? Maybe they were never sent as real letters at all. How far did he go to polish up his letters for publication? Critics suspect a lot of polishing, even as far as outright fabrication.

> Although Pliny may well have sent real letters in 96–98 resembling those of Book One, he evidently selected, revised and rewrote them with great care,

maintaining the fiction of authentic letters by avoiding explicit anachronisms ... though we can never know how much of Book One is original and how much is later recomposition, Pliny's own comments on revising for the sake of oratorical exercise provide a suggestive guide.[5]

What Pliny says about his speeches [7.9] is that, ideally, a revision after first delivery for general publication should retain a lot but add even more, insert some things and rewrite other things, as if grafting new limbs onto the existing body without sacrificing the original. If that is what he did with his published speeches, as he freely acknowledges, is that what he also did with his letters when he decided to publish them? He never says that he did not revise them: nor does he say that he did revise them. All he says is that the letters he chose were ones carefully written in the first place. Why then would he want to expend yet more effort in revising them?

His motives for extensive revision, some suggest, might have been two-fold – to improve how his letters looked as a literary collection, and to improve how they stacked up as a presentation of his life's work. In other words, so this criticism goes, when he saw how his letters were adding up as a historical portrait of his era and of himself and his reputation, perhaps he dived in and rewrote them as far as he needed to in order to rearrange the raw truth to make it look better. On that basis, we ought to be anxious about the whole collection, asking whether Pliny's so-called letters are literary constructs just like the poetic verses he wrote as part of the salon life of his time, no more real than his imitations of Greek verse forms.

> The letters are a creative self-dramatisation, a literary stab at self-immortalisation ... [their] self-conscious self-representation is the source of unresolvable uncertainties for Pliny's readers.[6]

On the other hand, Pliny specifically says in that first letter that he is not even trying to write history, even though his letters have been plundered for the historical nuggets that lie all around in his narratives. If he were writing history, he would not have been so irritatingly vague on the many details of his life that still baffle us. This has been called 'Pliny's habit of evasive display'.[7] But the attitudes and ethics expressed in his letters can quite credibly be taken as those of Pliny the man, if only because they are so revealing of his very human imperfections, such as his primness and his anxiety to please. A. N. Sherwin-White in his great Commentary on the letters sums it up well:

> Some regard the letters as entirely fictitious, written for the books in which they appear. Others speak of the letters as being written up from simpler originals.

But it would require an extraordinary ingenuity to invent so many convincing details ... [the letters] read as literary revisions of practical letters which have been polished in language and style.[8]

It is hardly surprising that Pliny, like many other authors, may have polished the style before publication. But that does not necessarily mean that he falsified his record. His letters are mainly to named and known people, refer to events known from other sources, describe his career in stages also known from other evidence, and engage with known controversies of his time. So to the extent that he polished perhaps more than he admits, he cannot have done it so comprehensively as to turn the letters into some new genre of fiction.

So his letters are to be taken as basically authentic, just as his country villas, his court cases,and his narrow escape from Vesuvius were authentic. But they are by definition Pliny's side of the story, his selection from a presumably much larger body of letters in his private archive. They give his 'spin' on events and people, to be scanned with a critical eye. In particular, we must be on the lookout for his persistent habit of self-promotion.

Few of his letters lack an element of self-praise.[9]

In particular, he used his letters as advertisements for his speeches and his skills as a speechwriter and orator, a sort of mailshot to get his spoken words into written circulation after the event.

How were the letters arranged?

The one thing that Pliny certainly did not do was present his letters in chronological order, as you might otherwise have expected. What he says in full in the first letter of Book One, written to his friend Septicius Clarus, a man of similar social status to Pliny and later Prefect of the Guard under the emperor Hadrian, is this:

You have often urged me to collect and publish any letters of mine which were composed with some care. I have now made a collection, not keeping to the original order as I was not writing history, but taking them as they came to my hand.

Few believe that his selection of letters was as casual as he makes out. As a result, much effort has been expended on determining just what his unacknowledged selection criteria were, and what literary artifices lie concealed beneath the smooth surface of the letters.

> It is now universally agreed that the arrangement of Pliny's letters is far from incidental. Indeed, each of the letters is carefully located, and various types [of letter] are distributed throughout the first nine books ... any study of the corpus must take into account where letters appear in relation both to the work as a whole and to each other ... even the briefest of the letters is a rhetorical masterpiece, carefully refined and placed within the corpus to create interlocking narratives about various aspects of Pliny's life, culminating in a complete portrait of their author, while at the same time masquerading as a casual collection.[10]

So the literary architecture of the letters has been the subject of intense but often sterile analysis that has obscured their actual content – what the historian Ronald Syme called a 'ruinous waste of erudition'.[11] Pliny's concern with formal presentation, both in his legal speeches and his (lost) literary compositions, is well attested and a fact about his life and his education. But our concern is not literary criticism, but Pliny the man, judged through the evidence of the content of the letters and other supporting evidence. If Pliny did pay more attention to the formal structure of his collection than he lets on, arranging it according to literary principles now only dimly discerned, that does not prevent us from unpicking his structure and re-ordering his letters according to the require-ments of biography.

Who did he write to?

There are a total of 105 named recipients of the 247 letters of Books One to Nine. The most frequently named recipient of Pliny's letters was his friend Tacitus, the orator and historian, with 11 letters. Next, with nine letters, came Calpurnius Fabatus, his wife's grandfather, who was from the same area of Italy as Pliny, around Comum. In all, Pliny wrote to 77 different people who can be otherwise identified, each receiving between one and 11 letters. For example, four went to Suetonius, the future biographer of the emperors. Relatives, by birth or marriage, make up only 16 of the correspondents. Some 28 of the people he writes to cannot be identified, leading some people to suggest that Pliny may have made up the names of some or all of these addresses to embellish an actual letter or even to head a letter which he made up for publication. We don't – and can't – know.

But it is noticeable, if unsurprising, that of the 77 we know something about, 48 were of senatorial rank, and most of the rest were in the lower segment of the Roman upper class, the class of equestrians. In other words, Pliny mostly, even exclusively, wrote to his peer group, although there is nothing in his letters to suggest any difference in tone between letters to the highest in the land and letters to the rest. This was the Roman rich and powerful in dialogue with each other – except that we do not have the other half of the dialogue. It is like listening in to one end of a telephone conversation. But if Pliny was writing to the rich and the powerful, it seems unlikely that he would totally fabricate some of his letters – it would so easily get known and bring discredit to the entire collection.

When were they first published?

There is much dispute about the exact dates of publication of each of the separate books of letters, in the Roman sense of 'publication'. As we have seen, dates are a persistent headache when discussing Pliny. The great German scholar Theodore Mommsen thought that the nine books were issued in quick succession from late 97 onwards, once the tyrant Domitian was assassinated and out of the way. But that equally great scholar Ronald Syme believed that none could have been published before 105, the date of the death of Regulus, the rival lawyer and great hate figure of Pliny's letters. So Syme suggested publication in four batches between 105 and 109. Previously many others had believed that the nine books were published in three separate 'triads', 3 x 3.

Sherwin-White, in his Commentary on the letters, suggested that Books One to Three appeared before Pliny took on the important and time-consuming job of Curator of the Tibur River in 104–6, with the rest appearing after he had left that post. Betty Radice suggested to the contrary; that the only time when Pliny had the leisure to sort out his letters for publication was after he was finished with the law case involving Varenus in 107, and before he left for the province of Bithynia-Pontus as the emperor's special envoy in around 111.

Part of the problem is that, in theory, each letter has not one but three dates attached to it. There is the date at which it was written, the date at which it was published, and the date of the events described in it – the so-called dramatic date. It is the dramatic date that matters most for a biographer. The trouble is that Pliny nowhere tells us what any of these dates are for any of his letters. The individual letters are not dated. Sometimes the date of the events referred to in them is clear from other sources, but more often it is not. So these dates have to be deduced, if possible, from the contents of each letter or from cross-refer-encing to other Roman authors such as Tacitus and Dio. It would be helpful to know all of those dates exactly, but we don't. The surviving copy of the Comum inscription, itself with gaps in it, helps to sort out the order of events in Pliny's life and some of the dates, but by no means all of them, and it leaves ample scope for debate and controversy about Pliny's life.

How did they survive?

Just like their writer during the eruption of Vesuvius in 79 CE, Pliny's letters only just survived the passage of the centuries. They might easily have got lost in the general destruction of Roman culture that followed the political collapse of the western Roman Empire in the fifth century. One way or another, most of the text that we now have, for all 10 books of the letters, probably dates back to a single ancient manuscript in codex form that survived in Paris, written out, so the experts say, towards the end of the fifth century and preserved there, by chance or design, for hundreds of years. Various copies were made of it in the Middle Ages, many of them incomplete or selective, so giving rise to a very confused manuscript tradition.

Not long after its rediscovery in the dawning age of the Renaissance, that priceless original manuscript in Paris was itself largely lost. Diplomatic pressures caused it to be transferred around the year 1500 from the library of Saint-Victor in Paris to northern Italy so as to be transformed, in Venice and elsewhere, into multiple copies by the new technology of printing, where it became a victim of the processes of print. Only a very small part of the original – a mere six leaves – survives in the Pierpoint Morgan Library in New York.

There was another risk. Over time the accuracy of the actual text of the letters must have suffered due to the laborious process of copying and recopying by hand that constituted both Roman and post-Roman methods of book circulation before the introduction of mechanical printing. But how much did the text suffer?

> As soon as Pliny's nine books of personal correspondence began to circulate in public about 100 A.D., the process of rewriting and corrupting them began. The law of human error soon took charge to the extent that what pass for Pliny's letters are undoubtedly only a distorted version of what he originally wrote.[12]

That is sobering, but perhaps unduly pessimistic. The printed copies made of the Paris manuscript in the years following 1500 were indeed often inaccurate. But by collating them with the more partial or selective versions also in circulation and dating back in some cases to the revival of classical learning under the emperor Charlemagne in the ninth century, scholars with a fine knowledge of the Latin language have painstakingly reconstructed what is regarded as a viably accurate text for the letters.

> Most texts of Pliny had holes in them somewhere, but fortunately they tended to have their holes in different places.

So the tale of the survival of the letters is itself a lesson in history and in human endeavour.

> The history of Pliny's text is a tribute to the tenacity of humanism, the will to seek and to find. When the corpus of letters had become so fragmented and lacunose, it took a lot of time and patience and the work of many hands to put Pliny back together again.[13]

Thanks to these brilliant scholars, medieval and modern, we can now concentrate, not on the accuracy of the text of the letters as we now have it, which is certainly good enough for practical purposes, but on the human story that emerges from the text and which is the subject of this biography.

Youth, class and that Plinian eruption

The striking thing about the early years of Plinius Secundus – once, that is, he had survived the eruption of Mount Vesuvius – is how soon in life he decided to follow the twin tracks of a legal career and a political career, within the context of the judicial institutions and political structure of imperial Rome. He could have chosen otherwise. He could have stuck to achieving success in the courts of law, and he could have chosen to stick with the lesser equestrian status as a Roman knight that satisfied his uncle, the elder Pliny. No one else in his family had climbed to the very top of the Roman status tree, as far as we know, to become a member of the Senate and a consul at Rome. But there is every sign that, almost from the start, Pliny was ambitious, or at least propelled forwards by an ambitious family and friends. Perhaps he was also sucked upwards by social pressure to fill the vacuum at the centre of Roman society, created by low birth rates among the top stratum and the nasty habit of periodic blood-letting. Pliny came from a wealthy provincial background.

His father figures

When Vesuvius, the volcano outside Naples, erupted so violently in the year 79 CE, Plinius Secundus was 17 years of age. That much he tells us [6.20]. So his date of birth could be either 61 or 62. His home town was Comum, modern Como, on the southern tip of Lake Como in northern Italy. He is vague in his letters about who his father was, as he is vague about many other details of his career. But the inscriptions help. His father was probably called Lucius Caecilius Secundus, son of Gaius, of the tribe Oufentina, a man of substantial wealth from the landed gentry of the area of Comum and a local magistrate. The German scholar Theodor Mommsen found Pliny's father elsewhere, in a certain Lucius Caecilius Cilo, son of Lucius, from the same area of Comum and also a magistrate, known from a different inscription. But this man, along with his concubine Lutulla, lived too early to be a plausible candidate for the honour of being Pliny's father. Either way, Pliny's father must have died when Pliny was still young, and when Pliny's name was not yet Pliny at all, but Gaius (or Lucius) Caecilius Secundus the son, similar to his father's name. What the evidence shows is that the Caecilii were members of a large family clan in the Comum area, with extensive estates and property.

After his father's death, Pliny tells us that under the terms of his father's will he then acquired a guardian, Verginius Rufus [2.1], a man of great standing at Rome. This was a key and indicative event in Pliny's early life, for it gave him not just a father-figure and protector but also a high-status patron. Verginius Rufus had been commander of the Roman troops in the Roman province of Upper Germany, had used his troops to put down a revolt against the emperor Nero by Vindex in 68, when Pliny was still a child of six or seven, and had then refused to allow his name to go forward as a possible successor to Nero as emperor. Pliny pays a moving tribute to this man on his death at the great age (by Roman standards) of 83. Verginius's funeral oration was delivered by none other than the famous orator and historian, Pliny's friend Tacitus. Pliny says of Rufus [2.1]:

> He lived on to read about himself in history and verse … he gave me a father's affection.

The connection between Verginius and Pliny's family was that they were close neighbours around Comum:

> We came from the same district and neighbouring towns, and our lands and property adjoined each other.

Pliny's early debut into the metropolitan life of Rome, leaving behind the comfortable but provincial life of Comum, is often ascribed to the influence of his mother's brother. This was the man we know as the elder Pliny, who was named Gaius Plinius Secundus. He later adopted his nephew, probably in his will, as his son. In the light of Pliny's subsequent career as an expert on wills operating in the Roman court of law that dealt with important inheritance cases, it is interesting that Pliny's own life was shaped so decisively by two successive wills, first his father's will and then his uncle's. He was himself living proof of why the Romans, or Rome's upper set, attached such importance to inheritance cases.

But it may well have been Verginius Rufus rather than the elder Pliny who set Pliny's sights so high. The elder Pliny was certainly an influential imperial official and a noted author of many books. He was also a friend of the emperor Titus. But he kept out of political life as the Romans practised it, and remained a member of the equestrian order, the lower section of the Roman upper class. It is hard to believe that this was not a deliberate choice, for the elder Pliny lived through a period of intense turmoil and danger at Rome. He kept his head firmly below the parapet, and then was killed in the Vesuvius eruption before he had time to offer his adoptive son much career support. Verginius, however, had a riskier career, but adroitly avoided the traps. He ended up being appointed as a consul no less than three times – the absolute pinnacle of the Roman status ladder. He was in a unique position to foster Pliny's career. So it may well have been Verginius, rather than Pliny's uncle, who shaped and nurtured Pliny's youthful ambitions by encouragement and direct support, and by some lessons in avoiding the traps of high office that proved useful at a later and highly controversial period of Pliny's career.

Pliny's birth name went through a further permutation once he was adopted by his uncle. It was only at this point that the name Pliny/Plinius enters his formal name-set. On adoption he became in full Gaius Plinius, son of Lucius, of the tribe Oufentina, Caecilius Secundus. This was something of a mouthful even for Romans, so that in the list of Roman consuls – the high office that Pliny also eventually rose to – he is named simply as C. Plinius Secundus. Of course, he remained plain Secundus to his friends and eventually to his emperor-friend Trajan.

His female (and other?) relatives

Pliny's mother was presumably called Plinia, being the elder Pliny's sister, and she was with him when he witnessed the great eruption of Vesuvius in 79 and survived it when the ash cloud crossed the Bay of Naples and threatened to smother them both. Pliny mentions her five times in his letters, but curiously never by name. Nowhere does he tell us anything much about her, what influence (if any) she had on him, and for how long she figured in his life. She must be presumed to have died when Pliny was still quite young, and well before he started writing his letters. So Pliny may have become a double orphan at an early stage of his life, losing both father and mother.

This imprecision in his letters about what his parents' names and identities were is striking to a modern reader. So is his failure to mention the fact that he had a sister named Caecilia, who also died young. We know about her because before his death their father paid for a temple of the imperial cult to be erected in her honour – a task that Pliny completed after his father's death. One must wonder whether Pliny's own relatively early death, probably before the age of 52, had some connection with the premature deaths of his father, mother and sister. But perhaps that is just how uncertain life and death were in the Roman empire. Since his uncle had no children, Pliny was early on deprived of any close relatives of his own generation. Equally, he became the sole inheritor and focus of family wealth and family ambitions.

Some, however, have taken this name, Secundus, Latin for 'second', as indicating that he was the second son of his father, and that there must have been a first son who, like their sister Caecilia, died young. But apart from the name there is no evidence for such a previous son, no mention of such a brother in all of Pliny's frequent references to his family. The name Secundus, however odd to be called 'Second' may sound to a modern ear, was plainly just that, a name repeatedly used by his family, like Caecilius.

So we may presume that Pliny became the sole heir of both his father's substantial estate around Comum and the estate of his uncle/adoptive father. In other words, he started out his career as a rich man, and you had to be rich to aspire to be a Roman senator. This status required a substantial property qualification as well as qualifications earned by holding high public office. So almost from the start Pliny had both wealth and connections; and he had or acquired ambitions to match.

Education – as a legal expert?

Backed by that wealth and those connections, Pliny had the sort of education that only rich men could afford, but for them it was the norm. Often labeled as an education in oratory, it was in fact a broad-ranging education in Greek and Latin literature, grammar and language, history, good manners, deportment and the art of public speaking. It was this that gave an upper-class Roman his polish, his self-confidence, his poise and his clear superiority (in his own eyes at least) over the general population. The avenue to the top began early. In Pliny's case, he tells us [6.6] that he studied in Rome under two of the best teachers of his day. One was Nicetes Sacerdos, a Greek from the city of Smyrna on the coast of what is now Turkey, modern Izmir, who presumably taught him both Greek language and Greek literature as well as rhetoric.

The other was none other than Quintilian, the eminent Spaniard, author of the famous handbook on oratory and education titled the *Institutio Oratoria*. Appointed by the emperor Vespasian as a professor of oratory with a salary paid from public funds, and later appointed by the emperor Domitian as tutor to his great-nephews and heirs-presumptive, Quintilian would have taught Pliny Latin literature, language, and the finer points of public speaking and self-presentation. It was an expensive education, the best available. Quintilian could well also have provided Pliny with entry into the exclusive households of Rome, including the most exclusive of all, that of the emperor. Pliny's subsequent relations with the emperor Domitian were to prove the most puzzling and contentious aspect of his career.

Nicetes was also perhaps a mixed blessing to Pliny. He later earned fame by using his skill as an orator to save his own skin. According to Philostratus, in his book *Lives of the Sophists*, Nicetes fell foul of a Roman official called Rufus, who was then in charge of Smyrna's finances. Later, Rufus was transferred to be commander of armed services in Gaul, and from this position of power brought charges against Nicetes before the emperor Nerva. But in a neat sidestep, Nerva told Rufus to try the case himself, since he now had the power to do so. Nicetes therefore had to travel all the way across Europe from Smyrna to Gaul, but was so eloquent at his trial before Rufus that Rufus himself, despite having laid the accusations in the first place, acquitted him in tears. A tall story, perhaps, but indicative of the oratorical wizardry of Pliny's teachers. Sitting at the feet of these men, Pliny would certainly have met many other adolescents who would become his friends, acquaintances, peers and useful contacts for the rest of his professional life in law and politics. Elite education in England and France, for example, was until recently very similar to this in content and purpose, and similarly based on intensive study of Latin and Greek.

In the light of Pliny's later career as a legal expert and advocate, it is interesting that this was not in any sense a specialist legal education. It was the same education that every other rich boy could receive, and anyway there were no specialist legal colleges or law courses from which Pliny might have graduated. This has caused many to complain that, despite the common career designation of Pliny in modern writings as a lawyer, advocate or barrister, Pliny was not really a proper lawyer at all, either in the sense of being a legal expert, or in the sense that, say, a modern UK barrister is both an advocate in court and highly expert in the finer detail of at least some aspects of the law. Pliny was trained as a public speaker, an orator, a term that makes him suspect in certain eyes as being merely a wordsmith, in contrast to the specialists in law, the real legal experts or jurists, who did not pretend to be orators but to whom Pliny appealed from time to time for a legal opinion.

But as his career progressed, Pliny must have learnt a lot about the law just by his experience in the courts. In particular, his activity in the court that dealt with inheritance cases (see Chapter 4) must have taught him a lot about finance and money. That at any rate is how his contemporaries must have viewed it, judging by Pliny's later public appointments to positions essentially in charge of financial affairs. He acted as an assessor in tribunals set up by the Prefect of Rome and by the emperor himself, and as prefect in charge of two of Rome's major state treasuries. He also appeared for one side or the other in legal cases of alleged high-level financial corruption (see Chapter 6). So it is unfair to conclude that his generalist education with a bias towards oratory necessarily debarred him from developing legal expertise or from the right to his common designation as lawyer and advocate. The most important thing about his training in oratory, however, is that it prepared him both for a career in the law courts and for a career in the offices of state, notably the Senate: he could go either way, or both, and he chose both. The Roman Senate was where both streams met. The Senate was both the supreme deliberative body and the Supreme Court, as far as the emperor of the day allowed it to be. This question, of how free the Senate and its senators could be to guide and comment on public life, was to be the big political issue of Pliny's life.

Pliny's education at the hands of Nicetes and Quintilian took place when he was still very young – *vixdum adulescentulus*, Pliny says [6.6], scarcely into his teens. His education did get one thing out of his system early on. Pliny tells us that at the age of 14 he composed a play [7.4]. We don't know what it was about, except that it was a tragedy, and in Greek:

> What it was like, I can't say – anyway, I called it a tragedy.

This was probably not much more than a school exercise, and he never repeated it, perhaps fortunately. But Pliny did retain a lifelong interest in the techniques of composition and literary style, particularly the verse form known as hendeca-syllables, with 11-syllable lines (see Chapter 12). He even published a volume of such poems. His intensive literary studies perhaps explain why, when Vesuvius erupted, Pliny had his head buried in a book (of Livy) and at first took little notice of what was going on across the Bay of Naples until rebuked by a friend of his uncle. Yet it was by far the most dramatic, catastrophic and famous event of his whole life, occurring while he was not yet out of his teens.

Ashes like snowdrifts: The eruption of Vesuvius

Like his collection of letters, Pliny survived to tell us his youthful tale: but only just. He might never have had a story to tell. But that story is familiar nowadays to millions of tourists to the classical sites of Italy. The long-dormant volcano, across the Bay of Naples from Misenum where he was staying with his uncle, blew its top, violently. The eruption figures in the work of other writers too, like Martial and Statius.[1] But Pliny's is by far the longest and best account. Pliny indeed was lucky to escape with his life when thousands of others, much nearer to the epicentre of the eruption, perished, including his own uncle, the elder Pliny. Whole towns were buried, their inhabitants burnt or asphyxiated. The volcano was Vesuvius; the date traditionally given for the eruption is 24 August 79 (but many now think it must have been in October); the time when the eruption started about 1 p.m.; the towns destroyed included Herculaneum as well as Pompeii. It was a unique and mesmerising event.

> Why is the AD 79 eruption of Vesuvius unique? It is not the largest explosive volcanic event in history, nor is it the one that caused the largest number of fatalities. The Vesuvius eruption is unique because no other eruption in history has had such a profound effect on our culture and also illustrated to us the terror and destruction of an awesome and sublime natural catastrophe.

Pliny's extended account of it has been described as:

> the first eyewitness report of a volcanic eruption as well as a historic landmark that signals the beginning of the study of volcanoes.[2]

Vesuvius had been dormant for at least 500 years – for so long indeed that no one then alive had any idea of what terrifying things it could do. The volcano had given off warning signs for months, but no one recognised them for what they were, or took action. Since that time the volcano has erupted at least 30 times, the most recent being in 1944. Pliny tells the whole story of the 79 eruption in two letters he wrote much later to his friend, the historian Tacitus [**6.16** and **6.20**], in case it provided useful information for the history books that Tacitus was writing. The relevant passages of Tacitus have been lost, but Pliny's two letters have survived. They are an invaluable eye-witness account of the eruption, and show how vivid a storyteller Pliny could be – a gift that recurs throughout his letters. The accuracy of his description has caused experts in vulcanology to use the term 'Plinian' to categorise this type of eruption. The two letters are reproduced in part or in whole in almost all the guidebooks bought by the thousands of cultural tourists who visit the excavations of Pompeii and Herculaneum each year, and have done so ever since the rediscovery of the buried ruins 300 years ago. Pliny hoped that these two letters would earn him some sort of immortality, and that they certainly have done.

How near Pliny came to death is arguable. But it was near enough to be a close-run thing. The prevailing wind just happened to be in a different direction, carrying the bulk of the ash cloud away from where Pliny was staying but towards where his uncle had gone on his rescue mission. When his uncle first set out, he offered to take Pliny with him.

> [My uncle] ordered a boat to be made ready, telling me I could come with him if I wished. I replied that I preferred to go on with my studies, and as it happened he had himself given me some writing to do [**6.16**].

If Pliny had not been so bookish, he might have suffered the same fate as his uncle: asphyxiation. On the other hand, his uncle was not a fit man. His breathing problems – he was overweight – meant that he was particularly susceptible to the choking ash that fell around him. Some of his uncle's companions must have got away, and Pliny might have done the same. Or of course he might not.

The fate of the elder Pliny

Pliny's uncle, his mother's brother, was a career imperial civil servant whose official duties ended with him being appointed admiral in charge of the Roman war fleet stationed at Misenum, at the north-western extremity of the Bay of Naples, some 30 kilometres from Vesuvius. His father being by now dead, Pliny and his mother were visiting the admiral at his home in Misenum when the catastrophe struck. The first of Pliny's two letters describes the story of his uncle and his death in the eruption. The second describes Pliny's own narrow escape. Many of the victims of the 79 eruption might in fact have escaped if they had realised the danger, but at first they saw no reason to panic.

> For several days past there had been earth tremors which were not particularly alarming because they are frequent in Campania.

When the eruption began, and alerted to the gathering humanitarian disaster, the admiral ordered his fleet to cross the bay in an attempt to rescue people trapped on the shoreline. It was a doomed attempt, as is graphically shown by the skeletons found on the old shoreline of Herculaneum. The ships could not get near them.

> Ashes were already falling, hotter and thicker as the ships drew near, followed by bits of pumice and blackened stones, charred and cracked by the flames. The shore was blocked by the debris from the mountain [6.16].

Repulsed, the admiral put in to shore lower down the bay, at the house of his friend Pomponianus. He became trapped there, went to bed, but was roused again when the downpour of ash and stones threatened to wall him into his bedroom. He went outside with a pillow tied over his head as protection.

> They were still in darkness, blacker and denser than any ordinary night … He stood leaning on two slaves and then suddenly collapsed, I imagine because the dense fumes choked his breathing by blocking his windpipe which was constitutionally weak. When daylight returned his body was found intact.

Others escaped, including presumably his friend Pomponianus, and were able to relay these details later to the admiral's nephew. Otherwise Pliny could not have known about them. The admiral has been admired ever since for his courage and his instinct to give what help he could, at the cost of his life. But some critics suggest that the nephew invented this humanitarian motive for his uncle when in fact his uncle was just motivated by scientific curiosity. He was after all the author of the bulky *Natural History* that has survived and has informed many generations since then. He was an almost obsessive researcher and writer, as Pliny's letters make clear [3.5], and his first reaction was to order out just one boat to allow him a closer look at what was going on. But there is no denying that, when the full scale of the disaster became more apparent, he ordered out his entire fleet of ships in an attempted rescue mission.

The bookish survivor

The odd thing is that by his own admission Pliny the nephew, having chosen to stay behind to concentrate on his studies, became so buried in his book that he almost ignored the escalating eruption of Vesuvius until he received that rebuke from a friend of his uncle.

> Up came a friend of my uncle's … and scolded us both, me for my foolhardiness and my mother for allowing it. But I remained absorbed in my book.

This friend promptly scurried off to save his own skin. Yet, despite the rebuke, and despite what he could see across the bay, and in the midst of all the volcanic fireworks, Pliny just got on with his studies.

> After my uncle's departure I spent the rest of the day with my books, as this was my reason for staying behind. Then I took a bath, dined, and then dozed fitfully for a while.

This nonchalance in the face of impending and visible disaster – the product surely of foolishness rather than *sang froid* – is extraordinary, maybe even a later affectation to emphasise his lifelong love of books. The scene of Pliny blandly ignoring the violent events observable through the window across the bay in favour of his books later became a favourite cameo subject for classical history painters. Foolish or not, the young Pliny and his mother stayed put, and as a consequence were almost caught when the tremors reached their vicinity and the ash cloud veered towards them.

> That night the shocks were so violent that we felt as if [the house] were not only shaken but overturned. We went and sat down in the forecourt of the house.

But even then his books reasserted their power over him.

> I don't know whether I should call it courage or folly on my part, but I called for a volume of Livy and went on reading it as I had nothing else to do. I even went on with the extracts I had been making.

A 'Plinian' eruption

Despite having his nose in Livy – perhaps a pretence, perhaps to calm his nerves – Pliny's description of the volcanic cloud he now saw across the bay of Naples has become a classic. From it comes the formal name of 'Plinian' for the type of eruption he saw, particularly his vivid analogy with 'an umbrella pine'.

> Its general appearance can best be expressed as like an umbrella pine, for it rose to a great height on a sort of trunk and then split off into branches.

Events then overtook his bookishness. Pliny's account of what happened next makes scary reading.

> The sea receded from the shore so that quantities of sea creatures were left stranded on dry sand. On the landward side a fearful black cloud was rent by

forked and quivering bursts of flame … The cloud sank down to earth and covered the sea, then spread over the earth like a flood. Ashes were falling in heavy showers. We could have been buried and crushed.

Accepting that they were in real and imminent danger if the buildings at Misenum collapsed on top of them, he and his mother decided to leave the built-up area, followed by a panic-stricken crowd. But the carriages they ordered for their escape to a more distant refuge kept sliding this way and that as the unstable ground lurched and shifted under them, so they were useless. Pliny's mother urged him to go while he could and leave her behind, because she was both older and slower, but Pliny refused. They left the road for fear of being trampled by the frightened crowd coming up behind them.

We had scarcely sat down to rest when darkness fell, not the darkness of a moonless or cloudy night but as if the lamp had been put out in a closed room … Ashes began to fall again, this time in heavy showers. We rose from time to time and shook them off, otherwise we would have been buried and crushed beneath their weight.

So Pliny and his mother changed their minds and determined not to leave the area until they knew what had happened to Pliny's uncle. They rightly feared the worst for him and for themselves.

On the landward side a fearful black cloud was rent by forked and quivering bursts of flame, and parted to reveal great tongues of fire, like flashes of lightning magnified in size … Soon afterwards the cloud sank down to earth and covered the sea. It had already blotted out Capri and hidden the promontory of Misenum from sight.

Eventually a yellowish sun broke through again.

At last the darkness thinned. We were terrified to see everything changed, buried deep in ashes like snowdrifts. We returned to Misenum. My mother and I still had no intention of leaving until we had news of my uncle.

So the danger passed, and unlike his uncle, Pliny survived. The whole incident shows Pliny's almost uncanny instinct for survival when braver and bolder men perish. Pliny's youthful close encounter with death at the hands of a major volcanic eruption lends dramatic colour to his assertion that later in life, when he was in his thirties during the darker years of the reign of the emperor Domitian, he survived on the political scene:

while thunderbolts were dropping all around me [**3.11**].

A metaphor drawn from his narrow escape from Vesuvius came naturally to him – whether accurately or not is another matter (see Chapter 7). All this had happened by the time he reached the age of about 18. But more was yet to happen to him at that early age.

First wife, no children

The other thing that Pliny engaged in at around that same time was marriage. Pliny tells us that he first married when he was still very young – *adulescentulus adhuc* [**1.18**], using the same word, *adulescentulus*, that he applied to his education. Or rather, he tells us that when still so young he already had a mother-in-law, who features in one of his dreams. So one may presume from Pliny's remark that he entered this first marriage at the latest at the age of 18 or 19, maybe no more than two years after his narrow escape from the eruption of Vesuvius – that is, in or about the year 81, and at about the same time that he kicked off his career in the courts at the age of 18. He was probably married to this first wife for at least 15 years before he became a widower and later remarried. The question of whether he went on to have two or three wives will be discussed later (see Chapter 9).

So it is remarkable that we do not know the name of his first wife or anything much about her, except that she bore no children (Pliny never had any children) and that she was the daughter of Pompeia Celerina, whom Pliny continued to refer to as his mother-in-law even after his first wife's death. Despite such a long marriage, Pliny's first wife made almost no impact on his letters, not even to the extent of him mentioning her name. It is similar to the remarkable absence of information about his mother, whose name we may presume to have been Plinia, as the sister of the elder Pliny, though Pliny does not say so. Plinia appears in those letters about the eruption of Vesuvius, but nowhere else. From this silence we may assume that she had died before the dramatic date of any of Pliny's letters, but again he does not say so.

The silence about his first wife may be explained, if not excused, in the same way – that she died before the dramatic date of the letters. But it is still a curious omission, to almost ignore both mother and wife. Some attribute the omission to the very male-oriented society in which Pliny lived. Pliny does, however, tell us a lot more about the wife he later married, Calpurnia, who mattered to him a great deal. Perhaps his first wife just mattered less. Perhaps also, at the time of his first marriage and at that early age of 18, he was more preoccupied with launching his career. His choice of career – as an expert in wills and inheritance – strikes a modern reader as an odd one at first sight. How, where and why did he make that choice?

Starring in the noisy Court of One Hundred Men

To understand Pliny, we must understand the law court in which he founded both this legal and his political career.[1] By the time he reached the age of 18, Pliny was no longer by Roman standards an *adulescentulus*. In addition to entering into his first marriage, he tells us that he also began his professional career when he was 18 [**5.8**], and began it where he meant it to continue, in the court that specialised in inheritance cases, the oddly-named Court of One Hundred Men, the Centumviral Court, often shortened to 'The 100'. What this strange court did, and why he chose it, tells us a lot about Pliny. But what is most remarkable is that, in the same story told in that same letter, he announces not just a double debut, into marriage and into the law courts, but a triple debut, into marriage, into the law courts, and into the inherent political danger of opposing powerful friends of the reigning emperor. Pliny's transition from adolescence to manhood was abrupt and drastic. He really was beginning as he intended – or was fated – to go on.

> I had undertaken to act on behalf of Junius Pastor ... I was very young at the time and was about to plead in the Court of 100 Men against men of great political influence, some of them also friends of the emperor. But I carried on [and] I won my case, and it was that speech that set me on the threshold of a successful career.

So we learn from this one informative letter that he began his career in this law court when still very young, that he began this career in the early years of the reign of the emperor Domitian, and that he began it by challenging opponents who were friends of the emperor and could be dangerous. Most of the rest of Pliny's career sprang from these early beginnings. Challenging already established figures was a standard way of making your name in Roman courts and politics. What is unique about Pliny's letters is that they give us a detailed insight into how this cut-and-thrust of Roman public life actually worked in practice, and how one man navigated its inevitable perils. So why was his chosen public arena that oddly named court, dealing with (to us) private matters of inheritance? Who were the One Hundred Men? What did he and they do?

In an attempt to be helpful by analogy with the present, the conventional description in contemporary reference books in the United Kingdom says that Pliny was called to the Roman Bar, then made his legal career and reputation, and indirectly much of his wealth, as a barrister practising in the Chancery Court of Rome, specialising in inheritance law. An analogy with the legal systems of other modern countries such as the United States would use different terms, such as advocate or legal counsel, but the essence will be the same. But analogies between modern legal systems and Pliny's Rome can be fatally misleading. Pliny did indeed appear in court acting for one side or the other in legal disputes over contested wills, inheritance problems and the interpretation of the laws of succession – in other words, the movement of money, assets, debts and obligations from one generation to the next, triggered by a death. But Rome's equivalent of London's Chancery Court (which, incidentally, deals with a much wider range of legal matters than just inheritance) was very different to any modern court, and Pliny's qualifications for acting in it were very different to those of any modern barrister, advocate or legal counsel.

Pliny's legal qualifications – or his lack of them

For one thing, as we have seen, Pliny had no specific legal training, only a generalist education. He did not go to law school – there weren't any. There was no Bar for him to be called to, symbolically or otherwise. His main qualification for acting in the law courts was that he was an exceptionally good public speaker. Otherwise he just had the same upper-class education as any other offspring of an upper-class Roman family that could afford it. The Romans in their own Latin language had no exact equivalent to barrister or legal counsel. They generally called men like Pliny *causidici* (speakers to a law case) or *patroni* (patrons acting on behalf of their clients in court) or just *togati* (men who wore their toga to court). They distinguished between speakers in court, like Pliny, and the experts in the letter of the law, the *iuridici*, who did not appear in court but if asked offered opinions about what the law said or meant. Some critics of Pliny have therefore dismissed him as a mere spinner of words who made windy speeches but was not a real professional legal expert at all. But that is to underrate both the importance of the court he acted in, and what it took to be successful in it. It also imposes on the Romans notions about professionalism that are appropriate to our own age but not to his.

How Pliny himself got drawn into inheritance law he does not tell us, but can be deduced from how most others got into this branch of the legal profession. Ambitious young men anxious to make their mark quickly, branded as *basilicani* (basilica men, since the hearings were held in a big basilica-style building in the centre of Rome), threw themselves into this court, much to both Cicero's and Pliny's annoyance in their later middle age when they were well past this struggle for early recognition. Pliny complains of their sheer 'effrontery':

> Boys begin their legal career with Centumviral cases just as they start on Homer at school [**2.14**].

It used to be different, he implies, more dignified, in his youth. But Cicero made exactly the same complaint in his day a century and a half earlier,[2] and it is hard to see how else Pliny could have started his own career. He too started in this court when scarcely out of his teens, and started his career by taking on men much more senior than himself. He too was in his day a *basilicanus*, a basilica-man with the gift of the gab and a fierce ambition.

The reason for this (to us) strange situation is that Rome's equivalent of a Chancery Court, by its constitution and by the way it operated, demanded effective public speakers. In fact, and oddly from a modern perspective, apart from the Senate in its capacity as supreme court, it was in Pliny's day the only Roman court that still demanded such oratorical skills. So a man of Pliny's evident ability as a public speaker – and of Pliny's evident ambition to become a senator one day – naturally gravitated towards this court, as did many others. Consequently, it was in the practice of inheritance law, not in the study of it, that Pliny had to learn about inheritance law.

Where 100 may mean 180

The reason for this conjunction, so odd to a modern eye, of inheritance law and public speaking skill is that the Court of One Hundred Men (in Latin the *Centumviri*) was just that – a court with 100 men on the benches, sometimes more. With onlookers and witnesses, there were a lot of people in the courtroom, which was open to the public. In two letters Pliny tells us that the entire list of eligible judge/jurors (the so-called 'album' of names) when assembled to hear an important inheritance case came to a total of not just 100, but a colossal 180 men [**4.24** and **6.33**].³ Even in more routine cases, when the list was divided into four panels for separate trials, Pliny would be addressing over 40 people. That is without adding in the spectators who gathered round to hear the fun in juicier cases. So, far from the hushed and low-key court rooms of today, Pliny could regularly have been addressing several hundred people at a time. This demanded not just oratorical skill but a strong voice, stamina, acting ability and crowd management.

The distinctiveness of the Court of One Hundred Men is further highlighted by comparing it to the modern Chancery Court in London (strictly speaking the Chancery Division of the High Court). This court has no jury at all. Cases are heard by a single judge, a *unus iudex* as the Romans would have called him. So it is startling at first sight that the Romans did not use a single judge in inheritance cases also. Inheritance disputes are often detailed, complex and legalistic, hardly suitable (one might think) for settlement by the majority vote of a large and probably emotional crowd of men acting (as we shall see) as both jury and judge. The Romans used the single judge in many other legal situations. Why not in inheritance?

At the sign of the spear

The origins and functions of the Court of One Hundred Men have been the subject of fierce debates between scholars. The court dated far back into Rome's history, a venerable institution whose very age and prestige may partly explain its survival to the days of Pliny and beyond, and partly explains why it was such a desirable place for a rising orator to show his talents. You were linking in to the exalted past. Its exact origins are however a mystery. Its symbol, displayed to announce that the court was in session, was the *hasta*, the spear. The spear became a synonym for the court itself. The poet Martial refers to:

> the solemn spear of the Hundred Men.⁴

Martial incidentally also wrote lines directly referring to Pliny working on his speeches for the ears of the Hundred Men, lines of which Pliny seems to have been rather proud, because he quotes them in one of his letters.⁵ Another poet, Statius, wrote the line:

> idle stands the spear that rules the hundred judges.⁶

Why the spear, nobody knows. The spear was used to signify auctions of enemy or confiscated property, equivalent perhaps to 'going under the hammer'. But how it got to be attached to the Court of One Hundred Men is as unclear as many other aspects of this strange institution. What is still puzzling to a modern inquirer is why this rather mysterious but specialist court, hearing disputes over inheritance, should have been such a focus of public attention at Rome and the scene of such TV-like courtroom dramas, antagonisms and soap operas, as narrated by Pliny with his evident gift for storytelling. Within the complex apparatus of modern legal systems, inheritance law is not only a highly specialised branch of private law but also one which only rarely hits the newspaper headlines or television screens. Such limelight tends be reserved for high-profile criminal trials and reaches the inheritance court only in exceptionally nasty or lurid cases. Not so in the Rome of Pliny's day. The Court of One Hundred Men sat in public, almost as regular street theatre, open to the scrutiny and enjoyment of all, with its star performers and bare-knuckle legal brawls.

The noise of the crowd

The scene for these Roman inheritance disputes was the Basilica Iulia, a large multi-storey building running all along the south-west side of the Forum, right in the heart of Rome. Several trials might have been in progress at the same time, in opposite corners of the rectangular Basilica. On top of that, each court was open to any member of the public to enter and listen – and applaud or boo. Often audience members were actually hired and paid to go along and cheer one side or the other in the case, and no doubt barrack the other side. Then there was the weather. If not exactly open-sided, the colonnades of the Basilica must have been an echoing place, subject to the climate of the day, hot, wet or windy. Roman writers themselves tell us of the hubbub and high noise level of the Court of One Hundred Men. Pliny himself makes weary comments about it, as well he might. The scene was as different as could be to the clinical and orderly atmosphere of an enclosed modern courtroom. The elder Seneca tells us:

> speakers have to concentrate and struggle to make their voices reach the judges' ears amid the competing hubbub of the throng.[7]

Quintilian reminisces:

> I well remember when he [Trachalus] was speaking in the Basilica Julia before Tribunal One and, as usual, four juries were being empanelled and there was

total uproar everywhere, he could nevertheless be heard and understood and (what was most galling for the other advocates) he was actually applauded in all four tribunals.[8]

Writing long after Pliny's day, and in a satire that must have had some relation to the truth (for otherwise satire does not work), Macrobius was highly critical of drunken judges who were so full of wine that they had to urinate all the time, both on the way to court and during the proceedings, and were then too sleepy to read the evidence and instead complained about the litigants:

Why should I be bothered with these silly people?[9]

Pliny himself, perhaps in a similar fit of exasperation, uses a private letter to his friend Novius Maximus to give vent to his own frustrations.

Audiences follow who are no better than the speakers, being hired and bought for the occasion. They parley with the contractor, take the gifts offered on the floor of the court as openly as they would at a dinner party, and move on from case to case for the same sort of pay. The Greek name for them is 'bravo-callers' and the Latin 'dinner-clappers' … Yesterday two of my attendants were induced to add their applause for three *denarii* each. For this sum seats can be filled, a huge crowd assembled, and endless cheering raised whenever the chorus-master gives the signal [2.14].[10]

Yet for all that, or perhaps because of it, Pliny admits in another letter to Valerius Paulinus that he really enjoys it all. It is grand theatre, *grand guignol*, right at the heart of the Roman Empire, and he loves being a star in it.

Rejoice on my account and yours: oratory is still held in honour. When I was on my way the other day to plead before the Court, there was no room left for me to take my place except by way of the judges' benches, through their assembled ranks, as the rest of the floor was so crowded [4.16].

Pliny then spoke for no less than seven hours, remarking in his letter:

It is for us to produce something worth being written and heard.

In other words, you had to give the crowd their money's worth. A 10-minute presentation would not do at all. Notice also his conjunction of 'written' and 'heard'. Pliny spoke his speeches, and afterwards distributed edited copies of the best of them, in pursuit of his ambitions as a literary man (see Chapters 12 and 13). In another case, an elderly man of high rank had disinherited his daughter Attia Viriola in favour of a new wife he had brought home. So the daughter sued.

Pliny acted for Attia. He tells us that all 180 men, all four panels, assembled to hear the case, and that both parties

> had a large number of seats filled with their supporters, and a close-packed ring of onlookers several rows deep lined the walls of the courtroom. The bench was also crowded, and even the galleries were full of men and women leaning over in their eagerness to see and also to hear, though hearing was rather more difficult [**6.33**].

This was clearly a celebrity trial of its day, maybe a test of women's rights, and Pliny enjoyed being the focus of the crowd. No other courtroom of Pliny's day offered such theatricals. No wonder Pliny refers to this court as 'his arena' (*harena*, literally 'the sand', just as in the floor of the amphitheatre where gladiators slugged it out) [**6.12**]. As a footnote to this case, Pliny tells us the curious fact that the four panels voted by panel – in other words, as if they were four separate juries. Then two panels voted for his side, two for the other side. Presumably there must have been a way out of this deadlock. But it opens up a possibility that on a simple head count a majority of the jurors might have voted one way, but the division by panel might have pushed the verdict the other way. Infuriatingly, Pliny does not tell us what the final verdict was in this case. Did Attia get her money? We shall never know.

Judge *and* jury

Here we must add a further strong word of caution. We must be very careful about the names and terms used to translate Rome's legal system into modern usage. As with the care needed in calling Pliny a 'barrister' or any equivalent in other modern legal systems, so too we must be careful about the use of modern words like 'jury', 'jurors' and 'judges', particularly in this remarkable and idiosyncratic Court of One Hundred Men. At Rome, in this law court at least, there was no such thing as a judge separate from a jury. Translators sometimes refer to the 'jurors' in this court, and sometimes to the 'judges' – confusingly, since these were one and the same people. The panels of men who, in trying to be helpful, we may call 'juries', were not juries at all in the modern sense. The panels were both judge and jury.

They not only found for or against a defendant, a bit like a modern jury, by majority vote. But they also decided the outcome – the penalty or award or settlement, again presumably by majority vote, as in the case cited above. Who exactly these judge/jurors were is not certain. But they were probably drawn from the equestrian class, like the boards of jurors, each a thousand strong, set up by the emperor Augustus in his reforms of the judicial apparatus in the earliest days of the empire. The judge/jurors in the Court of One Hundred Man may have been a sub-set of these boards.

So we see that the Court of One Hundred Men was quite different to anything known in modern law courts. There was no presiding judge to sum up and guide the jurors. The judge/juror panels in this Roman court did not retire to consider their verdict in peace and privacy, like a modern jury. They voted there and then, amid all that hubbub. In other words, the panel of 40 or more men drawn from the list of those servicing the Court of One Hundred Men was all-powerful in each particular case, and onto them Pliny would have had to concentrate his entire rhetorical skills to get the result he wanted – as too did the opposing legal team. Justice, even for the rich whose wealth made it worthwhile to enter into these costly disputes over inheritance, must have been a hit-or-miss affair, where the right counsel speaking on your behalf was crucial – send for Pliny, if you can afford him, or if he owes you a favour. But what hope then for the common man in the Romans scales of justice?

Pliny as mediator

In other contexts we do hear of justice being administered by a single judge, the *unus iudex*. But he could be more like an official arbitrator, indeed was often referred to as *iudex arbiterve*, a judge-cum-arbiter, a respected person (probably from the upper educated class) chosen from an official list (the *album*) and asked to mediate and resolve a dispute, if necessary by order, at what was probably a private hearing in a room in his house, away from the noise and distraction of the crowds.[11] Indeed, Pliny himself, with his legal experience, was often asked or expected to act as mediator or arbitrator, either between quarreling tenants on his various estates, or as in one curious case where he was asked to adjudicate on a complaint by a friend called Curianus who had been disinherited by his mother, even though Pliny himself was one of the other beneficiaries of that same lady's will. Wisely, Pliny took on two advisers to help him avoid the charge of partiality. Pliny ended up by giving his share of the legacy to the complainant Curianus in the name of fairness – only to get it back again when Curianus died and left him a legacy in *his* will [5.1].

How extensive Pliny's private mediation practice as judge-arbiter was, we have no idea. But as a man of standing – a *bonus vir* in Roman legal parlance, a recognised 'good man' you could turn to for mediation – he may have been in demand. The role of the *bonus vir* was 'commonplace and pervasive' in Roman society.[12] If so, this side of Pliny's career figures far less in his letters than the *grand guignol* of the open court.

Sideshow or the only show in town?

Pliny's letters give the impression that the Court of One Hundred Men was not just the best courtroom show in town, but the only one. However, in face of the apparent hurly-burly and even chaos that attended this court, many modern scholars have refused to believe that the Court of One Hundred Men was anything other than a bizarre sideshow to the real practice of Roman law. In this (they believe) the single judge was the key player, a magisterial figure upholding across the centuries the full majesty of that great edifice of Roman jurisprudence which found its final expression in the monumental sixth-century Law Codes of the great Byzantine Emperor Justinian. These Codes in turn had a profound influence on the later legal systems of all western Europe, and still sit at the back of legal systems in places like France and Scotland. How can all this have been built upon the crude histrionics of the Court of One Hundred Men? If this view is correct, it not only demotes the Hundred Men to a sideshow, it also demotes Pliny to a self-trumpeting bit player in this sideshow. But was it like that?

A remark by the writer and orator Tacitus, both a friend of Pliny and a legal colleague who himself used his oratorical powers in the Court of One Hundred Men, has been seized upon in support of this derogatory view of that court. In his *Dialogue on Oratory*, written about 102 but set in the years 74–5, Tacitus puts into the mouth of his character Maternus the opinion that:

> actions before the Centumvirate Court, which are now considered to outrank all others, used to be so much overshadowed by the prestige of other tribunals that there is not a single speech delivered before that court that is read today, either by Cicero or by Caesar or by Brutus or by Caelius or by Calvus, or in fact by any orator of rank.

This remark by Tacitus feeds into a wider traditional view that in the glory days of the Roman Republic men were men and made great speeches in the Senate and elsewhere because they had freedom of public expression, whereas under the degenerate dictatorial Empire they were muzzled and had nowhere better to use their oratorical skills than in this bizarre sideshow in the inheritance court. But, as so often in writing about Roman history, there are political overtones to debates about apparently practical details of procedure.

The fact is that the great Cicero himself, in the heyday of Roman oratory, spoke in the Court of One Hundred Men. His greatest prosecution and defence speeches may have been made elsewhere, in pursuit of a political career that was not open to Pliny or Tacitus in the changed and heavily restricted circumstances of the empire, but even so, that court was a respectable part of the Roman judicial system, worthy even of Cicero. It too required his great oratorical skills. He too enjoyed

> the crowd that collected, the anticipation aroused

by his appearances there.[13] But surely, ask the critics, in order to be worthy of the attention of the great Cicero as well as the less great Pliny, the court must at least have had a much wider remit and scope than just the dry clauses of some deceased person's will?

Remit of the court

The question therefore is, what was the exact scope and remit of this court? What were the subjects that Pliny had to know about in order to 'give judgement and wisdom to the Hundred', as Statius wrote of another advocate, Rutilius Gallicus?[14] About this, there has also been controversy. If the court was not just a sideshow, surely it must have had much broader jurisdiction than just inheritance? Cicero is brought into this argument also, in particular his comments in his long essay *About the Orator* listing the legal matters under review in the Court of One Hundred Men. Cicero's list is a long one.

> Usucapion [ownership by right of long possession], guardianship, clan membership, children born after a will is made, land expanded by sediment and silt, land formed mid-river, creditor–debtor obligations, property conveyancing, walls [party walls?], lighting, roof drainage, wills witnessed or contravened, and innumerable other things.[15]

This may suggest that a wide range of financial, property and land disputes also came under the jurisdiction of this strange court. If so, it would have been kept very busy. The modern Chancery Court in London also has a very wide remit.

It does deal with validity of wills (contentious probate), the administration of estates of deceased persons, trusts and the Inheritance Act. But its main business is elsewhere, covering insolvency, patents, intellectual property rights, breach of trust, charities and much else. Is there a rough analogy with Rome, showing a court with much wider responsibility than just wills and inheritance?

But no Roman author talks of the court in any context other than inheritance, and what Cicero almost certainly meant by his list is that, in order to speak with authority on inheritance rights, a 'barrister' like himself or like Pliny had to display and bring to bear a wide range of knowledge about incidental and relevant matters that commonly crop up in inheritance cases, which are rarely simple. If the court's basic remit were much wider than that, Pliny – a vain man – would surely not have passed up the opportunity to show off the impressive range of his expertise. But he does not. It is all about inheritance.

In a similar tone of disbelief, some analysts of Roman law have argued that there must have been a floor limit, a minimum sum below which inheritance cases did not go to this heavyweight court but were dealt with by simpler means, maybe by a single judge (a *unus iudex*). The trouble is that Pliny does not say so. Indeed, on the contrary, he complains about his time being wasted on trivial cases (*parvae et exiles*) [**2.14**]. He never refers to a floor limit, although it must be possible that for minor cases the judge/jury panels were far smaller than 40 in number. Only once does he refer to a case in which there was an attempt to settle out of court by negotiation. After failure to agree, even that case was then referred to the court [**5.1**]. When it came to money, and given the close connection between money and status, apparently nothing was too trivial for this court.

Under the eye of the emperor

The court was also important enough to warrant the attention of successive Roman emperors. Its magnetism for the crowds, and its importance in Rome's highly stratified social structure, may explain why successive emperors thought it necessary to intervene in its operations – and why for Pliny the court became an avenue for promotion to the very top of the social pyramid. Among the wide-ranging administrative reforms introduced by the first emperor Augustus was a change in the management of the Court of One Hundred Men. Suetonius (for whom, incidentally, Pliny acted in this court) tells us that the court used to be convened by men who had been *quaestors*, that is, men who had climbed some way up the Roman ladder of public office. Instead, Augustus shifted this task onto a group of men called the Board of Ten.[16]

The Latin name for them was *Decemviri Stlitibus Iudicandis,* and this archaic language (as in *stlitibus*) suggests both ancient origins and a wide jurisdiction, something like 'The Ten Men for Judging Law Cases'. The Ten were, however, just the remnant of a larger body that did once have much wider responsibilities, but were confined by Augustus to the Court of One Hundred Men. The Board of Ten were not presiding judges in the modern sense, but simply saw to it that the panels of judge/jurors were convened and properly chosen. They were minor magistrates, but with significant powers and a staff to force witnesses to come to court.[17] The significance of this body for Pliny's career is that he quickly became one of these same *Decemviri*, and his appointment to that office was the first step in his climb up the Roman ladder of public and political office and the ladder of social status[18] (see Chapter 7). So professionally, politically and socially, Pliny's power base was in the rough-and-tumble of this strange court, perhaps the nearest that Rome got to the bear-garden of a modern parliamentary debating chamber.

The importance of the Court of One Hundred Men was again demonstrated when the emperor Vespasian moved to reduce a huge backlog of law cases that had built up by appointing more men both to the Court of One Hundred Men and to other tribunals. These extra men were given 'extraordinary jurisdiction' because, says Suetonius, the lifetimes of the litigants were not long enough to get through their cases by normal proceedings.[19] Even the emperor Domitian, no favourite of Suetonius, comes in for praise for his attempts to keep the judicial system on course. Suetonius says:

> Domitian applied himself conscientiously to the dispensation of justice, frequently holding additional hearings on the tribunal in the Forum. He overturned judgements of the Court of One Hundred Men which had been biased by favouritism ... jurors who took bribes he demoted along with all their colleagues.[20]

Whether or not it was a good thing to have the emperor overturning court judgements may be open to discussion. But Domitian's actions do show what abuses, including bribery, Pliny may have been up against in arguing his cases. The direct interventions of emperors like Vespasian and Domitian confirm the importance of this court, while making some cases particularly difficult to manage – would any jury dare go against the emperor's wishes, whatever the rights and wrongs?

Why One Hundred (or so) Men?

Domitian's intervention also casts doubt on one of the modern theories put forward to explain why this ancient but cumbersome court retained its role and shape. Some suggest that it was to prevent bribery. It was much harder, surely, to bribe 40 men, let alone 180, than just one man, the *unus iudex*. But clearly Domitian thought that some had been bribed, and punished them for it. Cicero singles out favouritism, political power and bribery as factors that perverted verdicts.[21] Another theory is that revenge was more difficult for an aggrieved litigant if revenge had to be against 40 or 180 men. Perhaps. But no Roman author says so. We must look elsewhere for the possible rationale for the creation and survival of this bafflingly un-modern court.

The most plausible explanation is that the central objective of much Roman legislation was the fixing of financial compensation for a wrong committed, a penalty expressed not as (for example) imprisonment, which the Romans did not use as punishment, but as the right of the successful party legally to seize money or assets from the losing party, by force if necessary, there being no regular police force to do that job. Financial reparation was the central feature of the high-level extortion trials before the Senate in which Pliny was later to figure so prominently (see Chapter 6). This type of financial penalty is obviously not appropriate for cases of disputed inheritance, where there is no verdict of guilt or innocence and the important thing is to preserve assets and obligations to be handed on to the right party.

This might explain the existence of a separate court for inheritance matters, but not its size. That is attributed (subject however to much argument) to the complicated family and clan (or tribe) structure of Roman society, which meant that large numbers of people had an interest in how and to whom property was handed on. With the assets named in a will there also came obligations, such as donations, freeing of loyal slaves, debts to third parties, and religious and family obligations and responsibilities to the extended household and to the clan. Inheritance disputes today can be notoriously acrimonious, marked by bitter disappointment felt by one side or the other.

Inherited obligations could also be crippling. Not for nothing did Latin authors refer to *damnosa hereditas*, the penalties of inheritance. Many must have tried to get out of inheritance rather than accept it, but *semel heres, semper heres* (once an heir, always an heir) went the Latin legal tag.[22] A large and representative court may have seemed to the Romans the best way to ensure that all aspects of a disputed will were examined and settled in the least-worst way and to the satisfaction of the wider community. Such matters evidently roused great public interest, as the statistics below show, and created a lucrative career opportunity for Pliny and other talented lawyers. The numbers of jurymen and of cases show just how central a part the inheritance court played in the Roman legal system.

The statistics of Roman litigation

J. M. Kelly carried out a detailed analysis of the sixth-century Emperor Justinian's famous Digest of Roman law, which cites cases going back hundreds of years.[23] Looking first at the *responsa*, roughly equivalent to the modern 'counsel's opinion', he stripped out those to do with criminal law, state business like tax or the army, and pure procedure. The result was, from the Pliny perspective, startling. Of the 1,306 citations left, this was the breakdown:

Succession cases (wills, legacies, donations etc.)	761
Contract	288
Family law	114
Property	85
Free/slave status	33

Analysis of *rescripta*, basically decisions of the emperor carrying the force of law, showed a similar pattern. Of 414 citations, 257 were about matters of succession. Kelly comments:

> Probably no greater contrast could be found between the litigation patterns of the ancient world and the modern world … given how distressing it must have been to have family affairs aired in public, at the mercy of your opponent's barrister, the weight of succession cases is all the more remarkable.

Again unlike a modern court, character assassination of the opposing side was part and parcel of a Roman lawyer's armoury of attack weapons, and was part of the fun of these trials for the general public who came to listen, though it was much less fun for participants. The Court of One Hundred Men was anything but a marginal phenomenon in Roman society and law.

What Pliny earned as a lawyer

So did a high-profile court like that and a string of well-to-do clients also mean high fees for counsel? That Pliny inherited money and houses from his uncle and adoptive father, the elder Pliny, is clear enough (see Chapters 10 and 11). That he ended up much richer than he began is also clear from his descriptions of his out-of-town estates and his donations to friends and to his birth-place, Comum. But did he make that new money from his legal practice? Did Roman advocates earn fees? If not, where did Pliny's extra wealth come from?

Pliny himself refers to the furore aroused in Rome when the presiding *praetor* (the *praetor* was a public office, in time held by Pliny himself, whose incumbent could refer cases to the court and had overall responsibility for the proper operation of the courts in Rome) sent a message to the inheritance court when it was about to sit, reminding them of the decree of the Senate forbidding the taking of fees. Pliny quotes the decree as stipulating:

> All persons bringing cases before the court are hereby required to state on oath before their case is heard that they have neither paid, promised, nor guaranteed any sum to any person for his legal assistance [**5.9**].

The consternation that this caused suggests that it was a rule more honoured in the breach than in the observance. The case was postponed, the court officials were puzzled about what to do next, and the *praetor*, named Nepos, was criticised for setting himself up as a guardian of public morals. Who does he think he is? asked his critics. Pliny, however, takes Nepos's side. Nepos had

> put a check on disgraceful bargaining and [would] not allow a noble profession to sell its services in this scandalous way.

Tell that to a modern lawyer. Pliny does, however, add this rider:

> The buying and selling of counsel's services were expressly forbidden; but permission was given, after a case was settled, for clients to give their counsel a sum not exceeding 10,000 sesterces.

So it might be supposed that Pliny regularly picked up post-verdict gifts of 10,000 sesterces from grateful clients, at least if he won their case. But he says not. In another letter Pliny amplifies the *praetor*'s message by quoting a statement by another official, a tribune of the people, complaining that:

> counsel sold their services, faked lawsuits for money, settled them by collusion,

and made a boast of the large regular income to be made by robbery of their fellow citizens [**5.13**].

The tribune's complaint is the occasion for Pliny to display his own clean hands.

> How glad I am that I have always kept clear of any contracts, presents, remuner-ation, or even small gifts for my conduct of cases!

So we may conclude that lots of *basilicani* and *togati* made big money directly from their legal practice, illicitly or otherwise. There was no disciplinary body (except perhaps the emperor) with powers to disbar them for breaching the rules. But if we are to believe Pliny, that was not how he made his fortune. He made no money at all, he claims. All he got for his clean hands policy, he says, was teasing from his friends that the Senate's decree was solely aimed at him and his 'robberies and greed'. So, while we cannot accuse Pliny of telling lies about not taking fees and gifts, we must nevertheless suppose that grateful clients found other, legal ways of expressing their gratitude, in their wills perhaps or in reciprocal favours. But the general allegations made about case fixing and corruption in the courts, coupled with the repeated hints of bribery made by Cicero and others, do not augur well for the larger question of whether less well-off Roman citizens had much hope of objective justice.

Informers and ambulance chasers

Perhaps even more remarkable than the packed benches of judge/jurors and rowdy spectators at inheritance trials is that the Court of One Hundred Men was also the arena in which potentially dangerous political animosities were played out, either to the benefit or detriment of the litigants. Pliny refers to people who were reluctant to appeal to this court:

> They feared the fate they had seen overtake many another – that they might leave the Court of One Hundred Men with a criminal charge against them [**5.1**].

Under a suspicious emperor like Domitian, this apparently mundane court could be dangerous. It was liable to be the stage on which played some of the most notorious actors in the imperial puppet theatre, the professional informers, the *delatores*, men out to make personal gain from proving that a will was invalid. If successful, their fee – a percentage – would be paid out of the estate of the deceased. This hunt for pickings from a person's will, if carried on outside the courts, was known as *captatio* – legacy hunting – and was so endemic that a man who hunted legacies merited a special name, *captator*. In court, family matters as well as political matters came under attack (perhaps simultaneously) from this type of informer. This is perhaps another reason why inheritors needed skilled men like Pliny to help protect them from such attacks.

> As was the case under the Republic, in the imperial period *delatores* took advantage of laws concerning wills and inheritances … *Delatores* were notorious for contesting the legitimacy of inheritances in particular; the successful prosecutor could enrich himself, and the imperial treasury as well, since legacies deemed unlawful could result in the confiscation of the entire inheritance by the imperial *fiscus* (treasury), with a share going to the accuser.[24]

Apart from pure validity under the law, there were other complications of which informers could take pernicious advantage. For example, they contested wills which omitted the emperor as heir to part of the estate. It was a mark of respect to leave a gift to the emperor in your will; in deed it was almost a compulsory gift, since lack of it could be interpreted as treason. It was a sinister practice to which the emperor Claudius put at least a temporary stop. The historian Dio tells us that, in 41, Claudius ruled that no one who had legitimate heirs should name him as heir, and in 43 ruled out of court hostile allegations against people who had received citizenship during his reign but had not included him in their will. Dio also says that the short-reigning emperor Vitellius refused to disallow the wills of men who had fought against him and had died in the fight.[25] Suetonius confirms that at first the emperor Domitian took Claudius's line and:

> when inheritances were left to him by people who had children, he would not accept them … False accusations which aimed at the confiscation of property he punished, imposing severe penalties on the accusers.

Later, however, when things went wrong, Domitian changed his tune, says Suetonius:

> The estates of complete strangers were seized if one person could be found who claimed to have heard the deceased, when living, say that the emperor was his heir.[26]

So under Domitian *delatores* were once again active in the Court of One Hundred Men, and wills again became 'political'. Some argue that Pliny and Tacitus are wrong in their judgement about this alleged insecurity of wills under Domitian, and that Domitian just wanted to be mentioned in his friends' wills as a gesture of *fides*, due respect. Nevertheless it is clear that, in general, depending on the emperor's attitude, the validity of wills could be attacked by third parties, for potential gain, on a wide range of semi-political charges.

> Our sources may be taking out on Domitian what was actually a perennial and annoying reality in Rome, the persistence of *delatores* in denouncing wills rendered invalid in one way or another.[27]

The tax on Jews

In a context where normal tax-collection was at best erratic, going after rich men's property – and some of them were very rich indeed – was a perennial temptation for emperors in need of cash, and informers, *delatores*, were instruments for such raids on private assets. Such raids could take manifold forms. For example, *delatores* may have attacked alleged tax evasion in the area of inheritance, notably the 5 per cent estate tax (*vicesima hereditatum*). They also targeted the tax on Jews, instituted by the emperor Titus. Suetonius says that, under Domitian,

> the tax on Jews, in particular, was exacted with the greatest rigour. Those who lived as Jews without being registered as such were indicted, as were those who concealed their origins and did not pay the tax imposed on their race.[28]

Suetonius then tells the story of one old man who was forced to expose himself to a judge to prove whether or not he was circumcised. Among the wealthier classes of Rome, inheritance was no simple matter, and was in Pliny's earlier years inextricably mixed up with personal rivalries and political manoeuvers. To be an inheritance lawyer was also to be mixed up with wider matters of state, as Pliny's career was to prove. This emotive background explains why Pliny, in the panegyric to the emperor Trajan which he delivered early in Trajan's reign, singles out for praise (in a phrase that sounds odd to modern ears)

> the new security of wills.[29]

For the Roman moneyed classes, this new security of wills under Trajan was an important social and political gain. Far from being a sideshow, Pliny was operating in a particularly sensitive section of the Roman legal system where politics and the law overlapped and collided. It needed a man of resource and prudence to navigate and survive in this slippery arena of shifting sands. You could not always separate the law court from the emperor's court. Those men of ill-fame, the *delatores* who would denounce both rich men and their wills indifferently, were common to both, the techniques the same. To be a leading light in the inheritance court was also to be involved in Roman-style politics. This may partly explain why Pliny took both paths simultaneously, a career at law and a career up the ladder of political status. If one, then both.

Enter Regulus, anti-hero

One *delator* whose activities were finally curtailed by this new security of wills under Trajan was a man who had previously made a career and an immense fortune by going after both political victims in the Senate and other people's wills and inheritances in the Court of One Hundred Men. He is the half-sinister, half-comic villain of Pliny's letters, that extraordinary character called Regulus. Pliny repeatedly sparred with him both in court and in the Senate, and in his letters holds him up as the anti-hero whose vices serve by contrast to sharpen Pliny's virtues. Yet he was in many ways remarkably similar to Pliny. To understand Pliny, we need to understand Regulus.

Sparring with Regulus and 'the most immoral fraud'

Towards the beginning of the emperor Trajan's reign, around the year 99, when Pliny was in his late thirties, there took place at Rome an extraordinary scene of either well-deserved retribution or hysterical lynch-mob revenge, depending on how you look at it. This retribution/revenge was visited upon the most hated group of men in Rome, the informers, the *delatores*, men who made a living from ferreting out and reporting to the authorities potentially damaging information about men with money or status, and earning a reward for doing so, often in the form of a large chunk of the victim's assets. In the panegyric that he delivered in praise of Trajan, Pliny positively gloats over the fate of these figures from the shadows of Roman life. They were rounded up, bound, displayed in the amphitheatre for the massed spectators to yell insults at, put on boats, and cast adrift on the open sea.

This is Pliny's account, spitting uncharacteristic venom at these now safe targets – safe, because the new emperor, Trajan, unlike some of his predecessors, would have no truck with them:

> There we saw the informers marched in, like a band of robbers or brigands. Nothing was so popular as the opportunity we enjoyed of looking down at the informers at our feet, their heads forced back and faces upturned to meet our gaze [then] they were led to long-lasting punishment and retribution. Ships were hastily produced and they were crowded on board and abandoned to the hazards of wind and weather, a whole fleet of informers thrown to the mercy of every wind. What joy for us to watch the ships scattered as soon as they left harbour ... The real criminals were nailed to the rocks which had been the cross of many an innocent man: the islands where senators were exiled were crowded with informers.[1]

This vivid scene of hatred, revenge and undisguised gloating contrasts with the normally ultra-polite tone that Pliny adopts in his letters – except when talking about Regulus. Trajan was neither the first nor probably the last newly installed Roman emperor to seek immediate popularity by exacting state-sponsored punishment on such men. But their activities and rewards derived from the needs and insecurities of the state itself – that is, of the emperor in power at the time. They were more a symptom than a cause. The men rounded up and cast adrift by Trajan were most probably the smaller fry of the informer game, men who had little defence when a new regime turned against them. Notably absent from the boats dashed on the shores of rocky islands were any men of rank, any senators – such as Regulus. Yet senators too had sought imperial favour, political advancement and huge material reward by denouncing fellow senators to the emperor and bringing them to trial and condemnation, on trumped-up or exaggerated charges. An exhaustive list of all the upper-class informers and prosecutors that we know about from the time of the emperor Tiberius to the time of the emperor Domitian – roughly the first century CE – consists of a total of 109 names, who between them were party to 155 known or probable prosecutions – not far off two a year.[2]

Sinister buffoon

Among such senatorial informers, the most notorius, thanks to Pliny, is his fellow lawyer, Regulus. This sinister figure stalks the pages of Pliny's letters, part-buffoon, part-criminal, destructive, dangerous, morally dubious, elusive, untouchable, unscrupulous – and immensely wealthy. Or so Pliny tells us. Pliny hated and feared him. The fear and hatred was mutual. Regulus was a generation older than Pliny, well established in his chosen profession by the time Pliny entered the law courts. Regulus had been a part of or indeed the direct provocateur of some of the most famous political show-trials of his time. He may have regarded Pliny as an upstart compared to himself, or seen him as a potential victim. During the first half of Pliny's professional career, for 15 years or so, he and Regulus sparred and circled round each other like Roman gladiators, in court, in the Senate, before the emperor, but neither was able to go for the kill – literally, since the end-game might have been the death or at least exile and financial ruin of one or the other of them.

But Regulus himself was never brought to trial for his alleged misdeeds. When he had the chance, after the fall of Regulus's last major patron, the emperor Domitian, Pliny flunked the task. It was left to Pliny's writings and those of Pliny's friend, the historian Tacitus, to deliver the final thrusts on

Regulus after his death. Their writings are in effect a posthumous prosecution of Regulus substituting for a real one. They have made Regulus the most notorious of Rome's feared tribe of informers and private prosecutors who specialised in earning rewards – some say blood money – by bringing down the rich and the powerful, with a lucrative sideline in disputing wills for a reward, and in outright legacy hunting. Pliny particularly notes their targeting of wills, as he would do as a specialist in inheritance law. A man who targeted wills even merited a special name, a *captator*. Pliny accuses Regulus of 'the most immoral fraud there is' in his unscrupulous hunt for legacies.

> No will was safe from these men … [but now under Trajan] the Treasury is no longer a mortuary and a grim repository for blood-soaked spoils.[3]

Men like Regulus were closely associated with the political witch-hunts that shook upper-class Roman society in the century or so up to Pliny's day. They were the clearest symptom of a political system in which there was no independent state prosecution service, no independent judiciary, no clearly defined professional body to set judicial standards, no police force to detect and prosecute crime. A man like Regulus was, to his enemies like Pliny, a Judas Iscariot figure, earning his 30 pieces of silver by betraying or compromising people more eminent, more distinguished than himself. The shadow of Judas has hovered over Regulus ever since. When Regulus died, Pliny's verdict on him was terse, harsh, unforgiving:

> Regulus did well to die and would have done better to die sooner [**6.2**].

Pliny also quotes with approval a remark by a colleague:

> Modestus said in a letter which was read out before [the emperor] Domitian that Regulus was 'the vilest of two-legged creatures'. Modestus never wrote a truer word! [**1.5**]

What brings Regulus to life for modern readers, however, is not so much Pliny's vitriol as his vivid and satirical portrait of Regulus in action. Because of, or despite, his antipathy towards Regulus, Pliny also portrays him as a buffoon, a comic actor in court, a master of theatrical effects.

> He used to be pale with anxiety, would write out his speeches though he could never learn them by heart, paint round one of his eyes – the right one if he was appearing for the plaintiff and the left one if for the defendant – change a white patch over from one eyebrow to the other, and never fail to consult the sooth-sayers on the results of his case [**6.2**].

Then again:

> He has weak lungs, indistinct articulation, and a stammer, he is slow at finding
> the right word and has no memory, nothing in fact but a perverted ingenuity,
> and yet his crazy effrontery has won him the popular reputation as being an
> orator [**4.7**].

This pen-portrait once again shows Pliny's excellent eye for detail and storytelling. It may also contain a hint of admiration. Whatever else, Regulus was
quite a character, making Pliny look a bit dull and prim by comparison. But they
say that the Devil gets the best tunes. Precisely because Pliny devotes so much
hostile comment to Regulus, he stands out from Pliny's pages like a coloured
pop-up, more vivid than Pliny himself, as an emblematic actor in Rome's first
century of troubled autocracy and with lessons for posterity. Does he deserve
the implicit verdict of Tacitus, backed up by Pliny, that men like him brought
ruin on the empire?

In search of revenge?

So who exactly was this sinister buffoon Regulus? His full name was Marcus
Aquilius Regulus, and thanks to Pliny and Tacitus he is by far the most
notorious – and some say, misunderstood – of the 'dreaded tribe' of informers
and legacy hunters. Much is vague about his origins. He may have been
descended from the old Republican nobility, and so be superior to Pliny in the
Roman aristocratic caste system. Working back from the date when Regulus
launched his first prosecutions against prominent men, he must have been born
between 40 and 45, so probably during the reign of Claudius (41–54 CE). That
makes him Pliny's senior by about 20 years. We know that he had a younger
half-brother, Vipstanus Messalla, who came to his defence when he was attacked
in the Senate for his (mis)deeds. The high standing of his family is shown not
only by his half-brother also being a senator, but also by Regulus's own marriage
to Caepia Procula, daughter or possibly sister of a man who was proconsul of
Baetica (southern Spain) in 95, consul in 102 or 103, and proconsul of Asia.
Regulus was well-connected.

We do not know for sure who his father was. But he may have been a man
who held high office under the emperor Tiberius and who had been sent into
exile by the emperor Nero, with the result that his assets were lost, divided up
between his creditors. In short, Regulus was probably the son of a man exiled

and ruined. What is certain is that, as a young man around the age of 20 – much the same age that Pliny began his career in the courts – Regulus launched a series of prosecutions that brought down and caused the death of senators of high status. It was a campaign far more destructive than the normal public debut of a budding orator.

This campaign may have been motivated by his family having been ruined by the troubles visited upon his possible father, and Regulus may have been using these prosecutions, and the rewards they brought if successful, as a way of restoring his or his family's fortunes and/or as revenge. It certainly made his fortune. Pliny says that Regulus clambered out of poverty and achieved wealth by these dubious means [2.20]. Regulus's most vocal critic in the Senate, Montanus, put it another way. In the year 70 Montanus claimed that, because Regulus was already wealthy and did not need the money, he must have been motivated by something much worse than normal ambition – by greed and a thirst for blood. So the theory that he came from a distinguished family ruined by dimly perceived political events and then sought both revenge and restoration of family fortunes by this ruthless means is plausible but unable to be proved.

Regulus the prosecutor

The early career of Regulus as a youthful prosecutor and informer certainly merited the epithet 'thirst for blood'. This was, to use a modern phrase, 'predatory litigation'.

> As under the Republic, the normal method for an ambitious man to secure distinction and advancement was through the conduct of a successful prosecution ... Hence arose the dreaded tribe of prosecutors and informers.[4]

In the reign of Nero, Regulus successfully undertook the prosecution of no less than three eminent men of consular rank. One prosecution was against Marcus Licinius Crassus Frugi, consul in 64, who was put to death between 66 and 68. Sometime before 65 it was the turn of Servius Cornelius Salvidienus Orfitus, who had been consul in 51. Then in 67 it was Sulpicius Camerinus and the latter's son. All three consular men met their deaths as a result of Regulus's onslaught. The details of these prosecutions are lacking. But the hostility that they engendered lived on for the rest of Regulus's life, and that is probably why he sought shelter, when he could, under the wing of later emperors like Domitian who could use his dark services, but with less publicity, behind closed doors.

The most grotesque story told about Regulus comes, not from Pliny, but from Tacitus in his *Histories*, describing events in the year 70. He alleges that, at the time of the assassination of the emperor Galba, Regulus actually took a bite out of the head of the murdered Piso, the aristocrat who was briefly Galba's nominated successor and therefore emperor-elect of Rome, but who was also assassinated. Can this horrifying story be believed? Or is it just more satire on Regulus, the better to discredit him? If it is true, it shows where buffoonery crossed the line into baleful cruelty. The passage of Tacitus is worth quoting in full because its passionate denunciation of Regulus has rung down through history as far as the French revolutionaries of the 1790s and beyond.

> [Aquilius Regulus] had attained a detestable eminence by engineering the ruin of the house of the Crassi and that of Orfitus. It seems that as a very young man Regulus had volunteered to take upon himself their prosecution not in order to save his own skins but in the hope of gaining power ... [In the Senate there came] a fighting speech from Curtius Montanus, who went so far as to allege that after the Emperor Galba's assassination Regulus had rewarded Piso's murderer, and had taken a bite at the murdered man's head. 'That action, at least,' he said, 'was not forced on you by Nero, and no purchase of rank or safety called for such fiendish behaviour ... It was blood-lust and open-mouthed covetousness that made you dabble in the carnage of noble men. From your country's corpse you stole the spoils of consuls. Sated with 7 million sesterces and clad in the shining robes of a priest [Nero had given him money and a priesthood as rewards] in a career of indiscriminate destruction you trampled on innocent children, men old and distinguished, and women of high rank, blaming Nero for lack of vigour because he wore out himself and his prosecutors by attacking one family at a time. The whole Senate, you cried, could be rooted out by a single sentence.'[5]

Tacitus suggests that there were many other, unnamed, victims of Regulus. But Regulus survived the attack by Montanus, if only just. During the debate, the senators were asked to swear an oath to the effect that under the emperor Nero they had never profited from the downfall of other Romans. Several senators were then expelled from the Senate on the grounds that they had committed perjury. But Regulus wriggled out of that one, perhaps thanks to the intervention of Domitian, and Montanus was later himself sent into exile. Pliny tells us:

> at the next meeting of the Senate, the debate was opened by Domitian. He stressed the need to let bygones be bygones and forget the measures forced upon men by the previous regime [meaning Nero] [**4.44**].

One must wonder why Domitian, then prince of the realm and future emperor, saved Regulus in this way. But Pliny remarks that Regulus continued his activities as an informer under Domitian, but in a more private and discreet way, using secret rather than public denunciations – if anything, an even more sinister activity [1.5]. So Regulus may have been involved indirectly in one or more of the high-profile political trials that took place in the later years of Domitian's reign. Domitian may have had good reason to protect him. Under Domitian, Regulus

> helped with the prosecution of Arulenus Rusticus and proclaimed his delight in Rusticus's death by giving a public reading of his speech against him (which he afterwards published) where he used the words 'Stoic ape' … Guessing how strongly I felt about this, Regulus did not invite me to his reading.

So Regulus had been proud enough of his skills, and confident enough of his immunity, to give a public reading of his notorious Senate speech against Rusticus, pointedly excluding Pliny from the guest list. Even under the next emperor, the stop-gap Nerva, Regulus was still a dangerous man [1.5]. There is a story that Nerva died from a seizure brought about by an argument he was having with Regulus. True or not, it may show that Regulus was still close to the centre of power, at least until the accession of Trajan as emperor. That means that he enjoyed a run of 35 years in the thick of Rome's nasty game of political infighting. It was only during the second half of this long career that Pliny ran into him, head on.

Regulus the legacy hunter

Pliny not only reports Regulus's boasts about ill-gotten wealth, but also accuses him of another habit distasteful to Pliny and many others: legacy hunting, known by the Latin name *captatio*.

> Look at Regulus, who has risen by his evil ways from poverty and obscurity to such great wealth that he told me himself, when he was trying to forecast how soon he would be worth sixty million sesterces, that he had found a double set of entrails which were a sign that he would have twice that sum. So he will too, if he goes on in the way he has begun, dictating wills which are not their own to the very people who are wanting to make them: the most immoral fraud there is … This is the man who accepts estates and legacies as if they were his due [2.20].

Pliny cites several cases of Regulus's unscrupulous chase after legacies. In one case, says Pliny, Regulus visited the sickbed of the wife of Piso, that self-same man he had hated when alive and whose head Regulus took a bite from, according to Tacitus. By use of superstitious mumbo-jumbo and characteristic playacting he persuaded her that she was not dying. So in gratitude she added a codicil to her will giving Regulus a legacy. Later, she realised she was in fact dying, and in her last hours accused Regulus of treachery and perjury, since he had sworn in the name of his own son that she would survive.

In another case cited by Pliny, a rich man called Blaesus wished on his deathbed to alter his will. Enter Regulus, hoping for a legacy and imploring the doctors to keep him alive long enough to make a new will. Then, when the new will was signed, Regulus demanded to know how long the doctors would go on denying the man an easy death. But Blaesus was too smart, and left him nothing. This same letter [2.20] also details Regulus's machinations to get his hands on the fortune left to their son by his wife, who had hoped to by-pass Regulus, no doubt for good reason.

Laying traps for Pliny

After Nero's time, Regulus switched emphasis from Senate to the law courts and made his main public and professional career in the Court of One Hundred Men, Pliny's own stamping ground. That is where Pliny, the younger man, got to know and dislike him so much. Yet Regulus won praise there for his powers of oratory, and clashed with Pliny on several occasions. It went far beyond not inviting him to private readings. It was professional rivalry in the raw. Pliny reacted by treating Regulus partly as a danger, partly as a clown. Pliny accused Regulus of deliberately laying political traps for him during court hearings, at a period when Pliny may have been in danger because of his known or suspected sympathies with senators unhappy with Domitian's regime. Pliny's friendship with Modestus was a case in point. Here is how Pliny recalls one trap laid for him by Regulus when they were both in court:

> He must have remembered too the deadly trap he laid for me in the Centumviral Court, when Rusticus had asked me to support Arrionilla, Timon's wife, with Regulus against me. Part of our case depended on the legal opinion provided by Mettius Modestus, the eminent senator who had been banished by Domitian and was still in exile. Up gets Regulus. 'Tell me Pliny, what is your estimate of Modestus?' Now you can see the danger if I gave a

good one and the disgrace if I did not. I can only say the gods must have put words into my mouth [**1.5**].

The reason that Regulus had it in for Modestus was that scornful public remark made by Modestus about Regulus being 'the vilest of two-legged creatures'. That remark was made not just to any casual acquaintance but directly to the emperor himself. It was a serious step to take, hurtful and provocative and potentially very damaging. Some see this as not just a reason, but actually a justification for Regulus's hostility towards Modestus and by extension towards Modestus's friend Pliny. This was not just courtroom banter, and it may explain why Regulus persisted with the question three times – a 'treacherous question', says Pliny. But Pliny found a smart answer that got him out of trouble. He said to the court:

> I think it is quite improper even to put questions about a man on whom sentence has been passed.

That silenced Regulus. Pliny got out of the dilemma by neither challenging nor approving the sentence on Modestus, but by hinting that in repeating the question Regulus himself might be thought guilty of questioning Domitian's judgement in banishing Modestus. Thus the danger was shifted cleverly from Pliny back to Regulus. The anecdote is a vivid illustration of how a man as skilled as Pliny in the political language of his day could make effective use of audiences whose ears were attuned to detect veiled implications. Pliny was later to make extensive use of his skill in political double-speak in the lengthy speech he made in praise of the emperor Trajan (see Chapter 8). One may admire Pliny's verbal adroitness in avoiding the traps laid for him by Regulus, a man who everyone knew was acting as Domitian's informal *agent provocateur*. On the other hand, Pliny also adroitly left it to others like Modestus to risk all in openly protesting against the excesses of Regulus. Pliny was not a man to take such risks.

Regulus as a rival orator

About the only thing that Regulus and Pliny ever agreed on was that they had different styles of oratory and different approaches to the job of Roman-style barrister/advocate. Pliny tells us:

> Regulus once said to me when we were appearing in the same case: 'You think

you should follow up on every point, but I make straight for the throat and hang on.' He certainly hangs on to whatever he seizes, but he often misses the right place [**1.20**].

Pliny derides Regulus as an orator and as a writer:

> I have often told you about Regulus's force of character. It is amazing how he carries out whatever he set his heart on … Depravity gains strength from reckless abandon. Regulus is proof of this. He has weak lungs, indistinct articulation, and a stammer, he is slow at finding the right word and has no memory, nothing in fact but a perverted ingenuity, and yet his crazy effrontery has won him the popular reputation as being an orator … [His memoir of his deceased son] is more likely to meet with laughter than tears; you would think it was written *by* a boy rather than *about* one [**4.7**].

Some see this as a cruel insult to Regulus, made by a 'jealous, vengeful' Pliny. Only after Regulus is dead can Pliny admit to qualified regret.

> I often find myself missing Regulus in court, though I don't mean that I want him back again. But I miss him as a person who really valued oratory … [his use of soothsayers] may have been gross superstition, but it did show respect for his profession [**6.2**].

The real difference between the two men, according to Pliny's friend Tacitus, was that the oratory of Regulus was 'profit-driven and bloody' (*lucrosae et sanguinantis eloquentiae usus*).[6] Regulus (according to Pliny) stood for everything that Pliny did not. Pliny parades Regulus as the anti-hero of his letter collection, as the negative to his positive, so much the better to highlight by contrast the characteristics of a Good Senator – and of himself as an example of the Good Senator.

> Regulus bears the same relation to Good Senators that the Bad Emperors Nero and Domitian bear to the Good Emperors Nerva and Trajan … Regulus's two cardinal crimes, *delatio* [informing] and *captatio* [legacy hunting], invert the virtues of the ideal upper-class politician: Regulus the orator uses the justice system for injustice, and Regulus the friend is no friend. His political as well as his social activities are driven by money, not the abstract noble values which drive the activities of Pliny and his circle.[7]

Regulus was therefore a necessary figure in Pliny's life and in his self-justification and self-definition as a principled lawyer and a proud if priggish senator. Regulus is portrayed as essentially the dark side of Pliny himself, the man that Pliny might have become had he been (in his own eyes anyway) less principled.

Or was he Pliny's mirror image?

The awkward fact, however, is that the two men were in many respects remarkably similar – not negative to positive, dark to light, but mirror images of each other. Both were excellent public speakers, if with different modes of handling cases; both were advocates prominent in the same court, the Court of One Hundred Men, and in the Senate; both had literary pretensions; both were or became wealthy; both received much of their wealth in the form of gifts from clients; both, as even Pliny admits, valued oratory as a high art form.

> Regulus the *delator* resembles Pliny the prosecutor, Regulus the *captator* resembles Pliny the loyal friend who is always rewarded with legacies from his friends, and Regulus the careful writer and orator resembles Pliny the careful writer and orator … In practice, the virtuous advocate acts approximately the same way as does the vicious advocate; he is enlisted to make the client's case sound as good as possible, true or false, and not to apply moral wisdom … Under a Bad Emperor, at least, one might imagine that the most unscrupulous advocate is the most effective one.[8]

Indeed, at least one contemporary could not tell much difference between Regulus and Pliny – or was not in a financial position to say that he did.

The voices of Martial

Pliny knew Martial the satirical poet, indeed was his patron – or one of them. But so was Regulus. Martial did not dare satirise Regulus, even if Pliny did. Rather, Martial wrote about both advocates in equally flattering terms. If you take Martial at face value, there is little to choose between them, and no sign of that courtroom warfare that Pliny advertises. Martial can be viciously scornful about other Regulus-type informers, for example Vacerra:

> You are an informer (*delator*) and a slanderer (*calumniator*), a swindler (*fraudator*) and a shady dealer (*negotiator*) and a cock-sucker (*fellator*) and a gladiator-trainer (*lanista*). I wonder, Vacerra, why you don't have any money?

Martial accuses Vacerra of sitting all day in the public toilet, not because he needs to shit, but because he wants an invitation to dinner.[9] No such crude language about Regulus, who features flatteringly in no less than 11 of Martial's compositions. Regulus is 'under divine protection', and 'your piety is no less than the intellect that goes with it'; he is accompanied by admiring crowds when he has secured an acquittal, and is as great as Cicero as a defence counsel. Martial celebrates Regulus's 'eloquent lips', and refers particularly to the court where both he and Pliny speak, hoping that Regulus's young son will

> feel his father's glory [in] the clamour of the Centumvirate Court and the dense encircling crowd.[10]

Sadly or otherwise, the son did not live that long. But the language equates with the words Martial uses about the 'eloquent' Pliny, working hard for 'the ears of the Hundred Men'.[11] From Martial, you would not get any hint of the antagonism between the two men, of Regulus's true profession, or indeed of much difference between them. Martial had to write to earn money and make a living, and was in no position to pick and choose who his patrons were. He wrote about Regulus when Regulus was a power in the land, as (presumably) Vacerra was not. But Martial once again illustrates the social and political ambiguity surrounding Regulus and the role of informers.

Regulus the penitent

After the assassination of Domitian in September 96, Regulus seems to have become worried about his future and his vulnerability to retaliation. Pliny remarks, rather gloatingly:

> Have you ever seen anyone so abject and nervous as Regulus since Domitian's death? It has put an end to his misdeeds, which were as bad as in Nero's day, though better concealed [1.5].

Through a rather embarrassed intermediary, Regulus sought a reconciliation with Pliny, no doubt in a bid to ward off possible prosecution. When Pliny refused this indirect overture, Regulus engineered a face-to-face meeting.

> [Regulus] grew even paler than usual, and stammered. 'That question [about Modestus] was meant to damage Modestus, not you.'

Pliny rejected this overture too. Even when Regulus's son died before him, Pliny still shows little mercy.

> Regulus has lost his son, the one misfortune that he did not deserve, but doubtless no real misfortune in his eyes. [His mourning] was not grief, but a parade of grief. It is amazing how he is now besieged by people who all loathe

and detest him and yet flock around him in crowds as if they really loved and admired him … they court Regulus by his own methods [**4.2**].

So, with the death of his son, Regulus the legacy-hunter in his turn fell prey to legacy-hunters, and Pliny is not sorry. Regulus, however, had grounds to be nervous of Pliny's intentions. Pliny tells us that in 97 he did indeed think of prosecuting Regulus. But he realised that Regulus was still too powerful and still had too many friends to be easily attacked in court. One wonders who these friends were. Pliny remarks:

> I am well aware that Regulus is hard to get to grips with: he is rich, influential, backed by many people and feared by more [**1.5**].

So Pliny backed off. Instead, in 97, Pliny turned his attack on someone else, Publicius Certus, a sort of Regulus-substitute [**9.13**]. Regulus himself never faced a trial. The verbal attacks on Regulus in the Senate and elsewhere, however, may have had some effect. Some say that Regulus, like Pliny, made it to the high office of consul. But the evidence for that is thin, and it is more likely that he never advanced beyond the much more junior offices of *quaestor*, granted to him by Nero as early as 70 along with his 'blood money', and possibly *praetor* [**2.11**]. By the end, the new man Pliny as consul outranked the old aristocrat Regulus. Regulus himself appears to have died some time before 106, having survived unscathed all the attacks on him, except for those delivered by Pliny and Tacitus in the name of history. Did he fully deserve these attacks, or can Pliny and Tacitus be accused of character assassination? Under many regimes at different periods of history, the role of the informer has been defended as well as attacked, justified as well as vilified.

In defence of Regulus

When the French Revolution broke out in the 1790s its leaders were steeped in knowledge of classical Rome. Their debate about whether to encourage denunciations of supposed enemies of their Revolution was peppered with references to Rome's notorious *delatores* like Regulus. They knew their Tacitus better than most people today. This led them to try to differentiate between 'good' and 'bad' denunciations, those made in the public interest and those made for private advantage, by using different French words for interested and disinterested denunciations. *Dénonciation* was the good sort, *délation* the bad sort. But they had to admit that it was impossible to draw a hard-and-fast line between the two.

In the old Soviet Union, under Stalin, during the great purges of the 1930s, citizens were actively encouraged to inform on each other. Many thousands of people engaged in informing and sending denunciations of fellow citizens to the secret police – the KGB in Russia and, later, the Stasi in communist East Germany.

> There were two broad categories: voluntary informers, who were usually motivated by material rewards, political beliefs or malice towards their victims; and involuntary informers who were entrapped by police threats or promises to help arrested relatives ... many people wrote denunciations in the sincere conviction that they were performing their patriotic duty.[12]

So were there 'good' informers and 'bad' informers? This central question goes right back to Regulus. Were he and men like him regrettable but necessary for the maintenance of Roman state security, which in Rome's case in the first century meant the security of the emperor? Is Pliny therefore unfair to Regulus? Was he, unpleasant as he may have been, a saviour of the state, a good *delator* and not a bad one? By sniffing out potential or actual plots and conspiracies against the emperor's life and denouncing the conspirators, did he and his fellow *delatores* save the state from even more of those bloody civil wars that broke out, for example, in 69, the Year of the Four Emperors? In defence of Regulus, it has been said that Tacitus 'selectively maligns' him, and that such men as Regulus were

> by no means purely the instruments of tyranny ... the need for state security always created a demand for the prosecutor's services ... the *delator* played only a limited part in curtailing the freedom of others ... the *delator* is generally neither a criminal element nor a force for destruction but one that maintained stability through law enforcement and service to the Princeps [emperor] ... such men were a vital part of the government, bringing with their talents a certain *je ne sais quoi* which even someone as hostile as Tacitus understood was indispensible ... they protected the immediate security of the princeps and the state ... one person's justice may be another person's *delatio* ... it may be justice at work ... parallels or analogies with the Gestapo, the Stasi, the KGB, or McCarthyite zealots are inapplicable ... personal enmities and vendettas, court intrigue, genuine attempts to punish injustice – for the most part this is not the stuff of tyranny but of Roman law, politics and culture.[13]

Having no public prosecution service, the Roman legal system depended upon private prosecutions and accusations brought by people who laid information against others. So it was, some argue, a necessary part of Roman justice.

Pliny deplored the informers, but himself acted as a prosecutor. The Latin term *delator* was itself an ambiguous term. Was the word synonymous with *accusator*, a neutral term for a man who under the Roman legal system legitimately initiated a prosecution in the public interest? Or was it reserved for selfish, malicious prosecutions and 'informing' for personal gain and 'blood money'?

Regulus v. Pliny – a summing up

Thanks to Pliny's letters, the lives of Pliny and Regulus will remain forever intertwined. But despite the similarities between the two men, that does not make Pliny and Regulus the same. Pliny did not personally cause the deaths of people. Regulus did – at least three, maybe five victims, all important people who he brought down and ruined by his accusations and his informing. Pliny did not prosecute others for direct personal reward, whether financial or political, or to gain unofficial power through closeness to the real seat of power, the emperor, for example as a member of his *consilium*. Regulus did all three of these things. Regulus made a profession of accusing and informing. He was active in that role over a long period of time, whenever the character of the emperor made it profitable – that is, over a period of more than 30 years. Pliny had no such sinister career. If Regulus was indeed a product of the system, he was not an inevitable product. He chose to do it, as Modestus clearly stated in his speech to the Senate.

To excuse Regulus's activities as an inevitable or even desirable contribution to state security is not only to condone a sinister activity that has plagued many other totalitarian regimes since Pliny's day, but also by implication to call Pliny a liar in his allegations against Regulus. Even if informers are symptomatic of totalitarian regimes, as history seems to show, they are not inevitable symptoms. In the case of Rome, the emperor could encourage or discourage them, and individuals could agree or refuse to become informers. Even if *delatores* like Regulus made some contribution to the protection of the state as personified in the emperor, they did a bad job of it. Both emperors who encouraged them, Nero and Domitian, were assassinated. Pliny launched prosecutions against prominent figures, as Regulus did. But they were against corrupt provincial governors (see Chapter 6), and, as a result of Pliny's prosecutions, citizens in the Roman provinces may sometimes have got a better deal and at least some sense of justice being done. The morality of the two men was quite different.

A Roman verdict

It is surely to the Romans themselves that we can look for a final verdict on such men as Regulus. Emperors repeatedly turned upon them. The historian Dio, for example, has many stories about emperors punishing informers, at least of the lesser sort. In 41, Claudius condemned to death in the arena – a nasty fate – those who had laid information against others or who had borne false witness. According to Tacitus, even the emperor Nero, the greatest user of informers, punished less important informers.[14] Titus, when emperor, banished informers from the city. Even Domitian, user of informers, destroyed many of those who gave him information.

> The acts urged on them by Domitian were the pretext for their destruction. He said: 'If you don't punish informers, you create them.'[15]

It is ironic that Domitian of all people, who according to Pliny made use of informers like Regulus, should articulate this fundamental truism about informers. Then in 96, under Nerva, many of those who had been informers were condemned to death, but there was such a storm of protest and recrimination that Nerva was forced to call a halt. Some men were too powerful to be touched. But then came that further bout of retribution meted out by Trajan, over which Pliny took such gloating delight. But by then Regulus was well out of personal danger and Pliny was forced to admit that he was beyond prosecution, except in the court of history. There remained only one option: literary revenge on Regulus; and Pliny and Tacitus carried that out ruthlessly and deservedly, but at the cost of immortalising this colourful but dangerous man as surely as Pliny himself.

Pliny the prosecutor: Corruption and the limits of Roman justice

The climax of Pliny's career as a lawyer came with his lead role in a series of six high-profile corruption and extortion cases brought against Roman provincial governors on their return from office. In the main, Pliny acted for the prosecution – a sometimes dangerous and unpopular championing of the rights of provincial or subject peoples against some of the most powerful men in the empire, men who moreover were Pliny's colleagues in the Roman Senate and members of his own elite social peer group. It may seem a big jump from practising inheritance law before a specialist law court to taking the lead in public prosecutions before the Senate, which was the highest court in the land. But the link was simply money. Through his specialism in inheritance cases, Pliny became an expert on finance and the adjudication of claims about money. This expertise is what also took him later on to important jobs in charge of two of the main state treasuries, the Military Treasury and the Treasury of Saturn (see Chapter 7). It is also what took him, late in his career, out to the eastern Roman province of Bithynia-Pontus, to try to sort out the financial mess into which many of its cities had fallen (see Chapter 14).

Unfortunately for Pliny's reputation today, the credit he deserves for this demanding and onerous activity of checking corruption and extortion in high places has been overshadowed by the most famous extortion case in all Roman history, the prosecution in 70 BCE of Verres, governor of Sicily 73–71 BCE, by that master of invective, Cicero himself, over 150 years before Pliny's time. The time gap between Cicero and Pliny shows for how long, and with what limited success, the Roman Empire had grappled with the persistent problem of malpractice by the men it sent out to govern its regions. One of the biggest failures of the old Roman Republic that Cicero championed so vociferously, at the eventual cost of his life, was to control corruption and extortion by its provincial governors. Indeed, the failure to provide adequate justice for once conquered peoples may have been one of the root causes of the collapse of the Republican regime. Between 149 and 50 BCE, under the Republic, there were about 56 known trials that were or may have been for extortion, known in Rome as *repetundae* trials, signifying the attempt to get the money back – in other words, restitution. But of these only 17 at most resulted in condemnation and up to 30 resulted in acquittal.[1]

> The great demerit of Republican law was simply that it was not enforced: it did not guarantee good government because acquittals were too easily procured ... courts were partial or corrupt.[2]

Ethnic prejudice and the skill of the defence counsel and also played a part.

> A skilled defence advocate – a Cicero for example – could undermine provincial accusers by playing on the stereotypes of the foreigner, the primitive and bellicose accusers ... or the shifty Greeks ... With these would be contrasted the allegedly upright Roman character of the accused ... These techniques of persuasion were reinforced by the collective self-interest of rich Romans.[3]

The irony is that the often-criticised Roman imperial regime that followed the Republic did make serious attempts to curb such abuses through the agency of people like Pliny and his great friend Tacitus, the orator and historian. Tacitus himself admits, in the introduction to his book *The Annals*, that the Roman provinces got a better deal under the emperors than under the preceding republican regime.

> The new order was popular in the provinces. There, government by Senate and People was looked upon sceptically as a matter of sparring dignitaries and extortionate officials. The legal system had provided no remedy against these, since it was wholly incapacitated by violence, favouritism and – most of all – bribery.[4]

The normal penalties for conviction on *repetundae* charges were exile (*relegatio*) and at least partial confiscation of assets, over and above simple restitution of moneys extorted or corruptly obtained. But the problem did not go away, and was one reason for the increasing centralisation of the empire as emperors, motivated by self-interest in order to ensure that the provinces could pay their taxes, sought to enforce more uniform and accountable standards among its administrators. But their intervention brought a wry and very Tacitean comment from Tacitus. Telling how the emperor Tiberius sat in on court hearings, he remarks:

> As a result of his being there, many verdicts were reached in defiance of intrigue and pressures from powerful people: justice gained, but liberty suffered.[5]

In other words, it represented yet another stage in the centralisation of power, even if in a good cause. It is hard to see how emperors could have acted otherwise, especially in relation to the huge empire they governed.

> *Repetundae* prosecutions were essential and necessary for the effective workings of government and for establishing goodwill and stable relationships between Rome and her subjects, who could not prosecute cases themselves but who could hire a person from the Senate to do so.[6]

That is what they did. They could, for example, hire lawyer-senators like Pliny and Tacitus to represent them before the Senate as supreme court.

Senate and informers

But there was a tricky problem in doing this. There was a fine and blurred line between proper prosecution of corrupt governors and the activities of the notorious *delatores* discussed in Chapter 5. These were informers who sought to enrich themselves and gain imperial favour by engineering the downfall of powerful men by bringing more or less trumped-up prosecutions, sometimes on *repetundae* charges and sometimes with the charge of treason (*maiestas*) thrown in for luck. Both Pliny and Tacitus castigate such *delatores*, yet themselves acted for the prosecution in *repetundae* cases. The problem was that

> one person's justice may be another person's *delatio*.[7]

Pliny published his trial speeches after the event, but they have not survived and so we cannot judge them. Cicero's speeches against Verres have survived so that we can read them. Cicero plainly saw the Verres trial not just as justice done but also as an opportunity to promote his own political ambitions inside the Republican regime of his time. He had mixed motives, as every Roman of the time would have known. Politics and justice were never entirely unravelled from each other in the Roman system of government. That was a fundamental weakness in the system. But extortion and corruption trials like those undertaken by Pliny and Tacitus were a necessary step towards at least an attempt at better government, curbing the worst excesses of men in high positions who were otherwise unaccountable.

Pliny's letters on the one hand show the Roman judicial system of his day struggling to get to grips with this problem of corruption and extortion. On the other hand, they also show the shocking extent to which Roman provincial governors were still willing to take chances and succumb to the lure of easy money, despite the increasing probability that these progressively more self-assertive provincial communities would not take such corruption lying down but would retaliate in the Roman courts.

Another problem in Pliny's day was that the Senate had become the court in which such corruption and extortion trials took place. But it was not an impartial court. When it came to those provinces of the empire still governed by senators as opposed to nominees of the emperor, senators were judging their own. Inevitably, they were partial. Pliny himself frankly admits to mixed feelings. Despite acting in the main for the prosecution, he tells us how sad it is to see a fellow senator brought down by such accusations [**3.4**]. The statistics, however, despite inevitable shortcomings, do tell a sorry story of persistent corruption problems that spilled over from the Republican period into the period of the emperors. But they also speak of more determined attempts to curb these abuses.

From the time of the emperor Augustus to Pliny's time – a century or so – there were 40 cases we know about of prosecutions brought against provincial governors on some charge or other. Of these, no less than 28 were found guilty, as against seven acquitted. In five cases we do not know the result.[8] These totals can be read in two ways. Given the bias of the Senate in favour of its own, the crimes must have been extreme to secure a conviction and may indicate many more potential but lesser corruption cases which never got to court. But they do nevertheless also indicate some attempt to rectify a bad situation. One must suppose that these convictions had at least some deterrent effect. So the ruling class had been warned. But one may also suspect that too many corrupt governors still got away with it.

At a personal level, Pliny's role in a significant number of such trials shows him in a positive light, as no doubt he intended. We only have his version of events. But what was to prove significant for his later career was that the largest single number of prosecutions over that previous century, seven in all, originated from the one province of Bithynia-Pontus – the very province to which he himself was later to be dispatched by the emperor Trajan in an effort, only partially successful as it turned out, finally to clean up that province's chaotic finances.

Punishment or restitution?

There was a lengthy background to all this. With no state prosecution service, Rome relied upon provincial assemblies or cities lodging claims at Rome for the restitution of money improperly taken from them, acting through personal representatives and through a patron-senator-advocate like Pliny. The primary objective was redress for financial loss rather than the punishment of the convicted. But both came into play, and this confusion of objectives seems to have dogged extortion cases even in Pliny's day, despite a long history of trying to grapple with this endemic problem. As far back as 149 BCE, some 250 years before Pliny's time, the then Tribune of the People, Lucius Calpurnius Piso Frugi, had set up a standing court to try extortion and corruption cases, showing how persistent the problem was even then. Under the empire, the definitive statute governing this offence became the *Lex Julia Repetundarum*, the Julian Law on Restitution, passed by Julius Caesar in 59 BCE. It was a complex law with over 100 sections. Unfortunately, we do not have its full text. But with modifications it remained the basis for Roman law well into the imperial period. It laid down various penalties for the guilty beyond simple restitution of the moneys illegally extorted, notably exile or banishment (from Rome, or from Italy) and loss of civil rights.[9]

But by Pliny's time there had been various changes in procedure and scope. The standing court had lapsed and the Senate had taken over the job of hearing such cases as well as the once separate function of assessing the damages, a function carried out by nominees the Romans called *recuperatores*, recovery agents. Also, the liability to claims for restitution had been extended to members of the governor's family and to members of the governor's entourage, as will be seen in the complex cases that Pliny dealt with. Perhaps offsetting this extension of liability, the Senate seems to have taken to itself the power to vary the sentence on those found guilty, usually in the direction of leniency.

What exactly was, and was not, corruption?

But corruption itself was not a simple black-and-white affair, and that was Pliny's problem. Everyone did it – to some extent. As a governor, where did you cross the line between acceptable and unacceptable self-enrichment?

> Provincial governorships were widely regarded as a legitimate source of income (Cicero himself did well while governor of Cilicia) and very few cases of

maladministration were ever successfully prosecuted in the Roman courts. But it did happen.[10]

With Pliny, it did happen. But it was probably a matter of degree – an attempt to curb only the most blatant or excessive abuses. The majority of governors were probably sensible enough to follow the ruling about gifts (for which read bribes) laid down by the later emperors Septimius Severus and Caracalla and quoted by the jurist Ulpian:

> Only set some limit ... There is an old saying: not all, nor always, nor from all. It is too uncivil to accept from nobody, but contemptible to take from every quarter and grasping to accept everything.[11]

In other words, don't overdo the extortion and corruption. Then you will be safe. The standards required of public life in Pliny's day were not the same as the standards we seek (but often fail) to achieve today.

> Was all this a sign of unchecked moral and administrative malaise ... If we condemn Roman habits, are we guilty of misplaced smugness as to our own superiority?[12]

This, then, is the ambiguous and ambivalent context in which Pliny stepped up to the bar, or its Roman equivalent, to take issue with the shifting boundaries between acceptable and unacceptable extortion.

Case One: Pliny and the Spaniards

The first extortion case that Pliny took on was the prosecution of Baebius Massa, ex-governor of the province of Baetica, covering what is now southern Spain [**3.4** and **7.33**]. It appears that Pliny already had some connection with Baetica and had become in effect a patron or representative of the province. So the Senate appointed him and his colleague Herennius Senecio to act for the province. This was in 93, under the emperor Domitian, and so was early in Pliny's career and presumably with Domitian's approval. This may have some bearing upon that most puzzling of all questions about Pliny, what his relationship was with this difficult emperor. The year 93 was also the year of the great purge of alleged opponents by Domitian, and Pliny's colleague in this case Herennius Senecio was one of the men who, shortly after this trial, lost his life in this purge. To be closely associated with him at that time must have carried a degree of political risk. How much risk, we can't be sure (see Chapter 7). Pliny refers to the dangers that he faced during this episode, and he continued to be associated with Senecio's family, perhaps by way of atonement for not having done enough to save Senecio's life [**1.5**, **3.11**, **4.7**, **4.11**, **7.19**]. On the other hand, Pliny himself came through unscathed. It was Senecio who fell victim to the animosities stirred up by this case, not Pliny.

The animosities are plain to see. After time had been granted for the collection of evidence (the *inquisitio* stage), Massa was convicted, and the Senate passed a resolution that his assets should be put into official custody until the claims against him had been settled. But Massa – surprisingly, in view of his conviction – then asked the consuls to restore his property to him. Senecio told Pliny that they should oppose this. Then when Pliny seemed inclined to let the matter go – again surprisingly, but perhaps because he sensed danger – Senecio said that he, Senecio, came from that part of the empire, meaning Spain, and had been a senior government official there (*quaestor*), and so had obligations there and could not let the matter drop. Pliny, still fearing ill-will among senators, then agreed to support him, and in the Senate they jointly voiced to the consuls their opposition to Massa's move.

Despite his conviction, Massa was apparently still present in the Senate, and launched a counter-attack on Senecio (not on Pliny) for alleged professional malpractice, and sought leave to prosecute him for *impietas*, a form of contempt of court. Why a convicted extortionist could contemplate such a counter-prosecution Pliny does not make clear. But it may be because Senecio's move implied that the magistrates responsible for the sequestration of his property could not be relied upon, and this equated to a charge of defamation against them.

There was general consternation in the Senate, as well there might be, until Pliny came up with a witty and legally astute retort that apparently defused the situation and was much talked about afterwards (says Pliny modestly). Pliny asked why Baebius had not brought an allegation against him as well, since he and Senecio were acting together. Thus Baebius might be implying that Pliny, as prosecutor, was somehow colluding with the defence. Such a charge, if not substantiated, could itself give rise to a serious counter-charge of defamation (*calumnia*). Baebius was forced to withdraw.[13] Pliny later got a letter from the emperor Nerva congratulating him on his smart move in this legal chess game. But that came too late to save Senecio from the purge, and one must wonder whether Senecio's persistence against Massa had contributed to the Senate's animosity against him. Pliny's letters make it clear that Senecio had vicious enemies in the Senate, and Massa's behaviour suggests that he had enough supporters in the Senate to think he could circumvent his conviction and even continue to attend its sessions.

So on the one hand Pliny gained the conviction of Massa and would find his position as patron of Baetica called upon in a much bigger extortion case later on. On the other hand, this first case in Pliny's career as a public prosecutor showed up the flaws, uncertainties and dangers of operating before a non-impartial Senate in this fraught area of Roman law and process. It also touches on the most challenging question about Pliny – his relationship (or, should one say, his favoured relationship) with the emperor Domitian.

Case Two: Pliny and the Africans

The next major case in which Pliny became involved was much more shocking, not for Pliny's position or for the ambiguous role of the Senate, but for the scandalous extent of the malpractice that it revealed [**2.11**, **2.12**, **6.29**, **10.3a**]. Pliny as chief prosecutor in the case must therefore deserve credit for his part in trying to check such deep-seated criminality. Pliny had as his colleague in this case his friend Tacitus, the orator and writer, and the case became ever more complex as it went on. The importance of the case is underlined by the fact that the emperor Trajan presided in person.

The governor was Marius Priscus, and his eventual conviction happened in January 100, so the trial must have begun much earlier, perhaps in 98. Charges were brought against him by one important city of North Africa, Leptis, in modern-day Libya, and by some individuals. At first it looked simple. Priscus pleaded guilty to extortion and asked for the usual special tribunal to assess how much money he should repay. But then the case got more daunting. Pliny and Tacitus came to realise that Priscus was not just guilty of extortion but had also taken bribes to convict innocent people and even to put them to death. This was about the most serious abuse of power imaginable. They told the Senate of their findings, and a full senatorial inquiry was launched.

Two men who were alleged to have given bribes, Vitellius Honoratus and Flavius Marcianus, were summoned to Rome from Leptis. Honoratus was charged with paying 300,000 sesterces to procure the exile of a Roman *eques* (a knight, that is, a man of status) and, perhaps worse, the death of seven of his friends. Marcianus was charged with paying 700,000 sesterces to get another Roman *eques* flogged, condemned to the mines, and finally strangled in prison. These events suggest a nasty local squabble between rival factions in the city.

Honoratus died at about this time – perhaps by suicide to avoid conviction – but the trial of Priscus and Marcianus went ahead in tandem, even though of course the charges were different, one for having accepted bribes, the other for having given them.

Pliny tells us that, amid periodic uproar in the Senate chamber, he spoke for nearly five hours – or rather that he was allowed 16 water-clocks, four more than normal. One water-clock (the *clepsydra*) lasted about a quarter of an hour but could be set to run slower. He later gave a private reading of his speech to friends, since he regarded it as raising several matters of legal principle and precedent.[14] The defence normally got half as long again, so the whole process took a long time. In all, it was a three-day session of the Senate, and Pliny was later to claim that those three days were full of open and free debate, in contrast (he said) to the cowed Senate of Domitian's day when no Senator dared speak his mind.[15]

There seems to have been no argument about guilt, but about the sentence. Priscus was not only fined the total amount that he was alleged to have extorted, but also banished from Rome and Italy, while Marcianus was banished from Rome, Italy and Africa. Priscus complained that Pliny's hate-figure, Regulus, had first advised him, then deserted him. So justice of a sort was done, but too late for that unfortunate *eques* who was flogged and strangled, and too leniently to satisfy the satirist Juvenal, who complained in his writings of a meaningless verdict. Priscus, claimed Juvenal, still had his money and simply retired to a safe distance to enjoy it, while the province that complained got little.[16] Pliny may have taken grave offence at being mocked in this way (see Chapter 13), but the matter was still not over.

Also implicated by the evidence was Priscus's deputy, or legate, Hostilius Firminus. Evidence showed that he had assisted Priscus in his illegal activities, and had demanded from Marcianus the sum of 200,000 sesterces on his own account. Of this sum – shock, horror – 10,000 was for cosmetics (*unguentarii*). Again, guilt was taken as proven, but the argument was about sentence. Some said that, as an example and warning to others, he should be excluded from the Senate – a serious loss of status. But somewhat to Pliny's disgust a more lenient decision was reached. It was a clear example of the Senate looking after its own. Firminus was allowed to retain his seat in the Senate, even though this might mean him sitting in judgement on people charged with the same offence for which he had been convicted. But he was excluded from applying for any future governor jobs or other public offices, so perhaps that was punishment enough.

At least the Senate – under the watchful eye of the emperor – had taken some steps to curb the worst excesses by its members. It is also interesting to see Pliny and Tacitus in action together outside the literary sphere. But the case and the grossly illegal events it brought to light reflect badly upon the standards of Roman administration. Pliny and Tacitus, who were originally reluctant to take on the case, deserve credit for standing out for better justice for those who had suffered from these abuses of power.

Case Three: The Spaniards again

Late in 99 or early 100 the Spaniards from Baetica came back for more [**3.4**, **3.9** and **6.29**]. They sought the help of Pliny, by now their established patron, in prosecuting Caecilius Classicus, who had been governor of that province in 97–8. Pliny resisted at first, knowing from experience that prosecution carried its dangers. But he eventually agreed, having taken leave of absence from his official duties at that time as prefect of a state treasury and in the hope that three prosecutions would relieve him of having to do it ever again. As it turned out, this was a vain hope, and the fact that the emperor Trajan gave him leave of absence from the treasury suggests that Trajan both wanted this case to go forward and wanted Pliny to lead the case. Perhaps, however he phrases it, Pliny had little choice, and the timing of this and the previous trial suggests that Trajan was keen early in his reign to crack down on corruption among his governors.

As well he might. The Classicus case was almost as shocking as that of Priscus, and casts a similarly gloomy light on contemporary standards of Roman administration. It also showed the political realities of piloting prosecutions through a supreme body like the Senate which was both supreme court and the clubhouse of the most powerful men in the land, apart from the emperor. Trajan, as he was to show again when using Pliny to help at his own imperial tribunal (see Case Six) and in his later appointment of Pliny to investigate malpractices in the province of Bithynia-Pontus, seems to have seen the problem and been determined to remedy it. Pliny was evidently one of his chosen instruments for doing so.

What made things easier for Pliny was that Classicus was already dead, probably by suicide. This freed Pliny from the onus of doing what he most disliked about such prosecutions – bringing down a fellow senator. What made it even easier, at least *prima facie*, was that Classicus had – astonishingly in the circumstances – left behind a detailed set of accounts in his own writing plus a copy of a letter he had written to his mistress in Rome boasting that he had swindled the Baeticans out of 4 million sesterces, perhaps not a large sum as swindles went in those days but still a lot of money. He seems to have been driven by the urgent need to pay off creditors, but there was no doubt that he had behaved in a brutal and corrupt manner.

By his (probable) suicide Classicus evaded justice. There was some delay while Pliny conferred with his clients, who decided not just to pursue reparations from the family of Classicus, as they were entitled to do under law, but also to lay actual charges against his wife, his daughter and some members of his entourage. Now it was getting complicated. Pliny decided to unpack the different cases and divide the allegations made by the Spaniards into a series of cascading and interlocking trials. He and his colleague Lucceius Albinus – prosecutors seem always to have worked in pairs, but with Pliny usually in the lead as the mastermind – first of all proved the case against Classicus using the man's own damning evidence, as the basis for proceeding against the other accused. The Senate allowed his family to keep what Classicus had before he went off to Spain, but ordered that all money extorted in Spain should be returned to Spain. If necessary, such money was to be retrieved from Classicus's creditors, if he had used it to pay them off. This presumably meant that such creditors would then have a case for recovery against the rest of Classicus's family and estate.

Pliny and Albinus next moved against two important named accomplices of Classicus, Baebus Probus and Fabius Hispanus. Pliny remarks that he was afraid that the combined influence of these and the other accused might get them off and/or shift the blame onto humbler actors in the drama while they themselves got away with it [3.9]. Both Probus and Hispanus were men of influence, says Pliny, being Roman citizens and knights if not of senatorial rank. Their case also involved the setting of a potential precedent. The two men's defence was that they were simply obeying orders from their legal superior. Those who spoke for them expected this defence to succeed. But it did not. The Senate agreed with Pliny and, as punishment, banished both men for five years. So an important legal precedent was set, if not actually two precedents. One was that superior orders were not a sufficient defence; the other confirmed that knights as well as men of senatorial rank could be liable to prosecution.

In the next stage, two other men in the entourage of Classicus were charged. One of them, Claudius Fuscus, was his son-in-law, the other a tribune of a cohort (of soldiers), Stilonius Priscus. Fuscus was acquitted, but Priscus was banished from Italy for two years. Yet more defendants were then tried, some acquitted, the majority convicted, with sentences of banishment for fixed terms or for life.

This had clearly been a deep-rooted attempt to extort money from the Spaniards, with tentacles reaching down from the (now deceased) governor. But the affair was still not over. Classicus's wife, Casta, was among the defendants. Wives had been liable under the extortion law since the time of the emperor Tiberius. But she was later acquitted – in odd circumstances, as we shall see. Classicus's daughter Classica was also on the list of defendants. But Pliny doubted whether there was enough evidence to convict her, told the Senate so, and with its consent dropped the charge against Classica.

At this point things became even more complicated. One of the witnesses from Baetica laid an accusation of collusion between Casta and Norbanus Licinianus, a Spaniard who had been one of the people officially collecting evidence against Classicus and his accomplicies. This put Pliny and Albinus in an awkward spot. Norbanus had been one of those instructing them. If he was convicted of collusion, the whole cascade of cases might collapse like a house of cards with the bottom card pulled out. So they kept quiet – wisely as it turned out, for Norbanus had form. He had been a crony of the hated emperor Domitian, profited from it, and had clashed with Classicus before, when Classicus had banished him after the death of Domitian. The accusation was made that he had been chosen to collect evidence against Classicus, not in the name of justice, but in the name of revenge – a motive that turned a proper act of *delatio,* informing, into an improper one. Today's arguments about the rights and wrongs of whistleblowing are an echo of these arguments made nearly two millennia ago.

The Senate refused to allow Norbanus time to prepare his defence, or even to tell him exactly what the charges were. In a fit of open political (and barely legal) hostility, Norbanus was found guilty there and then. He was banished to an island, after two senators of consular rank had also come forward to accuse him of adding his name, slanderously, to the prosecution under Domitian of Salvius Liberalis. Norbanus's conviction for collusion was the reason why Pliny was surprised at the acquittal of Casta, with whom Norbanus was alleged to have colluded. Surely, in a case of collusion, either both were innocent or both were guilty? This sub-trial showed how passion and partisanship rather than logic could rule the Senate.

And still it was not all over. Salvius Liberalis himself now came forward, as a senator. Driven by his understandable animosity towards Norbanus, he accused the whole Spanish delegation of defaulting on its obligation to pursue all the persons named in their initial indictment. That must have included Classica. Once again, the whole interlocking pyramid of prosecutions that Pliny had constructed might have been in danger of toppling – as indeed in a modern court of law it might have done. But Pliny says that he successfully defended the Spaniards, the convictions stood, and finally this complicated case was over.

Pliny's description of it offers us a unique insight into how the Roman justice system worked in practice. The case or cases did, however, show how high-level political and personal animosities could complicate the search for justice for badly treated subjects of the empire, and the difficult job of those who brought prosecutions. The lack of an independent judiciary also shows through clearly. If this is how governors behaved in the provinces which senators rather than imperial civil servants were appointed to govern, it is hardly surprising that emperors took increasing control of those parts of the empire that were, nominally at least, still outside their direct personal rule. They did not want disaffected or potentially rebellious subjects, nor subjects so financially afflicted that they could not pay their taxes.

Case Four: Bassus, gifts and Bithynia

Pliny's hope that his career as an advocate in extortion cases was now at an end proved to be in vain. Early in 103 he was back in court again – that is, before the Senate – in another case of alleged extortion by a provincial governor [**4.9** and **6.29**]. This time, however, he appeared for the defence, a role which in principle he preferred. It gave him an easier life. The main significance of the case for Pliny, however, was that it introduced him for the first time to the acrimonious internal politics of the Roman province of Bithynia-Pontus, an unwanted intro-duction that was to determine the last active years of his life.

The accused was Julius Bassus. Bassus already had form in Roman politics – 'much harassed, notorious for his misfortunes', says Pliny. He had already been up before the Senate once, in the time of the emperor Vespasian, probably on a charge of extortion, but had been acquitted. Later he became a friend of the emperor Domitian, but fell out with him and was banished, only to be recalled by the emperor Nerva. Now he was on trial yet again, and it became clear that his previous ups and downs earned him a lot of sympathy among the senators. Bassus maintained that he was the victim of informers (*delatores* again) in Bithynia who hoped to profit from his downfall, and he blamed his prosecution on those elements who were stirring up riots in the province. If true, this scenario did not bode well for Pliny's eventual assignment to Bithynia a few years later. But it introduced yet again that ambiguous attitude towards informers, especially provincial ones. Was this legitimate whistleblowing, or the opposite?

The trouble with Bassus's legal position, as Pliny quickly realised, was that he had openly admitted accepting personal gifts (called by their Greek name *xenia*) during his time as governor of the province, and had made that admission to the emperor himself. Accepting gifts, except very small ones, was technically illegal. On the other hand, there was a fine and wobbly line between accepting gifts as bribes, and accepting gifts as part of the normal gift-exchange culture of the Roman world. Recall again that advice, quoted above, from the emperors Septimius Severus and Caracalla:

> Only set some limit ... There is an old saying: not all, nor always, nor from all.

Pliny was probably well aware that one man's gift might be another man bribe. The same present, whether of money or other objects of value, could look different to the giver – a bribe – and to the receiver – a goodwill gift. So there were grounds for suspicion. In any case, in order to preserve his own professional reputation, Pliny could not be seen to argue in open court that such gifts were not illegal.

He decided on a middle way and entered a plea of mitigation. To do so took him three and a half hours on the first day of the trial and a further hour and a half on the second day. This may seem excessive, especially as Pliny's colleague for the defence, once again Lucceius Albinus, also had four hours in which to speak – making nine hours in all for the defence. That was the allocated time limit for the defence as against six hours for the prosecution. To be fair to Pliny, he wanted to cut the defence short, but Bassus insisted that he and Albinus use up all their allocated time, perhaps because he thought the Senate would get so fed up with the case that its members would settle for the simplest and easiest verdict.

In the event, he was right. Once again the Senate did not argue about guilt – that was evident – but about the sentence. Some wanted the full sanction of the law; others wanted Bassus simply to make good the money he had extracted, but otherwise to suffer no loss of status. Pliny's nine hours of pleas in mitigation seem to have paid off, because Bassus was given the lesser sentence. Pliny comments that, in the eyes of some, this created the same anomalous situation as the Priscus case, leaving a man as a member of the Senate where he might be a judge of people accused of the same crime of which he had himself been found guilty. Bassus may have benefited from senatorial sympathy for his previous ordeals. Pliny himself thought that Bassus had behaved foolishly – he forgot to set a limit on what he took – but not with criminal motives.

But the undue leniency of the sentence, and perhaps the undue sympathy of the court, were demonstrated by the fact that all acts by Bassus in his time as governor of Bithynia were rescinded, and anyone implicated in his legal judgements was given two years to appeal against his verdicts – a sure sign that there was underlying serious guilt. In that limited sense, right prevailed. Pliny had done his job well, if not exactly in the cause of pure justice.

But once again the story did not end there. The ambiguities about whistle-blowing reappeared, as confusing then as they are now. One of the accusers of Bassus was Theophanes, himself from Bithynia and the man who collected much of the evidence against Bassus. He himself then came under attack in the Senate, just as had Norbanus in the Spanish case, the allegation being that Theophanes also committed offences under the extortion law while collecting the evidence. Perhaps he had taken money to bring accusations against Bassus, perhaps from those same informers (*delatores*) that Bassus had pointed to in the first place. Thus the case seemed to be coming full circle. But the presiding officers of the court, the consuls, decided not to pursue the accusation against Theophanes. However, it must have become clear that Bithynia-Pontus was not a happy place, as Pliny was later to discover for himself. And it got worse. Bithynia would not go away.

Case Five: Bithynia again

No more than three years later or so, in 106 or 107, Pliny was once again drawn into the affairs of Bithynia [**5.20**, **6.5**, **6.13**, **7.6**, **7.10**]. He was again on the side of the defence, but the case once again threw up grave questions about what exactly was going on in that fractious province. So when Trajan eventually sent Pliny out there to try and sort the place out (see Chapter 14), there was already plenty of evidence of trouble there, and good reason for Trajan to suppose that Pliny might know enough about it to act effectively. The man accused – though it never came to a full trial – was Varenus Rufus, and that is extraordinary enough. Varenus Rufus had been the one whom the Bithynians had first asked to prosecute Julius Bassus on their behalf. However, he withdrew from the case, and it passed to Pliny. Varenus had then been sent to govern the province, just possibly because he appeared to enjoy good relations with its leaders, only in his turn to be faced with prosecution. The Senate voted to go ahead with the collection of evidence and witnesses, the stage of *inquisitio*. But the whole affair became bogged down in complex arguments about procedure, including a direct approach by the Bithynians to the consuls and then to the emperor Trajan himself, before there was yet another extraordinary turn of events.

A second delegation from Bithynia turned up, asking for the case to be dropped. Pliny, when asked his opinion, diplomatically said that the true representatives of Bithynia should be given a hearing, begging the question of who were the true representatives. One may suspect that Pliny as defence counsel realised that the more delay and confusion there was, the better it would be for his client. Pliny did not actually make a full speech. After more wrangling the emperor undertook to find out what the Bithynians actually wanted. Then we hear no more.

Presumably the case was dropped, and Varenus never had to face a formal trial. But the case must have taught Pliny – and maybe Trajan – that Bithynia-Pontus was prone to faction struggles and animosities, and also that the Bithynians were litigious people only too ready to turn on their friends. That may partly explain why Pliny was so cautious when his time came to be governor of Bithynia and why he was so often keen to get the emperor's personal approval for the decisions he took there. He has often been accused of timidity and feebleness in exercising his responsibilities in office in Bithynia. But how ironic and distressing it would have been if Pliny, the specialist advocate in corruption and extortion trials, was himself prosecuted for such offences, even by malicious conspirators. As it transpired, of course, he was not.

Case Six: Sitting with the emperor

There was one final case of alleged misconduct by a government official in which Pliny became involved. Once again this was in the period 106–7. But there was one big difference. The trial was before the emperor himself, and Pliny was one of Trajan's advisors in the case, an assessor in the emperor's *consilium*, his advisory council [**6.22, 6.11, 6.31**]. Pliny was clearly very pleased with himself. It was an honour to help the emperor in person, and he got to have dinner with the emperor. He had previously acted as an assessor to the Prefect in charge of the City of Rome, but that was not quite the same as sitting at the emperor's right hand. The reason why this case came before the emperor personally may be that it was a dispute between two senators about their administration of a province, and did not arise from complaints laid by the people of that province. We do not know which province the two men had been administering, but once again it showed how dysfunctional Roman rule could be.

The governor Lustricus Bruttianus had reported directly to the emperor that he had discovered his companion (*comes*) and former friend Montanius Atticinus to be implicated in a number of crimes. Atticinus retaliated with counter-charges against Bruttianus. At the hearing it was proved that they had once been close friends, to the extent that Atticinus had handwritten Bruttianus's will. But Atticinus had bribed a slave belonging to a scribe of Bruttianus, and had thereby intercepted and falsified various documents. By this means he had allegedly redirected towards Bruttianus a criminal accusation made against himself. On the advice of Pliny and the rest of the advisory council, the Emperor found Atticinus guilty, and he was banished to an island. Presumably Bruttianus was acquitted, for he was commended for his honesty.

A verdict

What is our verdict on this series of cases in which Pliny was involved? We have to aim off for the fact that, in all six cases, Pliny was more or less on the winning side, and in his letters there is an overtone of self-satisfaction about his success ratio. Perhaps, if he had a worse record in court, he would not have written so much about these trials. On the other hand, it does show that the Senate, through its agents such as Pliny, Tacitus and Albinus, was sometimes prepared to take action against at least the worst cases of malpractice by its members when holding high office. Equally, there is clear evidence from Pliny of their inherent reluctance to do so, so that the evidence had to be compelling and the accusers determined. The trials reported by Pliny

> show senatorial solidarity still at work to limit the consequences of malpractice … group solidarity and some xenophobia appear still to operate.[17]

Overall, therefore, despite the guilty verdicts, or perhaps because of them, the cases cited by Pliny do not reflect much credit on standards of administration in the empire. At best, determined subjects could get rough justice. Pliny himself may, however, be granted a degree of self-satisfaction. The subjects of the empire needed the support of men like Pliny, high on the Roman status ladder, if they were to get any justice at all. Sometimes, it appears, they did. Pliny the lawyer emerges as an honourable man, very concerned with the good name of the

Senate and its members, and prepared to act against transgressors of the admittedly subjective code of honour expected of them. He comes over as

> a conscientious, truthful man, self-important but hard-working, somewhat vain but not ungenerous, clearly not given to self-analysis.[18]

These trials of prominent men do, however, draw attention to Pliny's failure to prosecute the one man who most clearly demonstrates the odds against justice at Rome, his arch-enemy Regulus. Despite Pliny's stated intention to do so, Regulus was never brought to trial. If these corruption trials show Pliny the professional lawyer in a good light, as we may agree they do, it is in the political arena and in the competitive scramble for high public office that dark shadows are cast over Pliny's conduct, character and reputation – fairly or unfairly.

Surviving Domitian: Among the flames of thunderbolts?

In parallel with his legal career, and no doubt drawing upon the prestige it brought him, Pliny entered into a lifelong if intermittent career in public office. This took him from the most junior magistracies to the pinnacle of senator and consul. In this climb up the rungs of office and the Roman status ladder, Pliny served two famous emperors, Domitian and Trajan. Outwardly it was a distinguished and successful career in which high office and Roman-style politics were inextricably intertwined. But the 'how' and 'when' of Pliny's upward progression lead us head-on into highly controversial questions about Pliny's personal morality, his ethical standards of conduct and his truthfulness about himself. His dealings with these two emperors go to the very heart of the debate about what sort of person Pliny really was, and what our verdict on him should be.

Domitian and Trajan were diametrically different emperors, if Pliny and other Roman authors such as Suetonius are to be believed. Modern authors have tended to follow their lead, but, in the case of Domitian, with reservations. Domitian, whose reign lasted a full 15 years from 81 to 96, is commonly written down as an evil, suspicious and bloodthirsty tyrant. Trajan, who became emperor in 98, is commonly written up as a laid-back, bluff soldier and the 'best of emperors' (*optimus princeps*). Pliny worked closely with both emperors and won advancement by doing so. The contrast he draws between his two masters, one bad, one good, marks a deep fault line in Pliny's own attempts at justification for the twists and turns of his public career. But the serious accusations he has to answer (as he seems to have been well aware) are different but complementary in the case of Domitian and of Trajan. This chapter deals with Pliny and Domitian. The next chapter deals with Pliny and Trajan. A final verdict on Pliny will have to consider both.

Pliny's version: a rocky road to the top

Pliny leaves us in no doubt about what he himself wants us to believe about his early and middle career, under Domitian. He emphasises in his letters that it was a far from smooth progression up the status ladder. On the contrary it was, he claims, a perilous and discontinuous climb to the top. In a famous statement about his life during the later years of Domitian's reign, he says:

> I stood among the flames of thunderbolts dropping all around me, and there were certain clear indications to make me suppose a like end was awaiting me [**3.11**].

The thunderbolt metaphor was one that Pliny liked, perhaps dating back to his narrow escape from the eruption of Mount Vesuvius. He repeats it in his praise-speech of Trajan. Talking about himself and his friend and professional colleague Cornutus Tertullus during those years, he says that they both

> suffered from that robber and assassin of every honest man [Domitian] through the massacre of our friends as the hot breath of his falling thunderbolts passed close to our heads.[1]

Elsewhere, he says:

> I was not brought to trial, as I should have been if Domitian had lived longer.

In another letter, he summarises his career thus:

> [It] brought me advancement, then danger, then advancement [**4.2**].

So, in his letters, Pliny keeps returning to this insistent theme of the personal danger that threatened him in mid-career, during the final years of Domitian's reign. Pliny's conclusive proof of this is the notorious secret dossier denouncing him to the emperor.

The secret dossier on Pliny

Pliny tells us that, after Domitian's assassination in 96:

> among the papers found among his [Domitian's] papers was a dossier (*libellus*) of information laid against me [**7.27**].

This dossier had been prepared, he says, by a notorious informer. In other words, he was only saved from prosecution by the assassination of Domitian.

Was this dossier real? Pliny was repeatedly worried by political traps laid for him by Regulus, that most infamous of informers. But, as far as we (or Pliny) knew, Regulus never laid charges against him. But somebody else did take direct action against him, says Pliny, and that was Mettius Carus, a man also singled out by Tacitus for his villainous activities.[2]

Carus had a dangerous record as an informer. Indeed, he publicly jousted with Regulus about which of them should get the credit for which victims of imperial purges. Pliny [1.5], with his love of a good but in this case very unfunny story, tells his friend Voconius Romanus that on one occasion – place and date unspecified – Regulus was abusing the purge victim Herennius Senecio with such violence that Carus intervened with what was presumably meant to be a macabre joke, saying:

> What are my dead men to you? Have I ever attacked Crassus or Camerinus?

Crassus and Camerinus were victims of denunciation by Regulus and condemned during the reign of Nero, while Senecio, the most prominent of Domitian's victims, was (presumably) condemned on evidence provided by Carus, so was one of Carus's 'dead men'. Elsewhere [7.19] Pliny records that when Senecio was on trial it was Carus who conducted the hostile cross-examination of at least one witness, Fannia, both wife and daughter of other victims of Domitian's anger. Carus was clearly a dangerous man, a skilled and successful informer with a track record in his nasty profession. So Pliny had reason to be nervous of him.

Of course we do not know what was in the alleged Carus dossier. With experienced informers like Regulus and Carus out there reporting regularly to the emperor, there may have been dozens of such dossiers crossing Domitian's desk. The one on Pliny may not have stood out for immediate attention. Pliny was not yet of consular rank, so may not have been worth Domitian's wrath. But he might have been. It is reasonable to suppose that the dossier was not favourable to Pliny. Perhaps it tried to prove guilt by association; that is, if Pliny was a friend of people like Senecio who had been found guilty of treason, he might be similarly tainted. After all, Pliny and Senecio had been colleagues in the prosecution of Baebius Massa in 93, so their association was well known to all, including Domitian. A dossier on a known close associate of Senecio is perhaps not surprising, if, that is, the dossier really existed; the historian Ronald Syme doubted it. The real facts of Pliny's career, Syme says,

> discredit another allegation: the incriminating document from the hand of Mettius Carus ... found ... after the assassination of Domitian.[3]

If you doubt Pliny's whole account of his public career, then it is legitimate to doubt the existence of the dossier. Conversely, if you doubt the existence of the dossier, you may see Pliny's whole allegation of political and personal danger as a figment. Did Pliny make the whole thing up, or at least grossly exaggerate it? Worse than that, Pliny's career can be reconstructed in such a way as to make him into a positive chum of Domitian, a favourite who, thanks to Domitian's patronage, flourished and progressed to high office while others perished or were forced into ruinous exile. Does Pliny emerge as a hypocrite whose attempt in his letters to re-write that part of his own history is exposed by consideration of the facts as a whitewash of his dubious career record?

The two faces of Domitian

Judgement about Pliny's career under Domitian is complicated by parallel questions about Domitian himself. Was he as bad as Pliny later made out, and is the famous attack on him by Suetonius in his *Lives of the Caesars* distorted by Suetonius's bias against him? Even if Pliny really was a favourite of Domitian, was that altogether or necessarily a bad thing? Suetonius remarks on a drastic change in Domitian while in power, from clemency to cruelty and from generosity to greed. But his account is marked by consistent hostility and special animosity towards Domitian, some argue.[4] If Pliny was promoted in the earlier and better years of Domitian, perhaps that was nothing to be ashamed of?

On the other hand there is no denying that, in Domitian's great purge of the years 93–6, his later years, during which Pliny may or may not have held office, many distinguished men died or were exiled.

> That Domitian was autocratic and oppressive is scarcely denied even by his defenders … Domitian's reign was characterized not by exceptional efficiency nor by increased concern for justice and welfare but by the censoriousness of a disciplinarian … the deterioration of Domitian's relations with the governing class was intensified by his lack of *civilitas*.[5]

Lack of *civilitas* meant inapproachability and arrogance, exacerbated by his wish to be addressed as *Dominus et Deus* (Lord and God). Was Pliny closely associated with Domitian during the emperor's later period, a time of virtual paranoia? Pliny openly admits to a bad conscience about the purge years. Like his friend Tacitus – but in the safety of retrospect after Domitian had been assassinated in 96 – he confesses that he and his fellow senators did too little to help save the victims of Domitian. In a famous passage [**8.14**], Pliny speaks of a Senate that was:

> apprehensive and dumb ... summoned to idle away its time or to perpetuate some vile crime and was kept sitting for a joke or for its own humiliation ... On becoming senators we took part in these evils and continued to witness and endure them for many years, until our spirits were blunted, broken.

Pliny's retrospective regret is echoed by Tacitus, but with greater eloquence. In a much quoted passage from his life of, and tribute to, his late father-in-law Agricola, the great Roman general, Tacitus writes:

> It was not his [Agricola's] fate to see the Senate House besieged, the Senate surrounded by armed men, and in the same reign of terror so many men of consular rank butchered, the flight and exile of so many honourable women ... our hands it was which dragged Helvidius to his dungeon; it was we who were put to shame by the look which Mauricus and Rusticus gave, we who were soaked in the innocent blood of Senecio.[6]

The names Tacitus cites are those of the more famous of the victims of Domitian, some of whom, like Herennius Senecio, Pliny claims as his friends. In all, according to Suetonius, Domitian sent at least 11 men of consular rank to their deaths during his purge of the (alleged) opposition to his reign, often referred to as 'The Stoic Opposition', and many others were tortured. It was a dark and uncertain time. Yet Pliny seems to have survived, perhaps indeed prospered. The question about Pliny is therefore stark.

Did he or did he not hold high office at Rome at the very time when high-ranking men who he claimed were his friends were falling victim to that purge of alleged opponents of the regime, thus rendering Pliny open to charges of collusion and cover-up? Far from being in personal danger, as he claims, was he favoured and promoted by Domitian, only then to vilify this same emperor after his assassination in 96 in order to obscure their close working relationship? In short, was Pliny a moral turncoat?

To pick our way through this minefield, we need to go back to the beginning and track through the stages of Pliny's public career as revealed, not so much by his own words, but by those inscriptions that chance has partially preserved for us to read and which fill in a lot of the detail to add to what Pliny tells us – or skates over – in his letters.[7] We shall see that the crucial question at every turn in judging Pliny is not 'what he did' but exactly 'when'.

Pliny's early public career

At roughly the time that he first entered the law courts at an early age as an
advocate, and at roughly the same time as he contracted his first marriage, Pliny
also began his ascent of the political career ladder. What the inscriptions show
is that Pliny's first public office, probably held in 80 or 81, when he was still less
than 20 years old, was as one of the oddly titled *decemviri stlitibus iudicandis*
– an old-fashioned term for a board of 10 men who supervised legal arrange-
ments. This was a normal pre-senatorial junior magistracy, held at the earliest
at the age of 17 or 18, with a tenure of one year. Some suggest that it was in fact
obligatory to hold this office in order to proceed any further towards becoming
a senator. But there appear to be plenty of examples of men who rose high but
did not hold this junior office.

Pliny, however, may have had a special reason to do so. The main job of the
holders of this office was to organise the panels of men who, drawn from the
approved list, the so-called *album*, formed the judges and juries in cases before
the inheritance court, the Court of One Hundred Men in which Pliny was
already specialising. So he was digging himself into his chosen career.

Pliny's next step was also common but not obligatory by this time in the
empire's history. This most unmilitary of men became a military tribune,
serving with the Third Gallica legion stationed in Syria. This post he held for
a year or more, probably in 82. He did not have to do any fighting, but spent
his time polishing up the financial expertise which was to characterise his later
life and career, by auditing the accounts of the auxiliary units attached to the
legion [7.31]. These accounts were apparently in a mess, as were, he claims, the
military units themselves. Pliny was very proud of his military service – he tells
us about it no less than seven times in his letters. He justifies his decision to
enter the military by saying:

> Young men began their early training with military service, so that they might
> grow accustomed to command by obeying [8.14].

But in the same letter he makes it clear that his service was under the emperor
Domitian, at a time when morale was bad in the military.

> It was a time when merit was under suspicion and apathy an asset, when officers
> lacked influence and soldiers respect, when there was neither authority nor
> obedience.

In Syria, or on his journeys to and fro, Pliny made some useful contacts and friends, notably the famous Greek philosopher Euphrates, whose home he visited. Euphrates told him in no uncertain terms:

> Anyone who holds public office, presides at trials and passes judgement, expounds and administers justice, and thereby puts into practice what the philosopher only teaches, has a part in the philosophical life and indeed the noblest part of all [**1.10**].

In trying to follow this maxim, Pliny was to be sternly tested, maybe even found wanting. But that was for the future. After Syria, Pliny returned to Rome, where he took the next step up the lower rungs of the ladder of public office. In around 84, he became *sevir equitum Romanorum*. This was a largely ceremonial job, one of a board of six men whose job it was to organise and lead the annual 15 July horseback parade of Roman knights through the streets of Rome. These were knights who qualified to have a horse provided and maintained for them by the state, a privilege of status granted by the emperor – and withdrawn by him. These riders were no longer military men but businessmen and others belonging to the lower segment of the Roman upper class. Some of them could apparently still ride a horse, if not at a cavalry charge. Many known senators had first held this office, but with many others we do not know whether they did or not.

Pliny's middle career and the vexed issue of dates

So far, then, we can only conclude that Pliny (and his advisers) set about his public career path in a conventional, purposeful but unremarkable way. All this was about to change however, and the controversy about Pliny begins at this point. To summarise: from those lower rungs of the Roman ladder of promotion, Pliny climbed ever upwards, apparently in the normal progression of increasingly important and prestigious public offices. His next step after *sevir* was the big one, the one that gained entry to the Senate, the important post of *quaestor*. Then Pliny moved up again, to the office of Tribune of the People, then to the legal office of *praetor*. There followed two appointments in charge of important state treasuries, and later a job supervising the rivers, water supplies and sewers of Rome. Meanwhile, after the assassination of Domitian and after the interim regime of the emperor Nerva, he moved up again to the eventual rank and pinnacle of consul in 100. On paper, it was a distinguished though not unusual public career path. But there was far more to it than that. To see why this superficially conventional career arouses such controversy, we shall have to unpick the detail.

It is all about dates, specifically the dates at which he held those various successive public offices. The offices are listed in full in Table 1. There is no issue about them. The inscriptions prove that he held them. But when? There are two main versions of the chronology and Table 1 sets them both out. The essential point is that one version of the possible dates is favourable to Pliny's reputation, the other decidedly unfavourable. Some dates are neutral. So to convict or absolve Pliny of the accusations against him, we must dissect the complex evidence about the dates of his various public offices, especially the several points at which Pliny clearly enjoyed Domitian's favour.[8]

That relations between Domitian and Pliny started off well is beyond dispute. Pliny himself admits that he owed much of his early advancement to Domitian, the emperor whom he afterwards was to damn as a vicious monster (*immanissima belua*).[9] All Pliny's early advancement took place under Domitian. He was even granted special favours by Domitian, notably being excused the normally obligatory one-year gap between the office of Tribune of the People and becoming *praetor* [**7.16**]. Here was a special mark of imperial favour: Domitian emerges as Pliny's early patron. Pliny had cause to be grateful to Domitian, though later he went to great lengths not to fully admit it. Can this

Table 1. Alternative possible dates for Pliny's public career

Event or office	(A) Possible dates favourable to Pliny	(B) Possible dates neutral for Pliny	(C) Possible dates unfavourable to Pliny
Birth		61–2	
Debut in law courts		80–1	
I/c jury panels		80–1	
Military tribune		82	
I/c knights' parade		84(?)	
Quaestor	86 or 87	Area of dispute. Was Pliny in high office in the later 'purge' years of Domitian's reign – or not?	89
Tribune of the People	88 or 89		91 or 92
Praetor	89 or 90		93
Military treasury	96–7		94–6
State treasury		98–100	
Consul		100	
Priesthood		103	
I/c Tiber and sewers		104–6	
Provincial governor		110–12(?)	

advancement under Domitian be reconciled with Pliny's claims to have been in great danger from the same emperor?

Pliny as *quaestor*

The first instance of Domitian's favour came when Pliny became a *quaestor*, his first office of any great political significance, since the job brought with it membership of the Senate. Not only did he not have to canvass for support for this office [2.9], suggesting imperial favour, but once in that office he was picked out to become one of the only two (or possibly four) of the total of 20 *quaestors* who were personally attached to the emperor as *quaestor Caesaris*. This post involved conveying messages (for which one might read instructions) from the emperor to the Senate, an important communications function in government. So Domitian must have trusted him, and Pliny must have got to know Domitian well. This again suggests imperial favour.

There is, however, a problem about the date at which he was *quaestor*. Take a look at Table 1. Was it 87, 88 or 89? The standard view has been that it was 89, a date which has knock-on consequences unfavourable to Pliny for the dates of the rest of his career under Domitian. But Syme, after much deliberation, opts for the earlier date of 87, a date whose consequences are more favourable to Pliny because it begins to place Pliny's appointments more into the earlier part of Domitian's reign, which even Domitian's harsher critics agree was a more benign period.

Pliny as Tribune of the People

After the normal two-year gap, Pliny was appointed a Tribune of the People. Nothing controversial about that – except that this promotion must have meant that Pliny was, at the very least, acceptable to the emperor.

Pliny as *praetor* – but when?

Now we come to the real crux of the matter. The next conventional step after Tribune of the People was to the office of *praetor*. The *praetor* was a really high office in the Roman social and political system, and the question of when Pliny held this office lies at the very heart of the argument about his character and truthfulness. The standard calculation has been that Pliny was praetor in the year 93, the very year in which Domitian's great purge of opponents set in, a date supported by the suggestion that Pliny had previously been *quaestor* as late as 89 and Tribune of the People as late as 91 or 92, as shown in column C of Table 1. Domitian excused him the normal interval of one year between holding office as Tribune and promotion to *praetor*, so, in addition to the favouritism that this demonstrates, Domitian could have been deliberately putting Pliny into high office at a time of great tension at Rome.

If Pliny was indeed *praetor* in 93, at minimum it proves continuing patronage and trust on the part of Domitian. In that case, Pliny's protestations of his being in danger at this time are exposed as fraudulent. Pliny may even be, and indeed is, accused of collusion in Domitian's crimes, since as *praetor* he would have been involved in the legal processes and staged show-trials involved in the purge. In other words, he might be held complicit in Domitian's repression. It gets worse.

Prefect of the Military Treasury – but when?

The next dispute is about the date at which he held the post of Prefect of the Military Treasury (the *Aerarium Militare*). Pliny does not mention this important job in his letters, but it is known about from the inscriptions. It is often assumed that this appointment, very much in the gift of the emperor of the time, was held by Pliny immediately after he left the post of *praetor* in 93, and that he held it for the normal period of about three years – that is, precisely during the last and worst years of Domitian's reign. The military treasury had been set up by the emperor Augustus in 6 CE to provide pensions for soldiers at the end of their period of military service, with a financial endowment and dedicated tax revenues. It was looked after by three former *praetors*, such as Pliny, and was especially suited to Pliny's experience of finance. It was one of those routine jobs in senior Roman administration that, if it went wrong, could cause an emperor a lot of trouble; hence the need for safe pairs of hands at this military treasury, such as Pliny could provide.

The problem is this. As the job at the military treasury by convention required an ex-*praetor*, did Pliny hold this important office immediately after being *praetor* in 93, that is, for the rest of Domitian's reign? In short, did Pliny hold high office continuously during those last and terrible 'purge years' of Domitian, moving seamlessly from one high-visibility post to another, clearly with Domitian's assent and favour? Worse still, as a treasury prefect he could have been the official receiver of at least some of the money and assets seized from Domitian's victims. Hence he would be guilty of collusion and complicity in Domitian's worst excesses.

The hostile view of Pliny

This is as bad as it gets for Pliny – the accusation of being a willing accomplice to the emperor he later characterised as a 'monster', virtually a partner in crime. If these dates are correct, far from being a potential victim of the regime, as he later claimed, Pliny must have enjoyed Domitian's special trust. He must have been a 'regime trusty' right up to the end.

> If Pliny in fact held high office during Domitian's last two and a half years, it casts doubt on his picture of the danger he was in after the execution and exile of his seven friends ... if he was in fact uninterruptedly in office during Domitian's last, worst phase, the 'terror', he must be held guilty of deliberately propagating a false version of his position in his writing.[10]

Syme seems to have had little doubt about Pliny's culpability. He writes:

> Pliny survived unscathed. Indeed, he prospered, for all his declaration that he now called a halt to his career. The inscription contradicts. Pliny was one of the prefects put in charge of the *Aerarium Militare* (presumably from 94 to 96, inclusive).[11]

An even sterner critic of Pliny writes:

> Pliny was no victim of Domitian's regime ... Pliny's distinction between his situations pre- and post-93 is not only artificial; it is false ... Pliny is discovered in a fresh office, as one of the three prefects in charge of the *aerarium militare* ... Pliny was one of the fortunate few, a fact that wreaks irreparable harm on his narrative of sorrow and disfavor after 93 ... Pliny would have good reason to gloss over this appointment in subsequent years. As prefect of the military treasury, Pliny would have certified the legality of wills and received fiscal delations [i.e. allegations from informers], so that if Domitian did persecute the upper classes out of personal hostility and for infusion into the treasury, Pliny is concealing the distinct smear of his complicity.[12]

This is the most damning charge made against Pliny, that of collusion or complicity. If true, this charge would undermine the whole edifice that Pliny later tried to construct about his moral dilemmas at this period and his fundamental decency as a man 'different to Regulus'. It would, in short, convict Pliny as a liar and a phoney.

In Pliny's defence

This hostile view of Pliny depends entirely on that issue of dates. So can the dates be reconstructed in another way? There is indeed a quite different view of the dates, a view more favourable to Pliny's reputation, as set out in column A of Table 1. The argument in defence of Pliny turns essentially on the date at which he held the job of *praetor*. Was it, or was it not, in 93? All other dates derive from this one. If it was 93, then the hostile view prevails. If it was not, then his own assertion that he stood aside from public office during Domitian's bad years might be true.

One clue is that at the time of his (and Senecio's) fateful prosecution of Baebius Massa in 93, Pliny nowhere says that he was *praetor* at the time, as he surely would have done if he had held that office at that date. Indeed, as the office of *praetor* was in the main a legal office, it seems highly unlikely that Pliny would have been appointed to conduct a high-profile prosecution when also *praetor*. Nor would he have agreed to conduct such a prosecution if asked, given that even when in the more junior office of Tribune of the People he had given up his legal work [1.23]. For that reason alone there must be doubt about that all-important date of 93 for his appointment as *praetor*.

So could he have been *praetor* at a different, earlier date? If Pliny had previously been *quaestor*, not in 89 but in 86 or 87, then the knock-on consequence is that he could very plausibly have been *praetor* some years earlier than 93, say in 89 or 90 – that is, well before the purge of his friends and others set in. If Pliny was *praetor* at that earlier date, say 89, then his advancement under the special favour of Domitian would have taken place at that much earlier and more benign period of Domitian's reign, before the 'great terror' set in. Such a dating would be much more favourable to Pliny and to his reputation. The alleged danger to his person could have come after he held that office, when he was no longer in post, and the danger could have been real. Recall Pliny's own statement:

> My career brought me advancement, then danger, then advancement [4.2].

Perhaps he was telling the truth. Moreover, Pliny's time at the Military Treasury could have been not under Domitian at all, but under Domitian's stop-gap successor Nerva, say in late 96 and 97. It did not always have to be a tenure of three years, as some have assumed. In other words, an alternative look at dates can support the view that there was a long blank interval between Pliny being *praetor* and his being prefect of the Military Treasury. During this period Pliny held no office, and the period out of office included the period of Domitian's purge. It was this period in which he could have been in some degree of danger, as he asserts. Moreover, if he was not in office during these years, he cannot have been complicit in Domitian's excesses. If that is the case, we are entitled to accept Pliny's very precise claim, made in his praise speech of Trajan, that:

> I was promoted by that most treacherous emperor *before* [my italics] he admitted his hatred for good men ... [but then] I halted, preferring a longer route when I saw what the short cuts were which opened the path to office: in bad times I was numbered among those who grieved and were afraid.[13]

In other words, he says, at that critical juncture when things turned sour between Domitian and some of his senior subjects, Pliny withdrew from public life, so could not be held guilty by association. But would he have dared to withdraw? The mere act of withdrawal could be taken as an act of treason, a blatant advertisement of the fact that you disapproved of the regime. But if that is the case, and if Pliny did withdraw, then that in itself may justify his assertion of being in danger at that time.

The curious case of the visit(s) to the philosopher

There is, however, one further but major obstacle to be faced before we can accept Pliny's own version of events rather than that of his critics. The proof that Pliny must have been *praetor* in the year 93 and in no other year turns on one otherwise unexciting event in Pliny's life, his visit (or visits) to the philosopher Artemidorus. If the date of 93 is confirmed by this event, as many believe, then that proves the hostile date sequence for Pliny's various public offices and tarnishes his reputation – the sequence set out in column C of Table 1. Pliny is thereby skewered by his own characteristic ambiguity in not telling us his own story in full. But is the Artemidorus episode as watertight as it may seem?

It is Pliny himself who tells us the story. To bolster his case with more evidence of the dangers he ran he appears to tell us [3.11] that, when he held the office of *praetor* (that is, some time under Domitian), he went to visit Artemidorus after philosophers such as Artemidorus had been expelled by the emperor. He also provided Artemidorus with an interest-free loan to pay off his debts when:

certain of his rich and influential friends hesitated to do so.

This, says Pliny, involved a degree of risk to himself because of the attention it attracted. But the risk was justified because Artemidorus was an old friend from Pliny's days as a military tribune in Syria in 82 with the Third Gallica legion. To rub it in, Pliny emphasises that this was also a dangerous time during which seven people he knew, members of the group known as 'the Stoic Opposition', had been put to death or exiled. Their offence was the holding of philosophical opinions as well as family traditions hostile to absolute monarchy. In the famous 'thunderbolt' statement, Pliny forcefully associates his generosity towards Artemidorus with that time when:

> Senecio, Rusticus and Helvidius were dead, and Mauricus, Arria, Gratilla and Fannia were in exile. I stood among the flames of thunderbolts dropping all around me [**3.11**].

So even visiting an exiled philosopher, implies Pliny, could arouse imperial suspicion, particularly as Artemidorus was the son-in-law, and presumably the ideological follower, of another famous Stoic philosopher, Musonius Rufus. The Stoic connection may have been significant and increasingly dangerous. Since we know that Domitian's purge broke loose in 93, at first sight this otherwise innocuous anecdote seems to confirm that Pliny was indeed *praetor* in that same year of 93. If it was a dangerous visit to make, as Pliny claims, that just goes to show that Pliny was both in office and in the good books of Domitian at that time. Otherwise he would not have dared to do it. This is the whole evidence and argument for believing that Pliny was *praetor* in 93. If it is valid, then the case against Pliny wins.

... but were there two visits?

Pliny's account of his relations with Artemidorus, however, may not be as straightforward as it looks at first. It is often assumed that Pliny's statement implies only one visit, and that would necessarily have been in 93, the year when, some conclude, he must have been *praetor*. But perhaps there were two visits to Artemidorus, made at different times. The first could have been when he was indeed *praetor*, not however in 93 but in 89 or 90, as suggested above, a time when it would not have been dangerous. The second visit could indeed have been in 93, but by that time he was out of office and it would indeed have been dangerous because of the alleged connection between philosophical dogma and political hostility to Domitian.[14] In a curious phrase, Suetonius tells us that Domitian banished all philosophers from Rome and from Italy.[15]

Aulus Gellius uses a similar phrase.[16] Various other classical authors also use words that can be taken to imply not one, but two waves of expulsion, the first from Rome only, the second from all of Italy, as Domitian closed in on 'the Stoic tendency'.[17] Dio remarks that:

All the philosophers that were left in Rome were banished once again.[18]

So Dio implies two sets of expulsions. Pliny is quite explicit that his visit to Artemidorus when *praetor* took him only as far as the suburbs of Rome, so that visit cannot have taken place once Artemidorus and his colleagues were exiled from the whole of Italy. Moreover, if he was holding high office in Rome at the time, Pliny could hardly have been away for long enough to travel further than the vicinity of Rome.

So a plausible explanation is that Pliny visited Artemidorus not once but twice, and that his statement in letter **3.11** is a sort of summary or telescoping, appropriate to a letter but not to a history book, of different events spread over a period of time. The first visit, made in 89 or 90 when he was *praetor*, may have carried some risk, but not much. The second visit, when Pliny lent Artemidorus a lot of money but when he was no longer *praetor*, carried much more (and undeniable) risk, since it coincided with the general purge gathering pace around him. Pliny's assertion about that is quite clear. Pliny deserves credit for taking that risk when he did, whether or not he was in office. But the main thing is that if there were indeed two visits to Artemidorus, then the case against Pliny falls, the date sequence favourable to Pliny, as set out in column A of Table 1, can stand, and Pliny's good name is just about cleared.

So there you have it. On one arrangement of the dates, Pliny stands accused. On another arrangement of the dates, he is exonerated. On one he is a liar, on the other he is (broadly) telling the truth. As with so much else to do with Pliny's political career, in the end you either believe his own account, or you do not. The evidence raises complex questions without finally answering them.

Personally, I give Pliny the benefit of the doubt. Accepting one version of the dates rather than the other, and accepting two visits to Artemidorus rather than one, plus all that flows from them, is the only way to make coherent sense of what Pliny says in his letters, written and published when there were many people still alive who would have remembered the events and known whether or not his account was true or false. Pliny surely would not have dared to risk that.

Aftermath: Small revenge

Pliny boasts that the aftermath of Domitian's assassination in 96

> was a splendid opportunity for attacking the guilty, avenging the injured, and making oneself known [**9.13**].

He told the widow of Helvidius that he was determined not to leave her husband unavenged, and claims that:

> I was moved to act not so much by personal obligations as by the demands of common justice, the enormity of the deed, and the thought of establishing a precedent.

But for all the fine talk, he was able to do very little. He did not dare to launch a prosecution against Regulus, nor did he pursue his accuser Mettius Carus. The man he did pursue in 97 during a fiercely argued session of the Senate was a relatively minor figure called Publicius Certus [**9.13**]. Pliny accused Certus of 'bloodstained servility', presumably for his part in the death of the younger Helvidius Priscus. Certus got off quite lightly. Before Pliny could even name him in the Senate debate he had provoked, he was met with hostile cries of:

> Tell us who is the object of this irregular attack!

And

> Let us survivors remain alive!

In face of this, his petition before the Senate was then scaled down by other speakers to a request that:

> if such flagrant crimes as those committed by Certus are to go unpunished, he should at least be branded with some degradation.

And so it proved to be. Certus was not formally accused or tried. Instead, he was removed from his office at the head of the state treasury, the so-called Treasury of Saturn, and was denied the office of consul which normally followed on from that important job. But even here there must be a tinge of doubt about Pliny's motives. It may not all have been about 'common justice'. When Certus died shortly afterwards, his successor at that important treasury job was none other than Pliny himself, along with his friend Tacitus. This would have been about the years 98–9. Pliny then went on, unlike Certus, to become consul, the pinnacle and objective of his career, in 100. So Pliny gained a lot from securing Certus's partial downfall.

To be fair to Pliny and his low-key search for justice, neither Nerva, Domitian's immediate successor as emperor, nor Trajan who followed him, seem to have had much appetite for retrospective justice or judicial revenge. Pliny got little encouragement from on high to scratch at old sores, and could not have done much without imperial encouragement. Also, too many people still in power had guilty consciences for what they did or did not do under Domitian. Moreover, Nerva was forced by the Praetorian Guard to put to death the assassins of Domitian. Domitian was popular with his soldiers, in part because he paid them well. So not everyone shared Pliny's hostility to that emperor – or else they were afraid of what the assassins knew.[19] Pliny, ever circumspect, knew not to push his luck.

Later, when Domitian was safely dead, assassinated in September 96, Pliny claimed these victims of Domitian as his friends, and made a show of helping those of them that survived, or their surviving relatives. From the safety of Nerva's and Trajan's reigns, Pliny rushed about trying to do what he could for the survivors, as a sort of expiation. The brother of the executed Rusticus asked Pliny to find a suitable tutor for Rusticus's two orphaned sons [2.18] and a husband for his niece [1.14]. Pliny writes extensively about his claimed friendship with the executed Helvidius, his speeches in vindication of Helvidius [9.13], and his friendship with Fannia, Helvidius's step-mother and herself a former exile. Was this all a sign of a bad conscience? Or something worse than that?

It was left to Pliny's letters, and to the histories written by his close friend Tacitus, to award some sort of retrospective justice to Domitian's victims. Pliny's letters meanwhile can be taken as at the same time truthful, and economical with the truth. Neither they nor the other evidence substantiate beyond doubt the main hostile accusations made against him. Nor, however, do his letters and deeds completely exonerate him. From his great early patron and guardian Verginius Rufus, Pliny had learnt well the lessons and arts of survival.

Tactically praising Trajan: 'You tell us to be free: We will be'

You might have thought that having wriggled his way out of the hostile accusations made against him for his activities under the 'evil' emperor Domitian, Pliny and his career would have reached calmer waters under the 'good' emperor Trajan, who took office in 98, after the assassination of Domitian in 96 and the death of the elderly stop-gap emperor Nerva. But not so. Perhaps paradoxically, exactly the same accusation of being just an imperial sycophant is provoked by his relationship with the 'good' emperor Trajan as with the preceding 'bad' emperor, the one accusation reinforcing the other.

The test for Pliny's attitudes and character under Trajan is the big speech he gave which we know as the *Panegyricus* – the Panegyric.[1] Nothing has earned Pliny greater scorn than this speech, which he delivered before the Roman Senate in September of the year 100 in praise of the emperor Trajan, in Trajan's presence. Hence the title it is given – a panegyric, a formal speech of praise, often called an encomium or eulogy. *Panegyricus* was not Pliny's title for it, but it has stuck. Its importance is two-fold. First, it is almost unique.

> It is the only complete speech to survive to us from the last of Cicero's Philippics in 43 BCE to the celebrations of the emperor Maximian's birthday in 289, a speech which itself draws upon the language and imagery of Pliny's praise.

Its style and structure were and are therefore of considerable interest for students of literature and composition. But second, the speech is also a historical document.

> Pliny's *Panegyricus* has always been considered both a very important document for recovering Trajanic Rome, and at the same time an immensely problematic source of information on the events it purports to relate. It provides us with a precious eyewitness report of a period which is documented with an almost singular poverty.[2]

But it is the tone and language of the speech that offended so many. Its repetitive and unctuous flattery of the emperor has stuck in the gullet of even the hardiest admirers of Pliny's collected letters. Badly constructed, overly verbose, fulsome, diffuse, cringing, too full of compliments for modern taste – these are only some of the pejorative adjectives hurled at this lengthy speech. How could Pliny, self-advertised opponent of tyranny, be such a creep? Could there be any excuse for the groveling tone? Did Trajan the plain and blunt soldier really demand such flummery and flattery?

And did the speech need to go on for so tediously long? In some people's eyes, Pliny's sucking up to the 'good' emperor Trajan in this speech is as bad as, or even worse than, his alleged cosying up to the 'bad' emperor Domitian. Thus Pliny is caught in a double denunciation. The bad taste left by the tone of this speech is only made worse, say the critics, by the equally groveling tone of his later letters to Trajan from the province that Pliny was later sent out to govern, as we shall discuss in Chapter 14.

A double agenda?

But is this scorn justified? Perhaps there is more to the *Panegyricus* than meets the eye of the reader already inclined to distrust Pliny. Perhaps the speech has not one, but two agendas half-hidden inside the flattery. One is to praise with a purpose. Writing about a different century but the same country, Italy, one author says:

> A Renaissance courtier, whether literary-minded or not, would learn to employ panegyric with skill, and the skill lies not in praising insincerely but in praising tactically.[3]

Pliny certainly 'praises tactically'. His tactic is to try to define, for the ears of both the emperor himself and for the members of the Roman Senate (and so for posterity) how free men may coexist with an absolute autocrat – the central and recurring political dilemma for the Roman Empire and many more recent autocracies, including those of the Italian Renaissance and of the twentieth century. The word liberty, *libertas*, appears no less than 17 times in the speech. What could liberty consist of when one man was all powerful? At the heart of this speech is an attempt to nail down what liberty meant in practical terms, and to do so in the heart of government in a public forum like the Senate where the Emperor will have some difficulty in worming his way out of it. To the extent that he succeeded, Pliny deserves recognition for political astuteness, even courage of a sort.

His second agenda, less obvious from the language, is to praise himself, if only by association and by implication.

> Pliny leaves little doubt that he is both close to the centre of power and well qualified to assess it … He goes even further, however, systematically (and often superfluously) displaying insider knowledge … the speech is not really about emperors or imperial rule. It is ultimately about Pliny himself … leaving [his listeners] with the impression of an important and respected statesman who is honoured by his peers.[4]

A convenient lie?

The definition of liberty, *libertas*, that Pliny offers is narrowly class-based, aimed at a specific audience, namely his listeners in the Senate. It is not about the general population of the Roman Empire at all. It is almost entirely about how the Roman senatorial upper class can co-exist with an absolute autocrat, and it involves both sides of the political bargain knowingly conniving in a lie, a Noble Lie or a Convenient Lie depending on how you view it. This lie is that freedom is not a right but a gift that can be conferred by the autocrat, handed down from above, and consists in the autocrat refraining from interfering in the lives of his more important subjects when both sides know that he has the almost unchecked power to do so whenever he wishes – unchecked, that is, except by assassination, as in the case of Domitian. It is not a modern conception of freedom, which is full of positive rights – of speech, of religion, of movement. It is a negative definition that Pliny offers, not a 'freedom to' but a 'freedom from', the voluntary absence of something, and that something was interference by the emperor in the lives and (even more importantly) in the wealth and assets of Pliny's own peer group. After the dreadful periods of recurring harsh tyranny that Rome had experienced in recent decades, as under the emperors Nero and Domitian, perhaps this was the most useful thing that Pliny could do.

Rising to the pinnacle: State treasury, then consul

How had Pliny's career moved on since the death of Domitian so as to bring him to this point where he acted, in effect, as the official spokesman of the senatorial upper class, to his own greater renown? We left Pliny in the office of Prefect of the Military Treasury under (we believe) the emperor Nerva, that is, after the death of Domitian. From there, Pliny moved on to another and more important treasury job, once again demonstrating his ability with finance. This new office was prefect of the so-called *Aerarium Saturni*, the Treasury of Saturn. This job was a normal final step towards the very top of the Roman status ladder, the post of consul.

This treasury took its name from the temple in which it was housed. Its role was to hold state documents of all kinds, including decrees of the Senate, and the actual cash belonging to the state. From it were paid any disbursements ordered by the Senate. It had been set up by the emperor Nero in 56, perhaps not coincidentally, since another of its functions was to receive property to which there was no heir, and the property of condemned men – of which there was no shortage under Nero. But under any emperor, to be its prefect it was clearly an important job.

Pliny elbowed his way into this job and into the rewards that followed from it. We have seen how Pliny, as a substitute for his avowed but unreachable target Regulus, tried to prosecute a minor figure called Publicius Certus. Certus was removed from office as head of the Treasury of Saturn and barred from the office of consul. Certus died shortly after, and his successor at the treasury was Pliny himself, along with Tacitus, in the years 98–9. Then, having done this treasury job well enough, in the year 100 Pliny received the ultimate reward he craved – promotion to the august rank of consul. And that was the occasion for this controversial speech.

Senatorial protocol or prostituted rhetoric?

The speech was in one sense routine. As an official duty, the senior of the two incoming consuls regularly thanked the emperor for their promotion to consular rank by means of a speech praising the emperor, called an *actio gratiarum*, a motion of thanks and acceptance. It was part of Senatorial protocol, and was itself an indication of how power at Rome flowed downwards from the centre. The emperor granted you this high office, and it was compulsory to say thank-you. It was an occasion at which

outward form, however false or tedious, had to be respected.[5]

If the emperor was in Rome, this 'tedious' ceremony may have taken place as many as six times a year, as each new set of consuls took office. We have no other examples of these acceptance speeches with which to compare Pliny's. Pliny himself must have listened to many of them during his career in the Senate. But just possibly Pliny's effort was more artful that most, and more artful than he has been given credit for by many of his critics.

It may be compared – but only with difficulty – to the more philosophical speeches composed by Trajan's other close friend, Dio Chrysostom, about the arts and duties of kingship, which may have been composed at about the same time, may also have been delivered to the emperor in person, and may have also survived in their written versions. Dio may even have been in Rome at the time of Pliny's oration, and Pliny was to meet him again during his later appointment as the emperor's special envoy to the province of Bithynia-Pontus, Dio's home territory. But there is no hint of any cross-references between the two, and, despite its verbiage, Pliny's speech is much the more interesting.

The long and the short of it

Pliny was certainly very proud of his effort. So much so that he decided to lengthen and elaborate it into a version suitable for general publication and invited some of his friends to come round and hear him read it. This is the version of the speech that we have. What relation it bears to the original speech as spoken in the Senate, apart from being longer, we do not know. What happened at Pliny's reading of the text to his friends suggests that this expanded version may be as much as three times as long as the original. Many readers of it today think that Pliny would have done himself a great favour by not lengthening it, or not nearly as much.

> It has fallen, not undeservedly, into almost universal contempt. Pliny would have been wiser if he had not expanded and developed the more simple version actually delivered in the Senate ... the speech is couched in the grand style, full of florid conceits and rhetorical artifice ... as wearisome as they are vacuous [but] it is probably his woolly repetitiveness which in the end reduces most readers to despair.[6]

Pliny at one point [55] almost gives the game away himself, and says openly to Trajan:

> Since adulation has exhausted any possibility of innovation, the only way left for us to do you honour is to venture sometimes to say nothing.

Many have wishes that he had followed his own instinct. But of course he could not. This was not one of those 'sometimes'. He had to give a speech as protocol demanded, and then decided to capitalise on the effort he had put into it. In a letter [3.18] Pliny tells us that:

> I thought it my proper duty as a loyal citizen to give the same subject a fuller and more elaborate treatment in a written version ... When I had decided to give a reading of the speech to my friends, I did not invite them by note or programme, but simply asked them to come 'if convenient' or if they 'really had time' ... the weather too was particularly bad, but nevertheless they attended two days running and ... they made me continue for a third day.

Not of course a whole day, but perhaps (at a guesstimate) an hour or so each day. So if the longer version took three normal sessions to read out, perhaps the speech that Trajan heard in one session was a third of what we now have. Lucky Trajan.

> Three hours of intensive glorification would be an inhuman ordeal for the most patient of rulers.[7]

But Trajan would certainly have seen the longer version as well, so Pliny must have been confident that his emperor would approve of its contents. Possibly Pliny was only saying what he already knew Trajan wanted him to say. Pliny also sent copies of the long version out to his friends, such as one to Voconius Romanus [3.13], probably in a deliberate attempt to ensure its survival as a work of literature. In the longer term, his *Panegyricus* certainly did survive and became an example to others of how to compose praise-speeches. We have it only because it was put at the head of a collection of 12 praise-speeches, the so-called *Panegyrici Latini*, all the rest of which date to several centuries later and may have been composed in Gaul. This grouping has provoked more than one caustic comment, such as:

> The *Panegyric* was preserved and became the parent and model for a prostituted rhetoric of the Gallic renaissance of the fourth century ... [Pliny] in his ideals of oratory seems to be hopelessly wrong ... [but] there are some terse and epigrammatic sentences which redeem it.[8]

A manuscript containing this collection was found in 1433, then lost, but not before copies had been made. So, fulsome or not, Pliny's composition – by far the longest of the 12, thanks to Pliny's extensive revisions – has had a long if chancy afterlife.

Blaming Domitian – tactically

Does his speech deserve this long life? Syme is typically cynical about it, dismissive of any substantive content in it and dismissive of Pliny's motives, especially in relation to Domitian.

> To enhance Trajan and exhibit his own virtuosity, Pliny evokes at great length the tyranny of Domitian. The facts were bad enough to tell their own tale. Such is the regularity with which he [Pliny] distorts them, that the reality underlying the rhetoric can often be surmised or disinterred. An official orator need not confine his loyal efforts to distorting the truth. It may sometimes be expedient to suppress it entirely.[9]

This dismissive verdict of course turns essentially on Syme's view of Pliny's earlier career during the years 93 to 96. Syme thought that Pliny prospered under Domitian, so that the hostile references to Domitian that echo like an insistent drumbeat punctuating the whole length of the *Panegyricus* are hypocritical. Pliny certainly lays it on thick about Domitian, demonstrating the oratorical gift which made his *Panegyricus* such a model for others. For example, talking about the imperial palace, he says:

> This is the place where recently that fearful monster [Domitian] built his defences with untold terrors, where lurking in his den he licked up the blood of his murdered relatives or emerged to plot the massacre and destruction of his most distinguished subjects [**48**].

Lurid stuff. Domitian had put to death both the sons of his father's brother, that is, his own cousins, who might have been rivals for his throne, and also a number of senators. Domitian therefore provides Pliny with a definition of what *libertas* is not. This is the point of another colourful passage in the *Panegyricus* in which Pliny tells how under Domitian people did not even dare to show their own preferences towards this or that gladiator in the circus arena. Comparing the present with the past, he says:

> No one now risked the old charge of impiety [i.e. treason] if he disliked a particular gladiator; no spectator found himself turned into the spectacle, dragged off by the hook to satisfy grim pleasures or else cast to the flames. He [Domitian] was a madman who used the arena for collecting charges of high treason, who felt himself slighted and scorned if we failed to pay homage to his gladiators [**33**].

Dead gladiators, like beasts killed in the arena and like men executed for treason, were dragged away by a big hook inserted into the corpse. If a true story, it nevertheless was a powerful metaphor for how the aristocracy felt about its arbitrary treatment by Domitian, at least in his later years in office.

Ending the 'servile war'

As a contrast to Domitian, Pliny praises Trajan for restoring the proper order of things, at least from the perspective of a Roman aristocrat. In particular, he commends Trajan for taking steps to keep slaves in their proper place. The hated Domitian had used slaves as informers against their owners and therefore upset the proper order of society by conferring power upon the powerless. Pliny says:

> Loyalty is restored among friends, a sense of duty to freedmen and obedience to slaves, who can now respect and obey and keep their masters … you have freed us all from the accuser in our homes … and suppressed what might be called a servile war … how welcome it is for those of us who remember that emperor [Domitian] who suborned slaves against the very lives of their masters [42].

In similar vein he congratulates Trajan [88] on keeping the imperial freedmen in their proper (subservient) place. Trajan had acted to re-secure the class boundaries that put senators at the top and slaves at the bottom. The aristocrats had suffered materially from autocrats who flouted the law and used slaves as their instruments, so the rule of law – even though the emperor could also make the law – became a keystone of Pliny's attempt to define, tactically, how the new emperor was reforming the functions and role of his high office. Pliny was no believer in equality. Praising a friend for his firm action in upholding the traditional class distinctions, Pliny in one letter pithily remarks :

Nothing is more unequal than equality itself [9.5].

This sounds like an epigram he learnt at oratory school. But it summed up his belief in firm class boundaries as a way of maintaining a stable society – a policy he is recommending to Trajan, and one that his audience would have found very reassuring.

Purifying the language

But before he can do all that, Pliny first of all has to scrub clean the language that he uses in his speech, or try to. It is a mistake to be too mesmerised by the flummery in the *Panegyricus*, copious as it is. Pliny was well aware – and says so – that the excesses of flattery aimed at the emperor had by his time so debased and corrupted the language of politics that it was almost impossible to sound sincere in praising even a good emperor.

> My vote of thanks should be as far removed from a semblance of flattery as it is from constraint … we should endeavour to say nothing about our ruler which could have been said of any of his predecessors … Away with expressions formerly prompted by fear … nowhere should we flatter him [i.e. Trajan] as a god and a divinity.

But Pliny has to make clear what he means by his attempt to purify the language of praise. In a telling passage, he explains:

> There is no danger that in my references to his humanity he will see a reproach for arrogance; that he will suppose I mean extravagance by modest expenditure, and cruelty by forbearance; that I think him covetous and capricious when I call him generous and kind, profligate and idle instead of self-controlled and active, or that I judge him a coward when I speak of him as a brave man [3].

When anything can mean its opposite, and when his audience had sat through many speeches in which exactly that happened, or was suspected, Pliny has to insist that he means what he says, as a preliminary to getting down to his real theme, that of using his new conception of liberty, *libertas*, as a way of protecting and promoting the interests of the senatorial class to which both he and his hearers and readers belonged. It is a paradox that, in claiming to do away with false and obligatory flattery, Pliny himself luxuriates in acres of supposedly sincere flattery to decorate his message, so that the message is difficult to discern. What is that message?

Pliny as political theorist

Trajan, says Pliny, is introducing a new moral order. It is one in which stage mimes and their 'perverted art' are banished [45] and philosophers are valued [47]. This is an implied contrast with Domitian's expulsion of philosophers from

Rome and from Italy, an episode that came close to home for Pliny since it put him in personal danger because of his long friendship with the philosopher Artemidorus – or so Pliny says (see Chapter 7). But in the main Pliny struggles to arrive at a notion of liberty that was more than just a change of emperors from a bad one to a good one, and independent of a particular emperor. He wrestles with that fundamental paradox – how to be free under an absolute autocrat whose word is law. So his *Panegyricus* can be read as:

> An exercise in political theorizing ... as it explores ways to conceive life as the Romans wish to live it, as free yet within the constraints of absolute rule ... a new conception of *libertas* ... at the least, in its invention of a conception of freedom that attends to the constraints created by severe asymmetries of power, Pliny's *Panegyricus* should be understood as a serious intervention in Roman political thought.[10]

So the Panegyric was about imperial ideology. Pliny tells us plainly what he thinks his speech is about. He declares roundly that Trajan

> is amending and reforming the character of the Principate, which has become debased by a long period of corruption. [53]

Pliny makes three bold assertions with special resonance for his hearers. The first assertion, astonishing in its implications, is that the all-powerful autocratic emperor is nevertheless himself subject to the law.

> You submitted yourself to the laws, the laws which no one designed for the emperor ... now for the first time we can say, not 'the emperor is above the law', but 'the law is above the emperor' [65].

At a practical level, Pliny's fellow senators, with their money, property, assets and status at stake, would have seen it as particularly important to know that they could rely on the law being upheld. Most of Roman law was about property, and respect for law by the autocrat was fundamental to the sense of security of the upper class to which Pliny belonged. What the men of wealth most hated was insecurity, the capriciousness that a wayward emperor like Domitian could exhibit.

The second assertion, almost as astonishing, is that the emperor is making himself accountable – literally. Pliny says:

> An emperor must learn to balance accounts with his empire, to go abroad and return with the knowledge that he must publish his expenses and account for his movements, so that he will not spend what he is ashamed to make known to all [20].

To make his point, Pliny was drawing on a field he was familiar with – financial accounts. But the suggestion that a Roman emperor should publish his accounts for all to inspect, is both unusual and implausible. Politically, it is on a par with Pliny's equally unlikely, if desirable, suggestion that the emperor was also subject to the law.

His third assertion is perhaps, to the modern ear, the most astonishing of the three.

> You tell us to be free: we will be (*iubes esse liberos: erimus*) [**66**].

How can someone be ordered to be free? To us it seems a contradiction in terms. But Pliny's claim must be seen in the Roman context. It had a very limited meaning. For senators, it meant a freedom to speak their mind without fear of reprisal during debates in the Senate. Pliny says exactly that.

> You tell us to express ourselves openly, and we shall do so ... open our lips long sealed by servitude.

No doubt senators would use this new freedom with discretion. It did not change the realities of power. Perhaps this new *libertas* amounted to little more in practice than the expulsion of the sinister informers Pliny so graphically describes. If so, it was an illusion of freedom, a kind of convenient political lie in which, if everyone colluded, everyone could be happy, or so Pliny suggests.[11] But taken literally and if put into practice, his three propositions would have added up to a revolution in the governance of the empire, a taming of autocracy. But Pliny was no revolutionary, and he probably had more modest if still tangible ambitions.

Liberty of the purse

Pliny's attempt to flesh out his conception of this new freedom was centred elsewhere, not on political rights, but on the very specific and practical financial bargains and privileges that Pliny, using the opportunity of this speech, was trying to negotiate with his emperor on behalf of the senatorial class to which he belonged, and which were his audience. No wonder those who missed his speech when delivered in the Senate flocked to hear him read out his extended version afterwards. A mere literary event it was not. It was all about money.

Pliny drew extensively on his own career and fields of experience, in the

Court of One Hundred Men dealing with inheritance cases and as prefect in charge of two of the state treasuries. He refers pointedly to the

new security of wills [43].

This is contrasted with the previous reign when the emperor's name was misused to give authority to forged documents which invalidated a rich man's will and so made the assets named in it forfeit to the state treasury. In striking phrases that demonstrate Pliny's powers as an orator, he says:

> It is a pleasure to see peace and quiet restored to the treasury, to see it as it was before the days of informers. Now it is a real temple, not a mortuary of citizens and a grim depository for blood-soaked spoils ... Men no longer go in fear of informers: instead they fear the law ... anyone may call your procurator or his agent to justice, to appear in court ... the same court serves the principate and the cause of liberty (*eodem foro utuntur principatus et libertas*) [36].

This is a particularly striking formulation. It equates and interlocks the security of wills, the end of the activities of informers, the right to appeal to the law, the interests of the emperor, and the cause of liberty (*libertas*). A heady mix. Pliny, as we have seen elsewhere, lays particular emphasis on the curbing of the activities of informers who sought personal gain from challenging the wills of rich men. This accounts for that extraordinary scene [34–5] which Pliny narrates in which boatloads of informers were bound, marched into the amphitheater to be abused by the populace, and then cast adrift at the mercy of the wind and waves to perish or survive on whatever rocky islands they are shipwrecked.

The 'new security of wills' would have been a big prize for the Roman aristocracy. It meant freedom from the insistent twin threats. first of informers seeking to profit personally from invalidating wills and, second, of an emperor encouraging these informers to bring treason charges just to enrich the state treasury. Pliny by this time knew a lot about both private wills and the public purse. It was *libertas* of a sort, a 'freedom from' this type of malpractice, and so a fundamental one for men of property.

Inheritance tax

There was another 'freedom from'. That was freedom from paying taxes, specifically inheritance tax, an area Pliny knew even better. He goes on at great length – four whole sections of the speech [37–40] – about the 5 per cent inheritance tax, the *vicesima hereditatum*. This was introduced by Augustus in the year 6, nearly 100 years before, as the main source of income for the military treasury, the *aerarium militare* of which Pliny also by now had direct experience as its prefect. What pleases Pliny is not having to pay it. Trajan had apparently extended immunity from this tax in the name of fairness, but also in the name, says Pliny, of preserving and fostering family ties by not letting inheritance tax debts owed to the state damage private family unity. In his profession, he had probably seen many families torn apart by squabbles over who should inherit what, or be liable to pay what.

Nevertheless, it all sounds like specious window-dressing. Trajan had also given immunity to small estates, and cancelled debts contracted before his reign began. Paying less tax, and not having to pay back your debts, is bound to be a popular policy for a new emperor seeking approval from the class most likely to support (or depose) him. Pliny dresses it up with all the verbal finery he can muster. Yet he is also infuriatingly vague about the detail of these fiscal reforms, which as a senior treasury official he would surely have known a lot about. Perhaps the detail would have pointed up the narrow class focus of Trajan's fiscal concessions. Pliny also stresses other things [**50**], such as the new safety of personal property, the restoration work on town mansions, the selling-off of surplus property by the state treasury. (To whom? To those who could afford to buy it, presumably.) But the key freedom, Pliny tells Trajan, and a key definition of *libertas*, was freedom from taxation, and Trajan had duly obliged. Why?

A troubled inheritance

Trajan had good reason to express his gratitude, by tax concessions and cancellation of debts, to those people who until his elevation to the purple had been his peer group and equals. In an extended and surprising passage [**5–8**] Pliny details the political troubles into which the Roman state had threatened to fall during the brief reign of Trajan's predecessor, Nerva, who died in late January 98, less than three years before Pliny's speech. The events of that time were therefore fresh in the senators' minds. It was a troubled time in which civil war threatened to break out all over again, as had happened 30 years earlier. There was uncertainty about the succession, a mutiny by the Praetorian Guard in Rome under its commander Casperius Aelianus, and the emperor himself was under virtual palace-arrest.[12]

You might have expected Pliny to stay silent about this unhappy period, by the end of which Trajan had emerged from almost nowhere to be Nerva's chosen (or enforced) successor, expressed by his formal adoption as Nerva's son and heir. But to the contrary, Pliny launches into a graphic account of the troubles, trying to disguise a political fix (probably between the senior generals of the army) by rewriting it as a story of the saviour Trajan riding nobly to the rescue of a state in peril – and contradicting himself as he goes along.

> He [Trajan] was not created by civil war and a country racked by the arms of battle ... you were reluctant to assume imperial power ... persuaded because you saw your country in peril and the whole realm tottering to a fall ... threatened with destruction ... rioting and mutiny had broken out in the army ... an emperor was besieged in his palace, arrested and confined ... army discipline broke down.

All this trouble was ordained, he claims, just so that Trajan could be called in as saviour of the state. Yet Pliny's words cover up, if only just, the obvious fact that Rome had been in trouble, that Nerva had little choice in the matter, and that Trajan had not been elected to the job by formal vote of the Senate but as the result of a peaceful *coup d'état*. Nevertheless, it was the men of senatorial rank who had thrust Trajan into power. It was time to show his gratitude to them, just in case those who put him there decided to un-put him.

But Pliny's story was also a pointed reminder that the principal function of the all-powerful emperor was to prevent civil war, to shield the state from chaos, and to be acutely aware that the most likely time for civil war to break out was the moment of succession between one emperor and the next. Wrap it up as he may in flummery, Pliny could hardly have delivered a more pointed piece of practical political advice, as numberless kings, princes, tyrants, emperors and czars have discovered both before and ever since Pliny's day.

In praise of praise

So we may fairly conclude that Pliny's speech in praise of Trajan, obligatory as it was and bound by rules of protocol at Rome, was not just a gratuitous exercise in obnoxious flattery, and should not be used as a weapon to discredit Pliny, still less to make him an object of mockery. There is a serious if self-interested agenda at work in the speech which makes it worthy of survival. It is about what freedom, *libertas*, might mean under an absolute autocrat, and about what type of *libertas* the autocrat should encourage among his senior subjects so as to secure his position as absolute ruler by implied consent. That is the real meaning of that otherwise extraordinary statement of Pliny's:

You tell us to be free: we will be.

This is an unadorned paradox, more than just a professional orator's flourish, that Pliny suggests must sit at the heart of any *modus vivendi* between an autocrat and his most powerful subjects. Freedom is not a right, but must be given, top down. When offered it, the senators must take it and the advantages it confers with good grace, as the best substitute available for the real *libertas* that they had lost a century or more before with the demise of the old Roman republic. Freedom thus conferred can be withdrawn. But the reward is that the senatorial class will enjoy tax benefits and security of their enormous assets and high status. The emperor will enjoy freedom from rebellion (rebellion such as Nerva experienced) and, at the extreme, from assassination (as experienced by Domitian).

It was a political bargain at the heart of the Roman state that Pliny was proposing to his listeners, who included the emperor, a bargain limited in scope to 'freedoms from' and limited in reach to the upper crust and their financial self-interest, but detailed with indicative examples and well coated in oratorical sugar. Quite clever really – in the circumstances and manners of the time – and it was a political compact that was to hold fast for decades after Pliny proposed it. His speech did after all come towards the beginning of that long period of the 'Five Good Emperors' (Nerva, Trajan, Hadrian, Antoninus Pius, Marcus Aurelius) that many, like the great Roman historian Gibbon, regard as the apogee, the golden age of the Roman Empire. Perhaps Pliny praised tactically to some lasting effect – lasting, that is, for about 80 years, until it all went wrong again at the death of Marcus Aurelius. Pliny, within all the flummery, may have made his point.

Love letters to Calpurnia: Marriages but no children

Unlikely as it may seem for a cautious and rather prim lawyer, Pliny is credited with being the godfather of a new genre of western European romantic literature, the love letter between man and wife: not letters to a fictional, idealised goddess, not letters to a distant, unattainable object of impossible desire, not even the lament of a rejected lover, but letters to an actual and accessible flesh-and-blood woman, the woman he is married to; in Pliny's case, his second – or was it his third? – wife, Calpurnia. But there is a different view, as there nearly always is with Pliny, about his famous love letters to Calpurnia. In this more cynical view, these letters were mere literary exercises, composed to show off his stylistic skills and familiarity with Rome's love poets by imitation and allusion. So they are on a par with at least some of his political letters, essentially made-up jobs. Real love? Forget it.

Yet it surely takes a hard-hearted reader not to respond sympathetically and romantically when, in the last of that trio of famous 'love letters' that he sent to her [**6.4**, **6.7** and **7.5**], Pliny writes to Calpurnia:

> You cannot believe how much I miss you. I love you so much, and we are not used to separations. So I stay awake most of the night thinking about you, and by day I find my feet carrying me to your room at the times I usually visited you; then finding it empty I depart as sick and sorrowful as a lover locked out.

So who was this Calpurnia whom he says he missed so much?

How many marriages?

She was not, for sure, his first wife. Pliny tells us that he married young, at the very start of his career (see Chapter 3). So married Pliny was – but how often?

This question may seem surprising in view of the fact that, in a letter to the emperor Trajan, he quite clearly says that he was married twice. That is the letter in which he thanks Trajan for having given him, as a special dispensation, the special privileges, mainly tax exemptions, normally granted to men of his social class who have three children. Pliny bemoans the fact that even after two marriages he still has no children, much to his regret. So we could conclude quite simply that he married twice, yet remained childless.

> Still more now do I long for children of my own, though I wanted them even during those evil days now past, as you know from my having married twice [**10.2**].

As some consolation, Trajan granted Pliny's request (made on his behalf by a mutual friend) for the tax exemptions. So Pliny got the privileges without having to go to the bother, which he alludes to elsewhere, of actually having to cope with children.

From Pliny's letter about his early years it can be inferred that he entered that first marriage at the age of 18 or 19, maybe two years or so after his narrow escape from the eruption of Vesuvius, that is, in about the year 81. Then in another letter Pliny tells us that not long after the assassination of the emperor Domitian in late 96 – that is, in the year 97 or possibly in 96 itself – he was mourning the loss of this first wife, whose name we do not even know.

> I was greatly distressed at the time by the recent death of my wife [**9.13**].

So this wife had recently died. Pliny must then have remarried quickly, within a year or so, because his letter to Trajan recording two marriages seems to date from 98, since it refers to

> the opening of your auspicious reign.

But was this next marriage to Calpurnia – or to someone else?

Did he have three wives?

That Pliny had no children is beyond dispute. But despite his apparently plain statement to the contrary, some believe that he was married not just twice, but three times. His marriage to the Calpurnia whose absence he laments would be the third of these. Pliny's own irritating vagueness on points of marital detail has given ample scope for this alternative version. Indeed, this 'three wives' version was for long the standard view. What is puzzling is that the letter to Trajan should be dated as early as 98. If Pliny had recently married again, how could Pliny be so certain so soon, or Trajan be so ready to agree so soon, that his new young wife was not likely to have children?

If the grant of special tax exemptions that Pliny gained from Trajan was at all meaningful, then it must surely mean that in 98 no children were likely. But we also know from Pliny's letters that Calpurnia at some point had a miscarriage. Pliny writes feelingly to Calpurnia's grandfather, Calpurnius Fabatus:

> You will be sorry to hear that your grand-daughter has had a miscarriage. Being young and inexperienced she did not realize that she was pregnant, failed to take proper precautions, and did several things that were better left undone. She has had a severe lesson, and paid for her mistake by seriously endangering her life [**8.10**].

So presumably both she and Pliny were in principle able to have children, or thought they were, in the early years of their marriage, even after the miscarriage. Pliny remarks to Fabatus:

> the gods will surely grant us children later on, and we may take hope from this evidence of her fertility, though the proof has been unfortunate.

In other words, how could Pliny in 98 be lamenting his lack of children and asking for special tax exemptions from Trajan when in his letter to her grandfather he so clearly expects that he will still have children with Calpurnia? Does there need to be a better theory to fit the facts? Did Pliny marry Calpurnia only later, after the Trajan letter and after 98, and was there another but short-lived marriage after the death of his first wife and before Calpurnia, so that Calpurnia became not his second but his third? If so, then the two marriages that Pliny refers to in letter **10.2** to Trajan are to these two previous wives, neither of whom had children, and were the evidence for Pliny's lament about his childlessness. Calpurnia was not yet on the scene.

This three-wife version has heavyweight champions, especially A. N. Sherwin-White in his famous Commentary on Pliny's letters. It may seem to solve a puzzle. But only at the expense of creating more questions. For one thing, if this hypothetical extra wife existed, we would know absolutely nothing about her except that, as with the other wives, she had no children. Then again, the grant by Trajan of tax exemptions that Pliny makes so much of should not be interpreted too literally. It was just an honour that the emperor could confer on his friends and allies, like so many other honours, when and if he felt like it.

In reality, there was no need for Trajan to withhold the grant of the *ius trium liberorum* [the rights gained by having three children] simply because Pliny might yet become a biological father. By Pliny's time the privilege had become a political reward. In addition, there is no other indication in Pliny's letters of a third marriage or of individuals with whom he might have become associated through such an alliance ... there is a dearth of evidence for a third marriage.[1]

It is also quite possible that Calpurnia's miscarriage, and its serious consequences, may have been the occasion for Pliny's request for this honour. Pliny's comment to Fabatus about the gods granting children later on may just have been designed to soften the blow to Fabatus, who was keen to have great-grand-children. Probably, unless some new inscription is found, we shall never know for certain how many times Pliny married. But there is no compelling need to invent a middle 'third' wife without, so far, any evidence at all for her existence. My belief is that Pliny married only twice, the second time to Calpurnia.

Why no children: Tedium and hard work?

But whether married twice or three times, it is still remarkable that Pliny had no children. Pliny was but one instance of that curious and oft-remarked phenomenon of how the Roman upper class failed to reproduce itself, even in times of comparative peace, and despite long-standing tax and other incentives to have at least three children. Under the Law on Three Children, the *Ius Trium Liberorum* introduced by the emperor Augustus, men with three children also were preferred for high office, and were exempt from the duty to act as a guardian, apparently thought of as an onerous obligation. Yet Pliny's uncle of the same name had no children of his own, and neither did our Pliny (though he says he wanted them). Nor did Pliny's friend, the author Suetonius.

Was it too dangerous politically to be the head of a family clan or dynasty? Was it greed, not wanting to share the money? Selfishness? Was childlessness – *orbitas* in Latin – a positive advantage because it attracted the flattering attentions of legacy-hunters, as it did for Pliny's arch-enemy Regulus after he lost his only son? Was it due to lead poisoning? The question has puzzled many and defies easy explanation. But what Pliny actually says, surprisingly for a man who professed to want children, is rather downbeat. He refers to the 'tedium and hard work' associated with children.

Carefully chosen and persuasive words as well as material rewards are needed to prevail on anyone to submit willingly to the tedium and hard work involved in bringing up children [**1.8**].

Equally surprising is his comment about his friend Asinius Rufus.

He has several children, for here too he has done his duty as a good citizen, at a time when the advantages of remaining childless make most people feel a single child a burden [**4.15**].

So alongside tedium and hard work there were advantages (unspecified by Pliny) to having no children. But we may guess at one reason that favoured Pliny. Whatever its social cause, childlessness among the ruling families at Rome did lead to wealthy new aspirants from the more important provincial cities being sucked into high society at Rome and being able to climb the Roman social ladder to the very top – and Pliny did just that. Arguably, other people's lack of children was to Pliny's career advantage, whatever he personally felt about it. It is hard to avoid the impression that Pliny himself was privately ambivalent about having (or not having) children, but felt obliged to keep up a public stance of wanting them, especially when dealing with the emperor. Either way, we may assume that Calpurnia's miscarriage put an end to their prospects of having children.

Calpurnia's virtues

So who was Calpurnia, and why did Pliny profess so much affection for her? Unlike his first wife, we do at least know her name and a bit about her. She would probably have been only around the age of 15 at the time of marrying Pliny, much younger than him – he would be about 36 or so. But such an age gap was normal in upper-class Roman society, and in many other societies before and since. Calpurnia lost both her mother and her father early in her life, and was put in the care of her aunt Calpurnia Hispulla, her father's sister [**4.19**, **5.11**, **6.12** and **8.11**]. Her aunt loved her brother's daughter, says Pliny,

more tenderly than a mother.

As with Verginius Rufus, there was also a local connection. Calpurnia's family came from Comum, like Pliny himself, and Calpurnia's grandfather Lucius Calpurnius Fabatus had been an equestrian office-holder under the emperor Nero but (if the identification is secure) had a narrow escape after being accused of complicity in the incestuous relationship between Junia Lepida and her brother's son. Tacitus tells us:

> So-called informers fabricated against Cassius' wife Junia Lepida accusations of black magic and incest with her brother's son. Two senators and a knight, Gaius Calpurnius Fabatus, were charged with complicity. But they avoided imminent condemnation by appealing to Nero. He was preoccupied with important crimes, and they were eventually saved by their insignificance.[2]

This might or might not be the same Fabatus. The implication, however, as with the elder Pliny, is that Pliny's family and peer group from the Comum area had been circling around the seat of imperial power at Rome for some time, but at some remove from it, out of serious danger thanks to their relative 'insignificance', until Pliny himself embarked on a senatorial career. But perhaps even then he, like Fabatus, was saved by his own relative insignificance?

Calpurnia therefore came from an appropriate social background. If then she could not give him children, what else did Pliny value about her? The answer to that tells us a lot about Pliny, if not, alas, about the real Calpurnia. Pliny praises Calpurnia's *summum acumen* and *summa frugalitas* – her high intelligence and care with money. These were conventional upper-class virtues in a wife, but important none the less for a man like Pliny with a public face to maintain. His wife must be a credit to him. But what he particularly likes, he tells her aunt, is her interest in literature, in particular literature written by Pliny himself. A true sign of devotion, one may think, if all Pliny's literary efforts were as bad as the ones he quotes.

> She keeps copies of my works to read again and again and even learn by heart ... she has even set my verses to music and sings them to the accompaniment of her lyre, with no musician to teach her but that best of masters, love [**4.19**].

So everything we know about Calpurnia is connected to Pliny's social and literary interests, almost as if she had no independent existence outside Pliny's orbit. Was it, could it have been, in any modern sense a love-match? Or just an arranged match to enhance Pliny's social standing?

> Like all Roman wives, Pliny's wife Calpurnia was crucial to his reputation – that is, her behavior reflected directly on Pliny's ability to control his private life. The more his wife resembled him and conformed to his precepts, the more credit would accrue to him, particularly as Calpurnia came to him waiting to be molded into the ideal wife he required.[3]

This idea of an older man taking on a much younger woman with an agenda to mould her into some preconceived object, Pygmalion-like, is repulsive, not to say fruitless, to the modern mind. But it ignores the upbringing that Calpurnia had already received from her aunt, Calpurnia Hispulla, presumably on similar principles of wifely subordination, and does not necessarily mean that Pliny just regarded her as a pliable object and nothing more. Pygmalion after all fell in love with the statue he had sculpted, and got a real woman as his reward. Perhaps Pliny did the same. As some evidence of this, she travelled with him when, in later years, he was sent out to govern the Roman province of Bithynia-Pontus, and he went to great trouble to get her back to Italy quickly when family trouble demanded her presence.

'Absence letters'

Unless we regard (as some do) his three letters written directly to Calpurnia as purely literary constructs, works of fiction, we may therefore accept that they evince a profound affection and longing for her that is one of the most attractive features of Pliny's character. These three letters are all very short, shorter than one might expect between separated lovers. But bear in mind that they were writing to each other once or twice a day, in an age long before telephones, for contact rather than for information. That is why these letters have been credited with being the first example of that new sub-genre, the love letter between husband and wife.

> The three letters blend together, for the first time in European literature, the role of husband and lover.[4]

Unlike letters that refer to her but were not written to her, they give Pliny the vehicle to show his marriage as filled with mutual affection. They are what are called 'absence letters' – letters that admit to the distress that separation is causing. Calpurnia is away from Rome, probably recuperating from her miscarriage. Pliny just says she is in search of better health, but the connection to her failed pregnancy seems likely. The letters that pass to and fro – we only have this small selection of Pliny's, none of hers – are a substitute for personal presence. Urging Calpurnia to write to him once or more than once every day, Pliny says:

> I shall worry less while I am reading your letters, but my fears will return as soon as I have finished them … I am always reading your letters and returning

to them again and again as if they were new to me – but this only fans the fire of my longing for you. Do write as often as you can, although you give me pleasure mingled with pain [**6.4** and **6.7**].

He makes his feeling especially clear in letter **7.5**, already quoted. It reads like a love poem in prose.

> I stay awake most of the night thinking about you, and by day I find my feet carrying me to your room … then finding it empty I depart as sick and sorrowful as a lover locked out [**7.5**].

The lover locked out is a familiar convention of love poems, Latin ones anyway – the *amator exclusus*. But we know and Pliny knows that he will not be locked out, and he surely knows it is a literary metaphor, popularised by such great Latin poets as Ovid. That is the ground for dismissing these letters as essentially works of poetic fiction. Sherwin-White, in his Commentary on the letters, sees Pliny's protestations as no different to his regrets at the absence of other friends expressed in other letters. They are, he thinks, well-worn literary clichés. But whatever the poetic model used, when Pliny says he buries himself in his work to try to forget Calpurnia's absence, there is no reason to disbelieve him.

> Here, for the first time, Pliny openly expresses the source of his desire, his *amor* for Calpurnia. It is remarkable that Pliny, who prides himself on his self-control, would admit to being enthralled by his love for his wife.[5]

It takes a steely academic mind not to agree that:

> The content and diction of the letter is drastically different from any others in Pliny's corpus; for here, Pliny seems not to be in control of his feelings or his actions.[6]

The fact that Pliny appears to draw on the language and conventions of Latin love poetry to express himself, as scholars have correctly pointed out, is neither unusual – on the contrary – nor an indications that the feelings he expresses are false or artificial. What better master to have than Ovid for expressing love and loss?

Little else is known about Calpurnia. We may conclude that she was still away in Italy when Pliny died – or is presumed to have died – of illness while still in office in Bithynia-Pontus (see Chapter 14). If so, it was not just a temporary but a permanent parting from the woman that Pliny was so desperate to stay close to. What happened to Calpurnia after that, we have no idea. But Pliny's second marriage had lasted, like his first, about 15 years. So we may safely assume that whatever external social advantages marriage might bring to an ambitious lawyer, and whatever private reservations he might have had about children, Pliny liked the married state, and especially liked Calpurnia.

How rich was Pliny? Assets, income and expenses

Pliny was a rich man. But how rich? He does not tell us exactly. Even so, he is the only senator of his time about whose finances we have detailed information, thanks to his letters. These show that he had a good grasp of what his assets and liabilities were, and whence they derived, as might be expected of an advocate who specialised in inheritance cases and who held a series of financial jobs in state service. So he offers a unique case study of the income, expenditure and property values of an upper-class member of Rome's ruling elite.

Comparison with rich men and women of today is difficult because of the hazards of equating the Roman currency units of the time, such as the Roman sesterce, with a modern currency like the US dollar or the UK pound. Inflation and shifting currency exchange rates mean that earlier attempts to translate Roman money into today's equivalent now look very out of date. But a recent 2011–12 exhibition at the British Museum in London made a valiant attempt to equate currency values then and now, based on comparative costs of living for a Roman and a British soldier. Pliny was no rank-and-file soldier, but this at least provides some basis for measuring his wealth in modern terms. From clues dropped by Pliny and other Roman authors we can also get a good idea of comparatively where Pliny stood on the Roman rich list, where his wealth came from, and what it enabled him to do and buy. Pliny himself is conventionally modest about his assets, as rich men are apt to be.

> My resources as a whole are not very great and my position in life is expensive to keep up (*modicae facultates … dignitas sumptuosa*) [**2.4**].

But the many and various financial transactions he records make it clear that he enjoyed making a display of his wealth, even boasting about it in a measured way. The upshot is that he clearly had a place on the Roman rich list, but by no means towards the top of it. Taking into account Pliny's substantial inheritances from his family and uncle, Sherwin-White in his Commentary on Pliny's letters made a bold attempt to audit Pliny's wealth:

> Pliny was well shod in worldly goods, if not in the first rank for wealth ... The grand total [of Pliny's assets] may have been not less than 12 to 15 million [sesterces] ... Pliny was in the second grade of wealth. But despite his complaints, he did not do so badly.[1]

Another assessment broadly agrees.

> A close consideration of the letters suggests that Pliny may have possessed at least twice the sum of 8 million sesterces that contemporary sources sometimes indicate as an appropriate capital for a senator ... we can reach a very rough estimate for the capital value of Pliny's landholdings of 17 million sesterces.[2]

Taking a median figure from these two estimates of 15 million Roman sesterces, the figures worked out by the British Museum would make Pliny's assets worth about £150 million sterling, or US$240 million, in 2011 currency values. By way of comparison, on the museum figures a Roman legionary was paid the equivalent of about £12,000 sterling a year, before deductions, a bit above average earnings. Such figures are not to be pressed too hard; there are too many variables in the calculation. But they do indicate substantial – but not unusual – material wealth for Pliny, both by Roman standards and by the standards of today.

Who were the super-rich?

How did this compare to the super-rich of Rome, whose riches put Pliny into 'the second grade of wealth'? Pliny himself tells us that Regulus, his fellow lawyer, arch-enemy and hate-figure, was rich [1.5] and was trying to work out how soon his great wealth would increase to 60 million sesterces [2.20]. He remarks wryly that by his devious ways Regulus might even get to double that, to 120 million. Such figures would dwarf whatever Pliny had. But if Tacitus and others are to be believed, it was not an unrealistic or unparalleled figure for the very top of the wealth pile at Rome. Even Regulus would have fallen short of the enormous sums allegedly accumulated by two other notorious informers (*delatores*) under the emperor Nero, Vibius Crispus and Eprius Marcellus. These two rose from social obscurity to wealth of 200 million and 300 million sesterces respectively.[3] A senator named Cornelius Lentulus is said to have achieved 400 million.

Even more notorious was Narcissus, the freedman serving the emperor Claudius, who also accumulated 400 million, but who was forced to commit suicide when Claudius died. Compared to these men, Pliny was small potatoes. Our surviving sources name over 20 men with fortunes larger or much larger than Pliny's during the first 100 years or so of Rome's imperial period. But there must have been many more we don't know about. One factor in this wealth measurement is that the super-rich often owned land outside Italy as well as within. Pliny did not. They also owned or acquired several houses and properties in Rome itself, where values were highest. Pliny had only one house there, so visibly did not belong to the super-rich. But it is notable that the route to stratospheric riches was often by the dangerous trade of informing and political denunciations, and Pliny's wealth and assets may have been much more typical of those held by the upper-class landed gentry hailing from outside Rome itself.

The political importance of money

In estimating Pliny's wealth, it is important to take account of the social and political value of money. Money at Rome was not just about purchasing power, not at Pliny's level of society. It was about the patronage it enabled you to wield (see below); but centrally it was also about your ability to hold various ascending levels of public office. In a rigidly tabulated system regulating political and social advancement, your proven wealth governed what offices you could aspire to. All the important public offices in Rome and in the other cities carried a minimum property qualification. It was the men of property who ran the day-to-day business of the empire – those who had a vested interest in its survival, stability and prosperity. There were fixed ratios between the minima required for the various steps up the ladder of advancement. These were 1:2:4:12.

> The juryman must have double the wealth of the town councilor, the knight twice the wealth of the juryman, the senator three times the wealth of the knight.[4]

These calculations were the basic numbers game of the oligarchic system of Roman government. The emperor himself was of course well off the upper end of the scale. For a senator, the minimum asset requirement stood at a million (or 1.2 million) sesterces. But many at each stage would have had much more than the minimum. Equally, emperors quite often helped out senators whose assets had fallen below the minimum, so as to keep them within the charmed circle of the rich and powerful – if they were men he liked or valued. It was one way in which the emperor used imperial patronage to keep control of his upper class.

What Pliny shows in his mentions of money is that, from the start, he himself had quite enough of it to clear all the hurdles of these minimum property qualifications, so that from the beginning he could set his sights on a senatorial career. But if in practice assets of 8 million sesterces were regarded, not as compulsory but as appropriate for a senator, then he cleared that hurdle with less of a margin than many others. So his remark about his *modicae facultates*, his slender means compared to his *dignitas sumptuosa*, the expense of high office, was not false modesty but may, in the context of this rich man's club, have had some justice to it.

Pliny's assets and income

His property assets

Rich Romans held most of their assets in the form of land. Pliny certainly did.

> Nearly all my capital is in land [**3.19**].

Pliny owned a number of houses, and estates containing at least a main house. From his remarks we can conclude that he owned at least six houses, although he does not say this in so many words. But he had a town house in Rome from which to conduct his professional business. It stood on the Esquiline Hill of Rome, but nowhere does he describe it. Then he had houses on or near Lake Como, doubtless on the ancestral lands of his family, and tells us in detail about two of them, while implying more than two in total. His longest descriptions, however, are reserved for his two really impressive country houses, one perhaps inherited and one perhaps bought during his financially successful career. One of these was at his estate not too far from Rome at Vicus Laurentium, on the coast near Ostia. The other was further away from Rome at his estate at Tifernum Tiberinum in the area of present-day Città di Castello, on the modern Tuscany–Umbria border in the salubrious foothills of the Apennine mountains. So the total of houses was six-plus. Why did he need six-plus?

Well, he did not exactly need six-plus houses. But he had or earned the money to invest. He would never give up the ancestral properties of his family, he says [**7.11**], but would rather enhance them. He needed a town house for his career; and naturally he needed places in the country to go to in order to relax and to show off to his friends. The estate in Tuscany he refers to as *mei Tusci*, my lands in Tuscany, where he went to escape the heat of high summer. He probably inherited this estate from his uncle and adoptive father, the elder Pliny. The other near Ostia was for easy access during the rest of the year, a place he could get to after a hard day's work at the office, a distance of about 17 miles. A rich man's justification, of course, but a total of six (or more) residences is common enough for rich people today, as it was for rich people then. The great Cicero is said to have had eight houses.

His human assets: Slaves

Pliny also had human assets. He owned a lot of slaves. Rich Romans did. Pliny's must have numbered hundreds. Slavery and slave labour were taken for granted in the ancient world. Pliny shows no sign of any moral repugnance about this, no bad conscience. On the contrary, he likes to tell everyone how well he treats his slaves, and probably, by the standards of his time, he did. His most chilling remarks is:

> Nowhere do I employ chained slaves [**3.19**].

The implication is that many other landowners did. Even so, for Pliny slaves are part of the equipment needed to work the land; each was a tool with a voice – what the Romans called an *instrumentum vocale*. He says that the new estate he is intending to buy will need a good type of slave, which will increase the expense. Elsewhere he refers to his domestic household slaves and how he treats them [**1.12**]. He says he is prepared to give them their freedom, and to respect any wills they make as long as the beneficiaries are within his household. In his own will, Pliny made provision for the support of 100 slaves who had been freed, perhaps also under the terms of the will. Under Roman law this scale of so-called manumission of slaves must have meant that he had at least 500 slaves in total. Probably most of these freed men were domestic slaves, since rural slaves were much less often given their freedom. So exactly how many slaves Pliny had in total must be a guess, but it must add up to many hundreds. This was an asset base of sorts, held in human capital. How much he paid for his slaves, if he bought them, or how he valued slaves who were born on his estates and who were therefore his property, we just do not know.

But there is a distinctive feature of Pliny's slave-holding that makes slavery in ancient Rome a more complex matter than, say, slavery in the American deep south. Some Roman slaves were highly educated and highly skilled, and Pliny had slaves in that category, to help with his routine correspondence and record keeping, and to help the literary efforts of which he was so proud. These men were household functionaries whose distinctive roles merited separate job titles such as *librarius, notarius, amanuensis, anagnostes* (roughly, librarian, note-taker, secretary, reader).

These slaves were assistants who wrote down the dictation of those who could afford to own them, and who read out texts, literary or otherwise, to their masters in business sessions, during travel, or at dinner parties and as entertainments. These literate slaves or ex-slaves were perhaps among the fortunate few compared to the generally brutal regime suffered by Roman agricultural slaves. Nevertheless, Romans of the upper classes apparently took for granted the presence of these human aides to writing, reading and entertainment. Pliny for example had a *lector* called Encolpius [8.1]. The poor man is spitting blood, laments Pliny, and Pliny's doctors are looking after him.

> It will be a sad blow to him and a great loss to me if this makes him unfit for his services to literature when they are his main recommendation. Who else will read and appreciate my efforts or hold my attention as he does?

But his letters make it clear that he depended on having a slave-secretary on hand at any time that he wanted him, just as his adoptive father had had before him. Dictation to such a skilled and literate secretary figure, probably repeated several times with successive drafts, was the key process of the literary composition that was Pliny's great hobby. High skill and slave status were not incompatible, though it is probable that such skilled household slaves had a far better chance of gaining their eventual freedom than did agricultural slaves .

One consequence of this was that slaves, if not already accomplished in the arts of writing or reading, were specially trained in these skills from an early age. In the slave markets they could be sold for appropriately higher prices that reflected their greater utility value. The idea that rich men could, as a business proposition, train skilled men for subsequent onward sale, or indeed breed slaves for sale in the market as if they were horses or pigs, is highly controversial because it is so repugnant to modern sensibility. There is no evidence that Pliny actively traded human cargoes in this way. On the other hand, he bought good quality slaves, as for example to fit out his new estate in Tuscany. So slaves were definitely part of Pliny's financial asset base, an investment, even if we cannot quantify their hypothetical value in the marketplace.

His income: From land

How much income did Pliny generate from his property? Pliny tells us that he drew an annual income of over 400,000 sesterces from his estate in Tuscany [**10.8**]. The figures he quotes for one estate around Comum, yielding 30,000 on a capital value of 500,000, suggest a yield from fertile land of 6 per cent [**7.18**]. That is the basis for valuing his Tuscan estate at between six and seven million. What yield he got from his estates round Comum he does not say, except that it was less satisfactory. Elsewhere he buys another estate for three million but worth five, the bargain price being due to a period of neglect by the previous owner. Pliny expects to turn it around and generate an income from it of 300,000 a year – again a rate of 6 per cent. This estate was probably adjacent to his Tuscan property, since he expects to economise by not fully keeping up the house that stood on it and by sharing staff and overheads. Significantly, he expects no trouble in finding the three million.

Sherwin-White concludes reasonably enough that Pliny's annual income from his estates must have been between 800,000 and one million sesterces, or up to £10 million (US$16 million) a year at 2011–12 values, giving him a yield of (again) about 6 per cent on his landed assets. Pliny visited his estates as often as he could, given his professional obligations in Rome, and although he sings their praises as places to relax, hunt and write his poetic compositions, in reality he was certainly not an absentee landlord. He could not afford to be. He needed this large income from his land to sustain his other activities in law and politics. Even then, the large-scale donations that he made to others, as either personal patron to individuals or as civic patron to townships, suggests that in addition to his income from land, Pliny must have earned money by other means. But how?

His income: Legal fees?

Did Pliny, for example, earn any money from his professional practice as a lawyer? Today, that would be an absurd question. About Rome, it is not. There was plainly a lively controversy in Rome about whether or not advocates should accept fees. As noted in Chapter 4, Pliny actually boasts that, unlike some other advocates, he does not take fees for his work [**5.13**, **6.23**]. This contrasts – according to a senator quoted by Pliny, gleefully it seems to the reader – with those advocates who fake lawsuits just to generate fees, settle them by collusion with the other party, or just sell their services to the highest bidder [**5.13**]. Pliny is claiming to be Mr Clean, not touching money so that he cannot be accused of being influenced by it.

It is hard to believe that grateful clients did not acknowledge Pliny's services in some financial way. Presumably he had large expenses in preparing his cases. Even if some of the cases he took on resulted from the obligations arising from his role as patron (to clients, to his home town, and perhaps to whole provinces of the empire), at minimum he must have expected some non-financial rewards for his services, perhaps by expanding reciprocal obligations that he could call in at a later date. But if he says he did not take actual fees, where did he earn extra money to supplement his income from land?

His income: Salary on the job

Pliny certainly did earn money elsewhere, perhaps a lot of it. The various public offices he held on his way up the political status ladder, like his official appointments in charge of the river and sewers of Rome and of two of the state treasuries, probably brought in a salary. Whether and how much Roman office-holders got paid for their time in post is an uncertain area. But Sherwin-White reckons on an annual salary of not less than and probably much more than 300,000 sesterces for the treasury jobs.[5] Nice work if you can get it. Since proconsuls of provinces were also salaried, up to one million a year according to Dio,[6] then we may presume (without knowing for sure) that other offices Pliny held, up to his last appointment as special envoy of the emperor Trajan to the province of Bithynia-Pontus, also carried large salaries.

His income: Money lending

Pliny also made money from usury – lending out money. This was regarded by some Roman authors (and by many since) as a shameful activity. But we may suspect that many rich Romans did it, some on a large scale, even if they kept quiet about it. Pliny is open about it. He says off-handedly:

I lend out a bit (*aliquid fenero*) [**3.19**].

Some translate this as Pliny borrowing a bit. But the verb he uses faces the other way – he lends. The actual rate of interest he charged would be guesswork, but he clearly made money from his money-lending. Loans to relatives, however, may have been interest-free.

His income: Gifts inwards

Pliny's gifts to others were balanced to a degree by gifts made to him, usually as bequests in wills. The gifts inwards that he tells us about, and for which he names the figure, total 1,450,000 sesterces. For example, a certain Saturninus, a fellow citizen of Comum, left him a complicated bequest which, after paying off certain obligations, was worth around 700,000 to Pliny.[7] There are several other bequests he does not quantify. A striking aspect of this very Roman habit of remembering your friends in your will is that some of the bequests Pliny received were due to his literary reputation. He says that he and Tacitus, close friends and professional colleagues as well as fellow authors, often received bequests of the same kind and the same value [7.20].

Gifts outwards: To people

Pliny had enough money to be generous in giving substantial amounts to other people. It is the Roman gift-culture in action. He gives to a certain Firmus the sum of 300,000 sesterces to raise him from the status of a local town councilor, with assets of 100,000, to the status of an equestrian knight, for which he needs 400,000 [1.19]. He gives 100,000 towards a dowry for Calvina, to add to the amount provided by her father, and cancelled her father's debts to him – 'it will not tax my finances', he says [2.4]. He gives a farm worth 10,000 to his nurse to provide her with security in her old age [6.3]. He gives 40,000 to Metilius Crispus for his equipment as a centurion – a post that Pliny got for him. This seems a very large sum – one must wonder what it included. Crispus then vanished without trace, without even a letter of thanks [6.25]. He provides 50,000 towards the dowry of the daughter of Quintilianus [6.32]. His gifts to individual friends and clients – those that he tells us about – are reckoned to have totaled at least 740,000. Pliny must have been generating a substantial surplus of income over expenditure to be dishing out these sums – and no doubt many others he does not tell us about – to people he favours. But that was not all.

Gifts outwards: To his home town

Pliny was a patron of his home town of Comum, and donated to it on a large scale. His lifetime gifts to Comum were substantial. He tells us that he has given 1.6 million sesterces to Comum, and will not begrudge another 400,000 even though there has been some dispute about this money [5.7]. Additionally, he puts aside land worth 500,000 to provide a fund for maintaining free-born boys and girls of his home town [5.7, 7.18]. So being a patron of Comum during his lifetime, as he was socially expected to do but probably far exceeding his basic obligation, seems to have cost him a minimum of 2.5 million.

Gifts outward: Bequests

Another measure of Pliny's wealth is how much he intended to give away at death. In his will, Pliny would probably have made bequests to relatives and friends, but if so, we do not know about them. His biggest public bequest was again to Comum, to provide for the upkeep of the 100 slaves to whom he had given freedom. This fund amounted to 1,866,666 and two-thirds sesterces, an oddly irregular sum probably intended to provide, when invested, a known fixed income per year. After the death of the freedmen, the fund was to switch to providing an annual dinner for the common people of Comum.[8] Pliny also bequeathed to Comum a sum larger than 300,000 sesterces for furnishing the public baths there, with a fund of 200,000 whose interest earned was to go towards the upkeep of the baths. He appears to have paid for the baths themselves already, cost unknown. He also bequeathed a monument at Hispellum.

Pliny the generous

Pliny had no children, so we have no precise idea what happened to his considerable assets when he died. His widow probably inherited much of the money left after donations, and passed it on to her relatives. He does not seem to have been ambitious for money in itself, but perhaps, never having known poverty, he had no need to be. He had enough to support the life of a patron, professional lawyer and high state official, with the proper proportion of leisure time in prestigious surroundings that was expected of a Roman grandee of the second grade. But his generosity is nevertheless striking.

> When his lifetime gifts to Comum totaling 1,600,000 sesterces are taken into account, it emerges than Pliny was easily the largest public donor in Italy among those the value of whose gifts is known ... Pliny's generosities appear pre-eminent among gifts by private individuals in Italy ... it must be concluded that Pliny was outstanding in the extent of his public generosity.[9]

Here we see a good side of Pliny, a benefactor generous beyond what was just expected of a man of his class. But perhaps also we can sense his need to give and receive the personal affection of which he was deprived by having no children.

His posh country villas: A literary house and garden tour

The subject that Pliny is most pleased to elaborate on in his letters – without descending into the sordid business of financial value – is the grand villas he owned. These he was only too anxious to proclaim to his readers and to the world. Land and property were the main physical assets of a rich man, then as in most eras, and Pliny was pleased with his built environment, as he tells us at some length and with evident pride in several of his letters. His descriptions of what exactly a grand country house looked like in Roman times are unique in Latin literature. They have provoked numerous attempts to re-create Pliny's villas visually, both in two-dimensional drawings and in three-dimensional models, and to resurrect their scale, architecture and spirit in real buildings around Lake Como claiming direct aesthetic descent from Pliny's designs.

Pliny owned a number of houses or estates containing a main house. He must have had at least six houses in total. We may suspect that he owned further properties that he does not tell us about. But by far his longest descriptions are of his two substantial country houses and their associated estates, one on the coast not far from Rome, the other further away in Tuscany. These were primarily financial assets. But there was also a strong element of ostentation and social prestige in these properties, and that is why he writes at such length and so feelingly about them in his letters.

> Whatever the tradition before Pliny's time, it fell to him to develop and perfect a new genre of letter. With his mouthwatering evocations of nature and the built environment, he devised what might be called the literary house and garden tour.[1]

These letters are, however, tours with curious omissions. For example, nowhere does Pliny mention Vitruvius. Vitruvius is the now-forgotten but once famous Roman writer on architecture who lived about 100 years before Pliny's time and whose textbook on Roman building design (and much else) inspired a great deal of the subsequent villa, temple and palace construction in Italy and the rest of Europe until quite recent times. There may, however, be a reason for this striking omission. Pliny's attitude differed fundamentally from that of Vitruvius.

> Vitruvius emphasized such dry technical information as siting, proper founda-tions, drainage, structure in general, and the use of the orders of architecture [i.e. column design] in particular.

Only rarely does Pliny even refer to a column at all, despite it being the iconic feature of Greek and Roman architectural structures. Foundations were literally and metaphorically beneath him. Pliny may have felt that such mundane technical detail was demeaning to his dignity as a Roman grandee, or more charitably he may have lacked the necessary technical vocabulary and training. He may also have had in mind Varro's warning not to get bogged down in fancy Greek terminology for the various bits of the house, since that suggested an unhealthy and un-Roman indoor lifestyle.[2] Indeed, one overall purpose of Pliny's literary house tours is precisely not to demonstrate building expertise but to demonstrate expertise in the use of leisure (*otium*) in:

> the *otium*-rich environments of his villas.[3]

His tours of his villas [letters **2.17** and **5.6**] are impressionistic, about atmos-phere and not about structure.

> Pliny thought mainly in flat, planimetric terms ... simple sequences of spaces ... Pliny rendered one-dimensional what are by nature three-dimensional arts of building and landscape architecture.

There is also almost nothing about commodities, furnishing, ornamentation or materials. When it came to landscape, his extended descriptions of his gardens are better at defining the shapes and colours of trees and plants, particularly his box hedges, than they are about their planting or upkeep. Indeed, Pliny's most lasting influence has been on garden design rather than house design.

> The garden settings often sound like rooms with the ceiling left off.[4]

Living/work/leisure spaces

There is only one letter that goes more into technical detail, mentioning columns, and that is the only one actually written to an architect, Mustius. Pliny tells Mustius that on one of his properties there is a temple to the goddess Ceres which is old and too small, and offers no shelter from rain or sun. So as a public benefactor he has to do something about it.

> Please buy me four marble columns, any kind you think suitable, and marble for improving the floor and walls. We shall also have to have made a statue of the goddess [**9.39**].

He also wants new porticoes for shelter. But there are problems with the site, with a river on one side and a road on the other. There is, however, a suitable field on the far side of the road, so will Mustius please draw up a plan? This is as near as Pliny ever gets to the mundane building specifications that define an architect's contract. Similarly, Pliny is oddly vague about the uses to which the different areas of his villas were put. But perhaps that was a characteristic of the rich Roman lifestyle. They thought of space and the uses of spaces in quite different terms to today. Most spaces were multipurpose, and there was much less demarcation between rooms with one purpose and rooms with another – for example, between work space and living room.

> The Romans lacked our distinction of place of work (office, factory etc.) from place of leisure (home). To judge by the reports of daily routine, particularly those given by the younger Pliny, the *negotium/otium* (work/leisure) distinction of activity within the house corresponds broadly to a distinction of time between morning and afternoon.

There is no sharp distinction between bedrooms and other areas, such as we take for granted today, nor any concept of a master bedroom.

> The younger Pliny seems to be closer to the upper-class norm in the casual way he describes the *cubicula* (sleeping areas) dotted around his villas: he has his favorites, but he makes clear that no single one is the master's bedroom.[5]

Pliny's villas were living/work/leisure spaces on a large scale, flexible according to the master's whim – and the seasons. Pliny left the building work to the building professionals, perhaps wisely if he knew little about structural problems or cared little about what was on the walls. His concern lay elsewhere.

> Readers through the centuries have puzzled over Pliny's vague use of architectural terminology. Rarely did he specify the internal decoration or architectural framework ... On one point however he allowed no ambiguity. At every step along the way of his literary house tours, he referred his correspondents to the orientation of the principal rooms: whether they enjoyed the prevailing winds; whether they were suited to winter or summer use; whether they were secluded or noisy.[6]

So despite the fame of Pliny's celebrated villa letters, and despite their being the only extended descriptions we have of a grand Roman country mansion, there is so little detail in these letters – what some have called an example of failed description – that the natural impulse to visually recreate them is frustrated.

> There is such an absence of method and such vagueness that any attempt to restore it [Pliny's villa] is merely an exercise in imagination.[7]

Despite that, there have in fact been endless attempts to reconstruct, in both two and three dimensions, both of Pliny's main country seats – at least 24 of the villa near Ostia and 10 of the villa in Tuscany, not to mention pictorial depictions of the lakeside houses on Lake Como.

> Numerous attempts have been made to reconstruct the respective floor-plans from the texts. Most have been plausible, but none demonstrably correct.[8]

But perhaps physical reconstructions, however natural to the curious modern eye, were not the point for Pliny. The point for him was precisely the user experience – the amenity value, the sun, the light, the shade, the quiet, the flexibility of use.

His houses on Lake Como: The joys of pure loafing

This emphasis on the amenity value of a house comes out strongly in Pliny's letter about his 'several' houses around Lake Como [**9.7**]. He is building extensions to two particular houses, one of which is at the water's edge, the other of which stands higher up on rocks. One he has nicknamed 'Comedy' because in the Roman theatre the comic actor traditionally wore flat shoes. The other he has nicknamed 'Tragedy' because a tragic actor wore thick-soled boots to give him extra height. These nicknames have become famous, as has his statement that from Comedy you were so close to the water that using a fishing rod you could catch fish from the bedroom, or even when in bed. Both of course had splendid views. But architecturally Pliny leave us little the wiser – and where exactly were these houses?

> The location of these long-vanished structures is a continuing source of speculation among local residents. Various legends have arisen over time that have helped foster a string of villas along the lakeshore, each claiming descent from Pliny.[9]

One clue to location has been thought to be found in the spring that Pliny describes in another letter [**4.30**]. This spring flows down from a mountain into a man-made grotto and then into the lake. But its remarkable feature is that it does not have a regular flow, but stops and starts again three times day, at regular intervals. Pliny speculates about the origin of this phenomenon. His uncle, the elder Pliny, also mentioned it in his *Natural History*. It must have been famous locally. But was it on his property? Pliny does not say so.

> Whether Pliny had one of his several villas here remains moot: nevertheless, Plinian associations quickly attached themselves to the place. By about the mid-sixteenth century the so-called Villa Pliniana at Torno had been built on the site and had incorporated the famous spring into the back of its loggia.[10]

Despite such reservations, today's fashionable resort of Bellagio and the modern village of Lenno, both on the lake, are strong candidates for the site of Pliny's two house he nicknamed Comedy and Tragedy, as they have been since Renaissance times.

> Lenno and Bellagio offer an arrestingly good topographical interpretation of the text.[11]

But what the text of the letter shows is not so much a map reading as Pliny's almost boyish enchantment with these places and spaces, a celebration of an architecture which, says one author, is devoted to the joys of pure loafing, the joys of *otium* – however artificial that pose may be.

His estate at Ostia

The two famous letters in which Pliny describes his two country estates nearer to Rome are exceptional in their length and detail, being two or three times longer than the average for his letter collection [**2.17** and **5.6**]. It is this detail that makes them unique in surviving Latin literature. Despite their short-comings on architectural matters, they do convey Pliny's appreciation of the interplay between built space and garden space. One villa was on the coast not far from Rome, and near to Rome's port of Ostia. The other was further away, on the modern border between Tuscany and Umbria. As with the Como villas, there has been much speculation about the exact site of these two villas, or even their reality.[12] But to cast doubt on their actual reality – unless you believe that Pliny made up a lot of his letters as a purely fictional literary exercise – is going a bit far, straining credulity. The space descriptions are just too elaborate, while his architectural terminology is not elaborate enough, for a crafted literary composition.

In neither case does Pliny use the term 'villa' to denote his property. But in the case of his seaside villa near Ostia he uses the term *villula* ('my little villa') for something that was far from little [**2.17**]. Again, it's a rich man's affectation. This 'little villa' was actually at a place called Laurentinum, 17 miles from Rome. This meant that he could get there after a busy day's work in the city, and access was easy down a side-road leading off the main road from Rome to its main port at Ostia. Pliny recommends getting there on horseback rather than in a carriage, presumably because the last part of the journey was rough going. Because of the proximity to Rome, there are a number of other villa complexes along the same coastline, he tells us, so he has neighbours. So where exactly was this coastal *villula*? Pliny may appear almost to give a postal address for it. It is, he says, south of Ostia, on the coast, 17 miles from the big city, and the second house away from the nearest village. But was it the second house to the north, or to the south? He does not say. Changes to the coastline and the landscape mean that exact identification is unlikely. But what is clear is that, far from being a remote scene of rural leisure, this 'little villa' was

> a residence on a shoreline next to a busy village in the midst of a string of millionaire estates … [in] a well-supplied luxury zone for villa owners.[13]

Having left us with an incomplete postal address, Pliny then plunges into a sequential narrative of the different room spaces to be found within his villa boundary. He takes us through 24 of them, not counting antechambers, some upper rooms, spaces split into multiple rooms, and multiple rooms associated with the bath-house, but including an arcade, a terrace, a pergola and a kitchen garden. Some '*villula*'. There is no need to repeat Pliny's entire description – read Pliny. But a possible interpretation of the ground plan is sketched out, helpfully, in the edition of the letters by Betty Radice relied upon in this book and itself based on a physical model held in the Ashmolean Museum in Oxford, United Kingdom (under restoration at the time of writing so not on view). Pliny singles out the garden.

> The garden itself is thickly planted with mulberries and figs, trees which the soil bears very well though it is less kind to others.

But in the main Pliny concentrates on the views from the rooms, the light, the sound of water and waves, the shelter afforded from winds and rain, the amenity value. He is keen to point out that he does not get any income from this estate, so it cannot have included a lot of land. On the other hand, it costs him nothing to run. It is, he specifies, largely self-sufficient and so cash-neutral. Provisioning it is no problem.

> The sea has admittedly few fish of any value, but it gives us excellent soles and prawns, and all inland produce is provided by the house, especially milk: for the herds collect there whenever they seek water and shade [**2.17**].

Where are the slaves?

The herds may be present, but there is one notable absence of living creatures – the numerous slaves that must have staffed and maintained both this villa and his one on the Umbria–Tuscany border. Pliny nowhere tells us how many slaves there were or what they did. His only reference is to a set of spaces that are normally used by his slaves and freedmen. But these are

> quite presentable enough to receive guests.

So the slaves and ex-slaves had nowhere to call their very own, and could consider themselves lucky to have, much of the time, guest-quality accommodation. As if Pliny did not have plenty of room for guests elsewhere.

> The aim of such marginalization, architectural and decorative, was to render the low-status areas invisible to the visitor. We may compare Pliny's descriptions of his own villas in which his minute account of 'every corner' passes wholly over the service areas.

As with his Tuscan villa, Pliny was anxious to accentuate the rest and recuperation, the solitude and the quiet, that he and his guests could expect. His spaces are not just quiet, but eerily quiet. In his description we have no mundane areas such as bustling but smoky kitchens, bulging storage areas, and tiled bathrooms and lavatories. But the reality must have been that there were lots of people, even if non-people, all around but especially in these 'invisible' service areas. Despite Pliny's boasts of solitude and silence, one result of the physical omnipresence yet social invisibility of the slave attendants was that there could not have been any privacy anywhere as we understand it today.

> What is to a modern observer most striking about the richer houses is the low priority given to privacy … it must have been astonishingly difficult for an upper-class Roman to achieve real privacy.[14]

There are indeed areas where Pliny was able to retire into seclusion if he wished, and which are constructed so as to shut out light, heat and noise. But he was private there by personal edict, not by means of physical doors. So when we look round Pliny's villas in his literary house-tours, we see them through the filter of what he chose, by social convention, to see or not to see, and of what he invites his virtual Roman visitor and his virtual modern tourist to see or not to see.

… and where was his wife?

The other notably absentee from Pliny's picture of this villa is his wife. Whichever of his two wives it might have been, she is simply not there, at any rate not so as to feature in his description. Still less is there any suggestion that she had any influence over the design or management of this villa, or (unlike some of Pliny's slaves) her own room or rooms. Since it was a villa used for quick getaways from Rome, it would be surprising if she was not there and did not have her own quarters. But Pliny does not say so. He does however remark, if only in passing, that his wife did visit his other villa, the one in Tuscany, where he dined alone with her or with friends. But again there is no hint of her having a hand in the design or management of the Tuscan villa either, or her own place in it.

My place in Tuscany

Pliny's house and estate in Tuscany – *mei Tusci*, he calls them, my assets in Tuscany – are altogether grander than the Ostia property, showing what great wealth even a moderately (by Roman standards) rich man could command. Where exactly was this estate? Original doubts about the possibility and desirability of trying to find it – especially if it was as much a literary as a physical construction – have given way to the findings of archaeology. Thanks to the discovery of brick stamps bearing the initials CPCS (C. Plinius Caecilius Secundus) and also others bearing the initials of the elder Pliny, the site of the estate is with some confidence identified as being about eight kilometres above the modern city of Città di Castello. But general excavations have revealed little to add to Pliny's description.[15] Unlike Ostia, Pliny gets a substantial income from this estate, mainly from grapes to be made into wine, and much of his very long letter about it is devoted to the land and its fertility, the trees and the river, the flowers and the mountain backdrop. His idyllic description makes it sound like a paradise on earth. It is a place where he can literally 'take off his toga', Pliny's equivalent of abandoning his formal business suit and tie for his leisure wear.

> I can enjoy a profounder peace there, more comfort, and fewer cares. I need never wear a formal toga, and there are no neighbours to disturb me. Everywhere there is peace and quiet. There I enjoy the best of health, for I keep my mind in training with work and my body with hunting. My servants too are healthier here than anywhere else [**5.6**].

So here his servants, his slaves for the most part, get at least a passing mention. But he is probably referring to his immediate entourage, the close personal servants he brought with him from Rome, as he tells us elsewhere. One must suspect that he is not referring to the numerous agricultural slaves permanently working this estate, who may not be chained (as Pliny tellingly and chillingly remarks) but probably had a hard life looking after his labour-intensive vines. It would be interesting to know how many slaves, and how many former slaves and freedmen, Pliny needed for permanent cultivation of this large estate. But he does not tell us, even though they must have formed a significant part of his capital investment there. It is also good hunting territory – an occupation that the bookish Pliny says he enjoys, an interesting side-light on his otherwise sedentary lifestyle. Pliny also remarks on the number of old people who live in the area, attracted by its healthy climate, a retirement park for the elderly rich.

In another letter, Pliny goes into great and even boastful detail about the 'profound peace' he enjoys at this paradise villa, almost showing off how little he has to do with sordid business or estate management. On a typical day he wakes, lets his mind rove over his current compositions, calls in a secretary who opens the shutters and takes dictation, goes out onto the terrace, does some more dictation, goes for a drive, has a short sleep on return, takes a walk, reads aloud a Greek or Latin speech (to aid his digestion, he claims), then another walk, is oiled, does his exercises, has a bath, dines with wife or friends while a good book is read aloud, then takes another post-prandial walk with good conversation.

Thus the day comes to a satisfying end [**9.36**].

A real day, or the idealised day of a country gentleman at leisure posing for his readers? If in this letter Pliny is boasting about his successful social aspirations, he backs it up by being equally boastful in his main letter about the sheer size of this house, using the same technique of listing all or most of its many rooms.

It is much bigger than the Ostia house. He walks us through no less than 32 separate built spaces in the villa, against the 24 for Ostia, with an implication that there might be more.[16] Also, quite apart from the farming land around, there is a full riding-ground within the villa complex.

> The design and beauty of the buildings are greatly surpassed by the riding-ground. It is planted round with ivy-clad plane trees … box shrubs grow between the plane trees and outside there is as ring of laurel bushes … between the grass lawns there are box shrubs clipped into innumerable shapes, some being letters which spell the gardener's name or his master's; small obelisks of box alternate with fruit trees … at the upper end of the course is a curved dining seat of white marble shaded by a vine, water gushes out through pipes from under the seat.

These excerpts cannot do justice to the full elaboration of Pliny's eulogy of this estate. Taken together, his Tuscan letters give us a glimpse of a near-Eden and of the leisure style in which a Roman aristocrat aspired to live – whether or not in actuality the estate and his life there were exactly as he makes out. These are, like so many of Pliny's letters, self-promotional rather than factual presentations. Their purpose is to impress the reader with Pliny's good taste and private fortune. But Tuscany, then and now, is an astonishingly beautiful place to live and relax. Here, as in other letters, Pliny is probably polishing the truth rather than perverting it.

Income from land and grapes

If he got no positive cash flow from his Ostia estate, how substantial was the income that Pliny derived from this Tuscan estate and its vines? Pliny tells us in another letter [**8.2**] that he sold the grape crop to dealers, but not for how much. The purpose of this letter is different. It is not written to boast about the size of his income. On the contrary, its purpose is to tell the world what a generous man he was in agreeing to pay a rebate to those dealers who proved to have bid too much for his grapes when the market went sour. This is cash out, not cash in. To emphasise his lack of interest in sordid business matters, in another letter [**9.20**] he states with careless nonchalance that he himself picks the odd grape, tastes the odd glass of wine from the vat, and sometimes visits the servants he brought with him from the city who in turn are the people doing the actual supervision of the labouring peasants.

Despite a poor harvest, Pliny can afford to take it lightly, or to appear to take it lightly. But if he is right about his merchants, the crops from this estate can hardly have been the mainstay of his income. In short, it is hard not to conclude that neither of Pliny's two villa retreats were the prime source of income for Pliny.

> In reality the harvest he reaped came from his writing. Pliny was pretty much a gentleman farmer: neither villa could have provided much beyond his own needs and those of his numerous servants.[17]

These estates would certainly have had great asset value. But they also had prestige value. He could entertain there as well as get away from it all. He could, by these elaborate descriptions of them in his letters, boast about them. He was keeping up with his peer group, the Roman grandees who also owned large properties. But if he did not, as he claims, take fees for his legal work (see Chapter 10) and did not draw a large income from these two estates, the question of where exactly he got his undoubted high income from remains baffling – unless it was from money-lending and the salaries attached to the various public offices he held, or of course from a variable mixture of all these sources.

Sight for sore eyes

Paradoxically, what both villas, so open to the sun and views, did provide for him was an inner room where he could be in complete darkness, a refuge from both light and noise. Some have speculated that this was because he had poor eyesight and his eyes hurt him. One of his letters refers to his eye trouble. He has just travelled in a closed carriage with the light shut out, and his rooms (he does not say at which villa) can be darkened by blinds and shutters. He thanks his correspondent for the gift of a chicken.

> My eyes may still be inflamed, but they were sharp enough to see how plump it was [**7.21**].

Pliny went to such pains to paint for his readers a vivid picture of his luxury hang-outs. But perhaps he could not see them very well himself.

A fine crop of poets: Pantomime in the salon

It is Pliny who, more than any other Roman author, shows us in his letters how the literary scene worked in his day and in the century or so straddling his lifetime. Some 55 of Pliny's letters touch on and illuminate his, and Rome's, literary life. That is almost one in four of all his non-Bithynia letters. This reflects how important literary activity was to him and to the social context in which he lived. His great hobby and relaxation was literature, either reading his own latest compositions out aloud to invited friends in verse or prose, or listening to their latest compositions. Not everyone need have shared that enthusiasm. For other members of the Roman elite, it might have been hunting that filled their leisure time. Pliny went hunting too. But even there Pliny the literary enthusiast was still at it, doing his compositions, notebook at his side. When at Rome however, it was the round of literary salons that Pliny frequented. In one letter he says proudly:

> This year has raised a fine crop of poets. There was scarcely a day throughout the month of April when someone was not giving a reading. I am glad to see that literature flourishes and there is a show of budding talent [1.13].

Pliny is frank about his personal self-satisfaction.

> There are very few people who care for literature without caring for me too.

He is also frightfully pleased when people recognise him as a famous writer rather than as a famous lawyer. He proudly tells a story [9.23] relayed to him by his friend Tacitus. At the races Tacitus got talking to a man sitting next to him who enquired who he was. Tacitus replied:

> You know me from your reading.

To which the man responded:

> Then you are Tacitus or Pliny.

Pliny is thrilled.

> I can't tell you how delighted I am.

Pliny also tells the story of the man who travelled all the way from Gades in Spain (modern Cadiz) just to see the great historian Livy, and then went home again [**2.3**]. Being a famous author meant something to Pliny.

Managing leisure

The paradox is that Pliny's portrait in his letters of the Roman upper class at its leisure, enjoying a relaxed literary life composing elegant verses and listening to the new compositions of their friends, is also a lesson in how to manage and organise your leisure time properly and with objectives. Leisure time is managed time – or should be. As with his literary house and garden tour (see Chapter 11), Pliny displays

> his marked interest in the proper use of *otium* (leisure).

Productive use of free time is a recurrent theme in Pliny's letters, but in particular it applies to his letters about the literary activities of his circle, and of himself.

> He devotes considerable attention to time and motion studies, worrying about the degree to which his own *otium* is productive rather than merely idle, and urging his friends, too, to put leisure time to best use. The prime leisure pursuit is always study and literary work, and in this respect Pliny subscribes to an elite tradition which includes Cicero's *otium litteratum* (lettered leisure) and Seneca's declaration that '*otium* without literary work is death'.[1]

In other words, leisure could be hard work. What you did with it demonstrated how far you had trained yourself towards a well-ordered and well-regulated life. It was not just about literary quality and chatting to friends. It was a serious business.

The pantomime letter

However, Pliny admits that he personally had a problem with his own attempt at a well-ordered literary leisure-time. That problem, he tells us, was how actually to perform his own literary readings to his friends and peers. In explaining his problem, he may be showing himself to be capable of poking occasional fun at himself; or of course he may be deadly serious. It is hard to tell. The letter in which Pliny sets out this personal dilemma is commonly and rightly known as his 'pantomime letter' – if pantomime it was. In it Pliny says:

> I am told that I read badly – I mean when I read verse. So as I am planning to give an informal reading to my personal friends, I am thinking of making use of one of my freedmen [i.e. an ex-slave]. The man I have chosen is not really a good reader but I think he will do better than I can as long as he is not nervous. He is in fact as inexperienced a reader as I am a poet. Now, I do not know what I am to do myself while he is reading, whether I am to sit still and silent like a mere spectator, or do as some people do and accompany his words with lips, eye and gesture. But I don't believe I am any better at mime than at reading aloud [**9.34**].

Pliny as a mime? The picture of the eminent and sometimes pompous Pliny, successful lawyer and senator, sitting in the middle of a dumb show, waving his arms and hands about, mouthing words he is not speaking, screwing up his eyes like a silent movie clown, to accompany a voiceover spoken by his ex-slave sitting no doubt on the edge of the raised dais, is surely either absurd or self-mockery. At the same time it tells us a lot about how Romans did literature, and about the close ties between literature and other forms of public performance in the law courts and in the theatre. How Pliny resolved his dilemma we do not know. It is one of the many cases in his letters where Pliny irritatingly fails to follow a story through to completion. But the plain suggestion that other people did adopt this curious division of labour between the voice of the reader and the gestures of the author shows us that literature to the upper-class Roman was a performance art where body-language was as important as words or content. Elsewhere Pliny remarks plaintively that

> a man who is giving a reading has the two chief aids to his delivery, eyes and hands, taken up with his text, so it is not surprising if the attention of his audience wavers [**2.19**].

Just as the law was in part a performance art, so too was literature. It was a disadvantage of reading, says Pliny, that the two main organs that anyone must use for reading, eyes and hands, were too occupied to be used for more theatrical purposes.

The gentleman's literary club

A Romantic poet, starving in a garret or declaiming verse on a windy street corner, Pliny was not. The famous 'panto' letter is only one of a series of letters in which Pliny provides us with a unique insight into how upper-class literary life functioned at Rome, how books were written, reviewed, distributed and used, and about the pivotal role of slaves and ex-slaves as the 'enabling infrastructure' of literary endeavours. As in the case of his country villas, Pliny goes to great pains to depict to us, the readers of his letters, an idealised world, this time an urban one in which well-bred Romans gathered together to engage in rarified intellectual pursuits in their spare time, and in comfort. They visited each other, praised and evaluated each other's literary efforts, collected copies of each other's new works, and mixed politics and administration with books and philosophy in a seamless mixture that recalls, no doubt deliberately, Plato's ideal rulers and philosopher-kings.

It was how members of Rome's elite liked to think of themselves and how they justified their right to rule the empire. Pliny was of course himself a member of this elite gentleman's club, and proud of it. But, in passing, his letters give us valuable practical detail about how the book trade worked at Rome, what authors did when composing, what booksellers and bookshops did, what libraries did, and indeed how an actual book was manufactured and distributed in an era long before the invention of printing and paper, let alone e-readers.

But a word of caution is needed. Pliny may have had a background political agenda in his enthusiastic write-up of the literary scene of his day. He may be reflecting his concern to both praise and sustain, after the repressive later years of the emperor Domitian, the claimed new freedom of expression under the new emperor Trajan, about whom Pliny composed his famous *Panegyric* (see Chapter 8). So Pliny may be presenting us with this idealised view of how he and others composed and launched their new literary works as an example of this new freedom of expression. He was, after all, a close friend as well as correspondent and appointee of Trajan, who would presumably read and approve of Pliny's collected letters. There may be a closer connection between the *Panegyric* and the letters than might appear at first sight. In reality, philosopher-kings he and his literary circle were not, and the odious Regulus (see Chapter 5) was not the only unscrupulous self-seeker among them. On the other hand, Pliny could hardly be telling outright lies about the leisure life of his generation.

Whether he and the high-class friends who figure in his letters were just amateurish dilettanti producing routine and repetitive platitudes, or whether in among the inevitable dross we can see emerging some of the great works of literature in the Latin language, is yet another question, one much debated. This was after all the so-called Silver Age of Latin literature – not a term much in favour today – producing authors valued and read down to the present time. So we cannot dismiss out of hand the cultural life in which Pliny was such an enthusiastic participant and commentator.

The Roman book launch: A *recitatio*

The central event in the life of a new literary work, as described by Pliny, was the *recitatio*, for which there is no easy English translation. It was a public reading before invited friends, part book-launch, part recital, part theatricals, part social get-together, part rite-of-passage.[2] It was also a performance of some sort – hence Pliny's worry in his pantomime letter about whether, and how, to perform. We can call it a public reading, provided we also remember its multiple aspects. It was the key event in the life (or death) of a new literary composition. It determined whether the new work either took off and found a place in private or public libraries and, just maybe, survived to the present day, or died a death among the many competing voices on Rome's literary scene. There was no organised publishing and distribution industry such as we take for granted today. In Rome's quite different cultural environment, the public reading was in effect the act of publication of a new work. Either people liked it and wanted copies, or they did not. Either it entered the comparative safety of the library shelves, private or state-owned, or it did not.

But even in doing literature, Pliny has to be sensitive to Roman upper-class conventions. He is careful about either entering into or setting up too many social debts on the lines of 'if you come along to my reading to listen to my latest composition, I will come along to listen to yours'. In the Roman culture of gift exchange and mutual obligation, some people came along to your reading session just because they felt obliged to do so, or for fear that if they did not you would not come to their next reading and there might be nobody there, which would be a social disgrace. So Pliny tactfully says of his next composition:

> I shall not read it to my friends, for I don't want it to seem that I went to hear them with the intention of putting them in my debt.

There could be other dangers too. Pliny tells the story of a historian who, at the end of a reading of his new narrative about recent political events, was asked by some members of his audience to refrain from reading out any more of it the next day, because of the imputations it cast upon certain contemporaries [**9.27**]. The historian may have been Tacitus, but Pliny does not say so. But it is a hint that history came close to politics, and could be a dangerous and sensitive subject for a public reading.

Audience (mis)behaviour

Pliny also admits that this literary version of a mutual admiration society had its own dangers. The audience, even if it came, could behave very badly. It sounds just like many modern meetings. But it gives Pliny a chance to show once again what may (or may not) be his sense of humour. He complains:

> People are slow to form an audience. Most of them sit about outside gossiping and wasting their time when they could be giving their attention. They give orders that they are to be told at intervals whether the reader has come in and has read the preface, or is coming to the end of the book. It is not until that moment – and even then reluctantly – that they come dawdling in. Nor do they stay for very long, but leave before the end, some of them trying to slip out unobserved and others marching boldly out [**1.13**].

It must have been a terrible affront to try to launch your new composition, over which you had sweated for months, in front of people who did not really want to be there, or who sent in a mere slave to hold a seat until a good bit arrived, if it did. Such bad manners, however, were not confined to the public reading. Pliny tells us that at dinner parties also people got up and left just when the food was over and a reader was about to read some edifying bit of literature. It did not happen to Pliny of course. He tells us [**8.21**] that he gathered a leisured audience in his dining room in the month of July, a quiet time in the law courts, sitting on chairs in front of the dining couches, and over two evenings read to them his latest verses in three different styles, inviting serious comment.

The audience too was supposed to be part of the performance. They were not just mute listeners – or were not meant to be, anyway. Pliny expresses indignation about a reading given by a friend of his at which three 'clever' (an insult, I suspect) persons

> listened to it like deaf-mutes. They never opened their lips, stirred a hand, nor even rose to their feet except as a change from sitting still. What is the point of this laziness and conceit, this want of tact and good sense? [**6.17**]

So the members of the audience were supposed to play a role by their atten-
tiveness, verbal comments, physical attitudes, and enthusiasm. But they did not
always live up to the ideal. Plutarch also lists other faults of an audience, such
as not sitting still, frowning, putting on a disagreeable expression, a wandering
gaze, physical contortions, crossed legs, grinning, lowered head – all these and
more are 'reprehensible', he says.[3] Even silence could be taken two ways – there
was attentive silence, and there was passive silence [**2.10**]. It was not easy being
a good listener, any more than it was easy to be a good reader or author.

Equally, some audiences must have endured terrible stuff. Juvenal complains
of the stale themes that the audiences suffered at these events; perhaps, for
once, he was not being satirical.[4] Worse, some of the audience might just be
paid to be there – hired 'clappers' whose role was to applaud on cue [**2.14**].
But there was also genuine applause, and cries (spontaneous or not) of '*effecte*',
'*eugê*', '*pulchre*', '*sophos*' – roughly, 'terrific', 'nice work', 'lovely stuff', 'clever!'. Or
there might be a background murmur or, contrarily, sometimes the silence
of concentration [**2.10**]. The noise was what attracted the emperor Claudius,
who happened to be walking past, unexpectedly – and perhaps disconcert-
ingly? – to join the audience at a reading. Suetonius says that Claudius himself
could only get through a reading of his history works by dousing himself in
cold water, and then had to put up with a bench breaking under the weight
of a particularly fat man, thus causing much laughter and reducing Claudius
himself to giggles.[5]

The *recitatio* as performance

How, then, did you organise a public reading to avoid embarrassment and to
maximise the life-chances of your new composition? It was not a simple event
to stage. First, you needed a place to hold it. If you had a suitable or dedicated
room in your mansion house in town, all well and good. If not, you had to beg,
borrow or hire a suitable room, theatre or hall. Pliny praises a friend of his called
Titinius Capito for lending his house for public readings [**8.12**]. The hall had to
be furnished with chairs and/or benches, at least for the important attendees, at
the reader's expense.[6] The seating of the audience was probably hierarchical, to
reflect the Roman sense of class and place in society, just as it was in the theatre.
Invitations, possibly even programmes (*codicilli* or *libelli*), had to be sent out.
Clearly you already had to be a man of some means to hold the event properly.
If you were not, then it had to be the street corner or the public paths where

you would try to get a hearing, shouting often into the wind or the rain to the indifferent crowd.

Then there was the question of dress. You did not just turn up. If the satirist Persius is to be believed (satire needs to reflect reality, if in a distorting mirror) you put on your best toga, all white and washed, and your best sardonyx ring, as befits a performance before a distinguished invited public. You were, after all, on stage and on show. Persius also refers to the quasi-sexual excitement aroused in the audience by a powerful reading. *Carmina lumbum intrant et tremulo scalpuntur ibi intima versu*, he says: 'the poems enter the loins, and intimate parts are scratched by the tremulous verse'. Persius is using a satirist's licence to use a (not very nice) sexual metaphor to depict the pleasure that educated Romans derived from a reading – if it was well done.[7]

Then, as we saw with Pliny's pantomime letter, there was the question of who should actually read the new work. Was it normally the author himself? Often we cannot be sure. Maybe it was the author – or maybe, in accordance with the story told by Pliny, the author was uncertain about his abilities as a public reader and got his slave or freedman or his professional *lector* (reader) to do it instead [**9.34**]. The *lector* was a trained and expert reader, despite (or because of) being a slave or ex-slave, and might well do it better and more expressively than his master. Splitting the role as Pliny suggests in his pantomime letter is amusing, even silly to our view. But it does show how important was the performance aspect of new book presentation. A mere reading it was not. The usual practice seems to have been to read or declaim some preface or introduction while standing up, but then to read the main text sitting down. This meant having a suitable chair and possibly a reading table or low lectern.

What is remarkable is that none of Pliny's accounts, satirical or otherwise, makes reference to the actual means of reading, to the unrolling of the papyrus scroll (the Roman equivalent of a book) or to the deciphering of the 'river of letters' that made up a Roman text in the era before punctuation came into regular use, or even to the regular movement of the eyes or the mental concentration needed. What Pliny talks about, in his pantomime letter, is essentially his body language. The reading was a physical, almost theatrical performance that relied on the visual as well as oral impressiveness of the speaker. The voice, the dress, the face, the eyes and the hands all played their part. That is what lay behind the poet Julius Montanus's remark that he could only borrow material from Virgil if he could also borrow Virgil's voice and delivery – without that voice, the text was almost nothing.[8]

Not the content, but the style

Surely then, say its critics, the public reading was all about style and not about substance. After all, how could the young Calpurnius Piso possibly have known much about astronomy, the subject of the new poem he had written and which Pliny went along to hear at a reading? Indeed, what could the audience have known either about the subject? For the young Piso, it was a sort of rite of passage. What Pliny rushed up to congratulate him on was his delivery, not his content [**5.17**]. None of Pliny's letters discusses the content. Presentation, vocal and physical, is what the audience appreciated. But that is hardly surprising, nor necessarily a bad thing. Oratory was after all the standard training of an educated Roman. It was the oratorical aspects that they felt on sure grounds to appreciate (or not). Moreover, if you were expected to sit through two hours or so of a platform presentation, as Pliny suggests, you had every right to expect more than a dry academic lecture. You expected some drama, some fireworks.

The content was a separate issue. It might be good, or it might be bad. That was for subsequent readers and subsequent generations to decide – by copying or not copying the text to give it a life-in-use. Virgil's stuff was good, despite Montanus's remark about it needing Virgil's voice for the complete experience, and it survived. Many other works were no doubt bad, even if stylish, and perished. But style in literature does matter, and it is not a dismissal of the public reading to say that style was what a Roman audience could (sometimes) get its metaphorical teeth into. Moreover, originality of material was not the objective. On the contrary, to recall and rehearse what others had said before was not considered antiquarianism or plagiarism. It was the very stuff of literature of all kinds. An author's hope might often be to rehearse the material better or with new effects. That is what the audience was listening for.

How long did a *recitatio* go on for?

How long could you expect people to sit still (more or less) and put aside other commitments in order to listen, attentively or otherwise, to a reading of your new composition? Nobody, not even Pliny, really tells us this detail. There is the famous story told by him about how he spent two days giving a reading of a revised and much expanded version of his *Panegyric* of Trajan, previously delivered to the Senate in the emperor's presence. Even then he had not finished it, so he was persuaded by an allegedly enthusiastic audience to come back for a third day to get to the end [**3.18**]. Elsewhere he refers to another two-day reading of one of his speeches, and to a three-day reading by his friend Sentius Augurinus [**4.5** and **4.27**]. This was no quick drop-in session.

But Pliny does not tell how many hours of each day these readings took, and anyway, the official praise-speech of the emperor was no ordinary reading. It might have been politic, even politically compulsory, for many people to be seen to be in the audience and to be seen to have sat through to the end. Estimates vary between one and three hours for an average day's reading. But these seem to depend more on subjective estimates of the staying power of a Roman listener (or his buttocks) than on any direct evidence. Nevertheless, with the great emphasis on gesture, facial expression, style of speech, oratorical flourishes and, one must suppose, pauses for applause or comment, an average reading of one to two hours seems reasonable. On the other hand, the potential Roman attention span was probably far greater than today's. Look how many hours Pliny spoke for in the courts, up to six hours, and before the Senate. So it might have gone on for much longer if there was good reason. We can't be sure. As so often, Pliny can be infuriatingly vague on the detail.

Being an author: The process of composition

Pliny's letters do however give us a clear idea of how a Roman author typically went about writing a new work. His account may be biased towards those who had money and status, but reflects a society where slaves, educated slaves, were available even to writers of more modest means. Composition of a new work was more of a process than a flash of romantic creative inspiration. Composition, Pliny shows, went in stages. This is his own summary of how he himself went about it, at least when at his country estate, and it was probably the same for all those who, like Pliny, Tacitus and Suetonius, had full-time day-jobs and enough personal wealth. Writers like Martial who had to earn a living by their pen (or stylus) may have worked differently – in the case of Martial, by getting money from social superiors like Pliny and Regulus. Pliny says:

> I work it out in my head … then I call my secretary, the shutters are opened, and
> I dictate what I have put into shape; he goes out, is recalled, and again dismissed.
> [Then] I work out the rest of my subject and dictate it [**9.36**].

Then (if at one of his villas) he may go for a walk, take exercise, read a book, go for a horse ride, go hunting but with notebooks to hand, and even, he groans, meet a few of his wingeing tenant farmers. A hard life. But taking all his letters together, Pliny does give a worked out idea of the multi-stage process of literary composition and distribution, and within that he makes clear the pivotal role of highly skilled slaves. The 'publishing cycle' of antiquity was a process quite unlike today's publishing industry, and we rely on Pliny for elucidating its stages.

Stage 1: The author, having thought about the next part of his new text, dictates a first draft of this new bit to his slave-secretary, or *librarius*. This is also the stage at which the author may indicate the extracts from existing works that he wishes to incorporate (acknowledged or not) into his new text. In Pliny's description of his uncle's working method [**3.5**] he says that the elder Pliny bequeathed 160 notebooks full of passages selected from other authors.

Stage 2: The *librarius* writes out this piece of dictation, and the author corrects it, and another written version is made by the *librarius*. This routine may be repeated.

Stage 3: This first draft is sent, privately, to one or two friends for comment.

Stage 4: A public reading is given to an invited audience made up of people the author would like to impress, or who are themselves authors attending out of mutual obligation. Comments may be given or expected.

Stage 5: Comments given at the reading are incorporated, or not, and a final text is created – the 'autograph' copy.

Stage 6: If the new book was dedicated to some important person, a copy, perhaps a de luxe copy in a special binding ('binding' here means the cylindrical leather tube into which the papyrus scroll was put) is sent out to the dedicatee. A copy also goes to at least some friends who ask for it, and perhaps to some state or private libraries.

Stage 7 onwards: Fame, fashion, chance, indifference, politics, war, fire, religion, time and modern editors determine the long-term fate of the new work.

Was Pliny's stuff any good?

Pliny is as generous in his praise of the work of his fellow authors as he is nervous about his own, no doubt for social as well as artistic reasons. About his friend Spurinna he writes:

He composes lyric verses in both Greek and Latin; they are remarkable for their wit, grace and delicacy, and their charm is enhanced by the propriety of their author [**3.1**].

About a man called Pompeius Saturninus he positively gushes:

His aphorisms are apt and ready, his periods rounded with a formal dignity, his vocabulary impressive and classical ... his histories will please you even more by their conciseness and clarity, their charm and brilliance of their style and their power of exposition ... he also writes verses in the style of Catullus ... I read him for recreation [**1.16**].

Like Pliny, Saturninus was also, and primarily, an advocate in court, and it is noticeable that Pliny mixes praise of his court speeches with praise of his writings, almost indiscriminately. The readings that Pliny himself gave were often of his own court speeches, and he remarks that:

when published they look better and more impressive in a good-sized volume [**1.20**].

To men like Pliny it is clear that there was no clear dividing line between speeches in court and writing literature. Both drew upon the same skill set, the same shared educational background. Men disgraced in politics could also redeem themselves in part by writing. Silius Italicus, for example, wrote a huge epic poem about the second great war against Carthage which still survives, all 12,200 lines of it. Pliny remarks that:

Italicus had damaged his reputation under Nero – it was believed that he had offered his services as an informer ... but he removed the stigma of his former activities by his honourable retirement [in which] he took great pains over his verses, though they cannot be called inspired, and frequently submitted them to public criticism by the readings he gave [**3.7**].

Inspired his verses are not, modern critics may agree. But Italicus also won praise for his term as governor of the province of Asia, and his career shows how in Pliny's social stratum politics, literature and the courtroom formed an almost seamless platform for public performance and personal reputation. When it comes to his own efforts, however, Pliny is suitably cautious. He has doubts about the merits of letters as an art form compared to speeches, and stresses their demerits.

There [in speeches] the tone is set by the expression, gestures and voice of the speaker, whereas a letter lacks such recommendations and is liable to wilful misinterpretation [**5.7**].

It is ironic, then, that Pliny should be best known, almost solely known these days, for his letters, compared to the verses which he wrote in his spare time and which he refers to with some pride but with some nervousness [5.10]. Pliny's letters themselves have survived over the centuries because of their educational quality as examples of how to write elegant and structured letters – the art of epistolography. But his own poetry and verses have not survived as a body of work, whether deservedly or not we cannot fairly tell – he only quotes two short fragments in his letters [7.4 and 7.9]. If we are to judge by these, the praise he generously heaps on his salon colleagues does not rub off on Pliny himself. One eight-line poem he wrote starts off:

> The beauty of wax is its power to yield
> To the fingers' skilful touch.

The other which he quotes proclaims:

> I found that Cicero could unbend his talent
> To play with polished wit on lighter theme.

Even allowing for translation problems, this is not immortal stuff. To one correspondent Pliny admits that:

> I have never felt confident in any one style [of composition] [9.29].

Pliny is also honest enough to acknowledge some quite disparaging criticisms of his work, if in a rather injured tone, and that is an attractive touch to his character. To his friend Lupercus he writes:

> I had an idea that you had criticised some passages in my writings for being pompous, though I thought them splendid, and what I imagined to be a full treatment of a bold enterprise you dismissed as redundant and exaggerated [9.26].

'Redundant', 'exaggerated', 'pompous' – hard and harsh words, but if that was the view of a friend, perhaps it was true generally of Pliny's efforts, and quite likely true of many others besides Pliny. But we cannot be sure.

After all, this era of Roman history did produce among the inevitable dross a fine and varied crop of valued authors, as Pliny says in his 'April' letter: Tacitus, Martial, Juvenal, Suetonius, Statius, and not least Pliny himself – as a letter writer if not as a poet. Of these writers, Martial, Tacitus, Suetonius and Pliny all knew each other personally. Pliny and Tacitus were close friends. The writing lives of all of them at least overlapped. Pliny was at or near the centre of this group. Because of what they wrote about Roman history and society, Pliny's literary circle has been profoundly influential on our view of classical and imperial Rome, and on political theory and practice right down to the French Revolution and beyond. How did Pliny's circle function?

His literary circle – who's in, who's out, where's Juvenal?

However informative Pliny's letters may be about how he and his friends set about 'doing literature', there are several surprising omissions and gaps in what he tells us. Despite his many references to readings of new compositions given either by himself or by one of his friends, he is sparing on details about who actually attended his own readings and whose readings he went to. He does say that he is very choosey about who he invites to his literary events.

> I do not invite the general public, but a select and limited audience of persons whom I admire and trust [**7.17**].

But who exactly formed this 'limited audience' and how were they selected? Pliny rarely tells us, and it would be illuminating to know whether any of the other well-known authors of his time were ever in his audience. But again, Pliny does not tell us. Indeed, the question goes wider than that. For another oddity is the omission from his letters of the names of several famous authors of his time whom Pliny could be expected to write to, or know, or know about and discuss. Was his literary circle determined more by social and political status than by creative merit? Was it an upper-class dilettante club rather than an exchange of true wit and talent?

That Pliny knew a lot of important people, and that they shared an interest in literature, good, bad or indifferent, is clear enough from his letters. These people may have formed some sort of literary circle or book club. But it is hard to believe that their conversations were confined to the finer points of poetic composition. These men included real 'big beasts' on the Roman scene, important social and political figures such as Arrius Antoninus, twice consul (in 69 and 97), proconsul of Asia, and father-in-law of the future emperor Antoninus Pius. As a hobby this man wrote epigrams and iambic mimes in Greek [**4.3**], which Pliny tried his hand at translating into Latin [**4.18**]. Another grand figure was

Vestricius Spurinna, a veteran military general and writer of lyrics in both Greek and Latin. This man was also twice consul, had taken part in the civil wars of 69 on the side of the contender Otho, and for his exploits on the field of battle had a statue dedicated to him at the request of the emperor Trajan [1.5, 2.7, 3.1]. His high social status was such that Pliny's arch-enemy Regulus chose him to act as his intermediary in an attempted reconciliation with Pliny. In this same circle there figured Passennius Paullus [6.15], a descendant of the poet Propertius. For such men there was no incompatibility, such as there might be today, between public action as general or governor and writing poetry. Whether these men came to Pliny's readings, or he to theirs, Pliny does not specify, although it is reasonable to suppose that they did exchange social visits if not lyrical verses.

But in two other cases Pliny does tell us more clearly who attended what. Titinius Capito was an intriguing figure who for years was at the heart of Roman government as the man in charge of the emperor's correspondence (the job known in Latin as *ab epistolis*) under no less than three successive emperors, Domitian, Nerva and Trajan. He wrote a book about the deaths of the victims of Domitian's purge, and if anyone knew the truth about that bloody episode, it would have been Titinius Capito. He attended Pliny's readings whenever he was in Rome, and Pliny reciprocated by going to his readings,

> as is my duty or urgent desire [8.12].

Pliny also says that for three days he had been at a series of readings given by Sentius Augurinus of short poems that Sentius had written. These poems, says Pliny, exhibited

> delicate charm and tender feelings … wit and polished perfection [4.27].

Sentius Augurinus was a friend or relative of both Antoninus and Spurinna and was later appointed under the emperor Hadrian as proconsul of Macedonia, so he was another important personage. But what Pliny really liked about Augurinus's three-day reading was that one of the poems was in praise of Pliny himself, and Pliny does not waste the opportunity to quote it as an example of Augurinus's 'wit and polished perfection'. It reads:

> My verse is light and tender, as Catullus long ago,
> But what care I for poets past when I my Pliny know?
> Outside the courts in mutual love and song he makes his name;
> You lovers and you statesmen, to Pliny yield your fame!

Even in translation, this is banal stuff, and the best that might be said is that

Pliny's pleasure at being flattered in this way outweighed his critical judgement. This is not the only case where Pliny displays an almost child-like delight in being praised. On the other hand, perhaps it is typical of the pedestrian and self-congratulatory stuff that, in the main, was poured out at the literary-social salons attended by Pliny and his circle of important men in which their social standing was as important as, or even more important than, their literary abilities.

Pliny praises the young Piso [5.17] and his reading of a poem entitled *Legends of the Stars*. Given Piso's distinguished ancestry, it was not a recital that the class-conscious Pliny could have missed, even though Piso can hardly have known much about the stars. It was all a bit like a mutual admiration society. Pliny mentions [6.15] one reading he did *not* attend – the one at which Passennus Paulus, that descendant of Propertius, incautiously referred to a man who was actually sitting in his audience. This man promptly denied the reference so that Paulus got, says Pliny, 'a chilly reception'. Another reading he did attend was the one where he complains about the audience sitting like deaf mutes [6.17] but tactfully he does not tell us whose reading it was. Elsewhere [6.21] he tells us that he attended a reading given to a small audience by one Vergilius Romanus – whether small because select, or small because few people were interested, he does not say.

In other words, we know of only four people by name whose readings he attended, and few of the names of people who came to Pliny's readings. Given the reported intensity of the literary activity of Pliny and his friends, this is surprising. Even in the case of Suetonius, the future author of *The Twelve Caesars* and an acknowledged colleague and friend of Pliny, Pliny is familiar with his earlier writings [5.10] but nowhere says that he either attended readings by Suetonius (if he gave any) or that Suetonius attended his readings. Similarly, despite flaunting his friendship with Tacitus, Pliny gives no hint that they attended each other's readings – assuming that Tacitus gave any.

Pliny and Statius

A further oddity is the patchiness of Pliny's references to writers he might have been expected to know personally or at least to have commented on in letters to friends. The poet Statius, for example, is not mentioned, although he and Pliny may have had a common friend in Vibius Maximus to whom Statius dedicated a poem, a lyric ode.[1] From Statius it appears that Vibius wrote a world history, and that might put him among Pliny's literary set. So there may have been a literary if not a personal connection, and the careers of Statius and Pliny certainly overlapped. Statius was active until about the end of Domitian's reign and gave popular readings of his epic works in the big auditoria of Rome. But just as Pliny disliked noisy public events like the horseraces in the Circus Maximus, which had not the slightest attraction for him, or so he says [**9.6**], so too he may have shunned the big, crowded, theatrical recitals that Statius specialised in. But the lack of any mention at all is odd.

… and Juvenal (a mutual dislike?)

More remarkably, Juvenal is another author not there at all in Pliny's letters. There has been much speculation about why Juvenal, more famous than Pliny over the centuries since they lived, is absent from Pliny's narratives. Then again, Pliny himself is absent from Juvenal's narratives, at least by name. So the omission was mutual – but was it on purpose? One problem here is that the dates of Juvenal's life are far from clear. Publication of Juvenal's works is generally put in the period 110–30, so after Pliny's time and therefore not perhaps of concern to Pliny. But their lifetimes certainly overlapped. Juvenal had a verse-letter addressed to him by his fellow satirical poet Martial[2] and Pliny certainly knew Martial.

Juvenal's satires could well have been in private or draft circulation long before the formal publication dates ascribed to them. So we may speculate that Pliny either knew or knew about Juvenal but chose to ignore him and the type of rude satirical verse Juvenal wrote, so different from the refined and polite exercises in versification that seems to have been typical of Pliny and his fine friends. Perhaps there was a serious class division also. Juvenal just did not have the social status to be invited to Pliny's house, and Pliny did not think it proper to attend a reading by Juvenal, if Juvenal ever gave any.

On the other hand, there may have been actual mutual hostility, a dislike by Juvenal of Pliny, a dislike that was reciprocated. It has been a great game among scholars to spot in Juvenal's verses thinly veiled barbs aimed not precisely at Pliny but at his family and friends, as a sort of flank attack. Two references in particular may indicate such hostility. One is Juvenal's allegation about a certain lady called Hispulla that she was fat and immoral:

A bull fatter than Hispulla … Hispulla is crazy for a tragic actor.[3]

Now there was a Calpurnia Hispulla who was the aunt of Pliny's wife Calpurnia, and who looked after Calpurnia after her parents died. The two women were very close. Was it the same Hispulla? Some say it was, or could be. Some say not. Pliny also had two other ladies called Hispulla among his friends, widow and daughter of Corellius Rufus. It was not a common name. Could it be one of them? Or maybe it was the very fact that it *could* be any one or all of these three that was the whole point of Juvenal's jibe, and that is what got up Pliny's nose. But something else might have offended Pliny even more. Juvenal openly pours scorn on one of Pliny's most important court cases, the trial that Pliny and Tacitus conducted against Marius Priscus in the year 100 on charges of corruption while a provincial governor. Priscus was found guilty. But Juvenal was not impressed, calling it a meaningless verdict.

> After all, what's disgrace if their money is safe? Marius in exile starts boozing in the afternoon and savours the anger of the gods, while you, Province, the winner of the case, are in tears.[4]

Juvenal probably had a point, and the tone suggests that this satire was originally written very close to the time of the trial itself, while memories of it were still fresh. If he then showed it around, as Romans did, the prim and reputation-conscious Pliny may not have taken kindly to such open mockery of his legal efforts. In the messy political circumstances of the time, he had done his best. But Juvenal might have seemed to undermine the edifice of justice delivered that Pliny sought to build as his memorial.

> We may conclude that the two men were antipathetic, and that Juvenal revenged himself by side-hits like these while Pliny maintained a lofty silence.[5]

Other such side-hits have been spotted by literary hostility-hunters. Juvenal's mocking description of the villa of a rich but mean man is taken to be a veiled jibe at one of Pliny's villas. There are others. Juvenal has a go at a woman called Calvina, who allegedly sleeps with a rich man's slave for the money. There was a Calvina who was a relative of Pliny to whom he gave 100,000 sesterces as part of her dowry [2.4]. Juvenal also has a go at a certain Gillo who sleeps with a wealthy older lady, again for the money. Gillo was part of the name of Pliny's step-father-in law [9.13]. Procula is mocked by Juvenal as either a giant or a dwarf. Procula was the name of a lady from modern Padua that Pliny respected [1.14].[6] These may be pure coincidences, or they may not. Cumulatively, and whether or not you accept all these alleged side-swipes, some of which are more far-fetched than others, there is enough evidence to make hostility between the two men very likely. Putting it another way, Juvenal in his satires took side-swipes at large numbers of his contemporaries and elders. So if his active life overlapped with that of Pliny, as we may suppose, and if Pliny was half as important as he himself claims, then Juvenal may be expected to have had a go at him, somehow.

Patronising Martial

The supposition of at least a class difference between Juvenal and Pliny is supported by Pliny's attitude to Martial. When Martial died in Spain, having returned there to his native territory from Rome, Pliny [**3.21**] tells us that he gave Martial his travelling expenses – surely an act of patronage *de haut en bas*, from top man to lesser man. Pliny praises Martial as:

> a man of great gifts, with a mind both subtle and penetrating

and adds that Martial was one of his dearest friends. But then the truth comes to light. Pliny admits that one forceful reason why he liked Martial was because Martial wrote flattering verses about him, one of which he then quotes but implying that there were others.[7] The mutual admiration society was at work again. Only this one poem survives, and Pliny is able to quote it from memory. In an elegant but flattering tone suited to an offering from client to patron, it refers to Pliny working hard all day preparing his speeches for the Court of One Hundred Men. But there is no suggestion that Martial was ever invited to Pliny's literary gatherings, nor that Pliny attended any readings given by Martial.

There was more than a division of literary genre between the two men. There was also a less crossable class divide that friendship did not transcend. Perhaps that is why Pliny felt able to drop a heavy hint that in his opinion Martial's work was not of lasting value. The class divide was such that Martial had to admire Pliny, but Pliny did not have to admire Martial. He would not dream of saying anything so negative about his grand equal-status friends and their literary efforts, which he often praises to the skies as a social rather than critical acknowledgement. But about Martial he says (artfully putting words into his correspondent's mouth):

> You may object that his verses will not be immortal: perhaps not.

The irony of course is that Martial's artful verses have survived, been widely admired, and have amused countless generations since his death, while Pliny's verses, if not his letters, died with him.

The curious case of Silius Italicus, informer and poet

In one letter Pliny writes at length about the self-imposed death by starvation of Silius Italicus, in a tone that is respectful but at the same time keeping a careful distance between himself and Silius. Silius was a much older man than Pliny, and Pliny tells us that he gave readings of his epic verses while giving no hint that he, Pliny, ever attended those readings. On the other hand, Pliny must have read them, for (as with Martial) he permits himself an adverse comment, quoted in full in the previous chapter.

His verses cannot be called inspired [**3.7**].

But it is noticeable that Pliny's main interest in Silius is that this man had damaged his reputation by offering his services as an informer under the emperor Nero, but had retrieved his reputation by his conduct after Nero's death and when in retirement. However, Pliny also points out that Silius pointedly absented himself from Rome rather than attend Trajan's first triumphal entry into the city as emperor in 99, and, even more pointedly, Trajan actually gave him permission to be absent when a public figure of his eminence might have been expected to attend as a mark of respect and loyalty. Something is going on here – a hint perhaps from Pliny for those attuned to hear it that not all was well with Silius even at this later date. As with Regulus and Carus, and so with Silius Italicus, these informers and their (mis)deeds, and the degree of danger they had posed to Pliny himself, are a perennial theme of the letters.

Pliny and Suetonius

Two extremely well-known Latin authors are prominent in Pliny's letters, however: Suetonius and Tacitus. But there is a stark contrast between Pliny's treatment of Suetonius, as evidenced in the letters, and his treatment of Tacitus. This contrast once again shows the nuances of the Roman class system at work. While Pliny admired both men, there is a marked difference between his attitude to one and to the other. Suetonius was about 10 years younger than Pliny, having been born in about the year 80, probably in Hippo Regius in North

Africa, the same town that eventually became the seat of St Augustine. It appears that Pliny got to know Suetonius through his literary endeavours. In one letter [5.10] Pliny urges Suetonius to publish (that is, to circulate) his writing, implying that Suetonius was shy of doing so. Pliny had been bombarding him with his, Pliny's, hendecasyllables, verses with 11 syllables per line, and there is a playful suggestion that if Suetonius wanted to stop this bombardment he had better push his own stuff out into the world to displace Pliny's. Pliny's respect for Suetonius's literary capability is also shown by the fact that the famous 'pantomime letter' [9.34], in which Pliny seeks advice on how to conduct himself at a reading of one of his compositions, is addressed to Suetonius. In other words, Suetonius was someone whose opinion he valued on a matter close to Pliny's pride and self-esteem.

In another letter [1.18] that is not as innocent as it appears at first sight, it transpires that Suetonius knew Pliny well enough to confide in him a bad dream that he had. This seemed to portend that he would lose a case that was about to come up in front of the Court of One Hundred Men. This was of course the very court in which Pliny specialised as an advocate. Pliny does not say that he was acting for Suetonius, but clearly he was, because he says in his letter that to allay Suetonius's fears he will apply for an adjournment of the case, even though such adjournments are not normally granted. So here in this legal context Pliny and Suetonius are in the classic patron–client relationship that prevailed in the courts of Rome, and Suetonius is asking for a special favour from Pliny, which Pliny says he is in a position to obtain for his client. There may have been intellectual equality between the two men, but not social equality.

That the case nevertheless went against Suetonius may be implied by a letter closely grouped with the previous one in which Pliny seeks another favour for his friend/client Suetonius. Pliny asks a friend of his to ensure that Suetonius pays a fair price for a small property he is interested in – that is, that he does not get a bad deal. Pliny can ask this because the seller of the property is a friend of Pliny's friend. The friend-of-a-friend connection was strong enough in Roman society that Pliny can expect this favour. Pliny implies that this will be Suetonius's first property – a 'scholar turned landowner' – and will presumably give him some financial independence. Pliny is frank about who will be doing a favour to whom, and what social obligations will arise from the favour done.

He will be in my debt and I in yours [1.24].

That is how the Roman system (and many others) worked, and this was by no means the only favour that Suetonius asked of Pliny. Indeed, it is almost as if, in publishing the exchanges between himself and Suetonius, Pliny was deliberately advertising his powers of patronage to show what an important man he was. In another letter [**3.8**], Pliny not only says that he had obtained a post of military tribune for Suetonius (favour one) but also agrees to get this post transferred to a relative of Suetonius when Suetonius apparently decided that he did not want it after all (favour two). Here, once again, Pliny the grandee can confer favours on his chosen clientele. There were more.

Pliny says that he respects Suetonius both as a friend and as a scholar. Even though Pliny was not to know that Suetonius would later write his famous biographical series *The Twelve Caesars*, Suetonius wrote a long list of other works, now largely lost, on a huge range of topics such as Greek games, the Roman year, Roman customs, names of seas and rivers. At least some of these must have been penned during Pliny's lifetime. But in view of Suetonius's later career in imperial service under the emperor Hadrian, perhaps the biggest favour that Pliny obtained for him was to recommend him to the emperor Trajan and to ask for Suetonius to be granted the so-called privileges of three children [**10.94**]. Like Pliny himself, Suetonius was married but had no children. But Roman law imposed various penalties and obligations on the childless and those with few children, from which those with three children or more were exempt. It was a mark of special imperial favour to confer this fictitious status of parent on the childless. Trajan in reply to Pliny says that he rarely grants this exemption but, as a favour to Pliny, he will do so.

Pliny's letter was written from Bithynia while he was Trajan's governor/ plenipotentiary in that province. This is the evidence for the suggestion that Pliny took Suetonius with him to Bithynia, as a member of his staff – yet another sign of patronage. It is reasonable to conclude that Pliny, by securing a degree of financial independence and preferential tax status for Suetonius, and by recommending him to the emperor, probably laid the foundations for Suetonius's subsequent career at the very heart of the imperial system of government, not unlike the Titinius Capito referred to earlier. Suetonius rose to hold three important if ill-defined offices in the imperial civil service, successively in charge of the emperor's correspondence, archives and libraries (the jobs called *ab epistolis, a studiis, a bibliothecis*), until he fell out of favour with the emperor Hadrian and was dismissed, allegedly because he got too close to Hadrian's wife. Later he may or may not have been restored to imperial service. But it is supposed that his time in the imperial archives may have given him his material for *The Twelve Caesars*, a lively work whose colourful stories and personal and political anecdotes about Roman emperors have dominated our view of imperial Rome ever since – more so than Pliny's much plainer and less gossipy prose.

Pliny and Tacitus

No less than 16 of Pliny's letters are addressed to Tacitus or talk about him. Pliny's letters to Tacitus have been called

> one of antiquity's most notorious one-way conversations.[8]

At first sight, Tacitus is the senior partner in this dialogue, in which of course we do not have his side of the conversation. He was the elder man, born some four or five years before Pliny, and preceded him up the status ladder of Rome. He made consul in 97, some three years earlier than Pliny. Pliny admired Tacitus and sought every opportunity to associate himself with him, as if the great man's reputation would somehow rub off on Pliny. They were both famous advocates in court, and acted together for the prosecution of the ex-governor of the Roman province of Africa, Marius Priscus [**2.11**] (see Chapter 6). But theirs was far more than a professional relationship. Tacitus, delivering a funeral oration, is 'a most eloquent orator', says Pliny [**2.1**]. Tacitus is the master, Pliny the pupil [**8.7**]. Theirs is a 'lifelong friendship' in which Pliny emulated Tacitus. They swapped books for comment, and had their names often mentioned together [**7.20**]. As proof of this, they were often left identical legacies in other people's wills – a peculiarly Roman way of honouring and equating two people. Pliny likes to associate his name with that of Tacitus.

> I can't tell you how delighted I am to have our names assigned to literature as if they belonged there and not to individuals, and to learn that we are both known by our writing [**9.23**].

It appears to be Pliny who is anxious to be included in Tacitus's history books, not (as far as we can tell) Tacitus who wants to be in Pliny's letters. Pliny openly admits that he would like to find a place in Tacitus's narratives [**7.33**] and it is for that reason that he sends to Tacitus an account of his prosecution of another ex-governor, Baebius Massa. Moreover, it is to a request from Tacitus that we owe the most famous of all Pliny's letters, the two letters in which he describes the eruption of the volcano Mount Vesuvius in 79 and the death of his uncle, the elder Pliny, in that eruption [**6.16, 6.20**]. With a token show of false modesty – 'not important enough for history' – Pliny responds to Tacitus's request for information with a detailed description of the eruption and his uncle's failed attempt, at the cost of his own life, to rescue people from the fatal shore. Clearly Pliny leapt at the chance to figure, by invitation, in Tacitus's proposed narrative. But we don't know if he ever did. That part of Tacitus's *Histories* covering the year 79 has perished, so Pliny's shot at immortality by that route failed. Fortunately for him, and for all the modern guidebooks to Pompeii that quote Pliny with or without acknowledgement, Pliny's two letters did survive and have given him the immortal fame he desired.

This picture, drawn from Pliny's own writings, of Pliny giving constant precedence to Tacitus has played into the hands of those for whom:

> Tacitus is a great mind and author of a 'possession for all time', Pliny at best a second-rate survivor in the lottery of manuscript tradition.[9]

But the two men had more in common, and were more equal that even Pliny himself was willing to acknowledge in public. Moreover, Pliny's own reputation as an author has improved to the point where he can no longer be assumed to be inferior to Tacitus. They also had one driving motive in common. That was to avenge the victims of the emperor Domitian and in the process offer some explanation of their own conduct – and failures – under that regime. Their way of doing so differed markedly, one providing a simpler narrative concentrating on a happier present, the other a more complex narrative dwelling on the horrors of the past. But the common ground would have given them much to talk about. We may even picture the two friends

> sitting together in Pliny's villa, cheerfully sipping their Falernian wine, swapping clichés about life and morals, and from time to time patting each other appreciatively on the back.[10]

On the hunt

There is, however, one cautionary footnote to the letters from Pliny to Tacitus, which warns us not to think that these two men spent all their spare time doing literature and sipping wine together. Both of them went hunting too, as did most of their social peer group. Pliny tells Tacitus with some pride that he has just caught three wild boars despite being busy writing in his notebook [1.6], and he implies that Tacitus also hunts. This is confirmed in another letter [9.10] in which Pliny protests against advice from Tacitus to honour Diana, the goddess of wild places, equally as much as Minerva, goddess of urban craftsmen, actors and writers. But there was a problem about that, explains Pliny, and it was not on the creative side.

There is a shortage of boars.

So for the moment he can only deal with Minerva. With not enough wild boars to hunt, he will have to make do with poetry. The unlikely image of the bookish Pliny as a keen wild boar hunter is a useful corrective to the picture he himself strives so hard to put across to us of a refined literary society devoted to rarified poetic pursuits. It was the pursuit of wild boars that equally stirred the blood. There was clearly a lively and close relationship between Tacitus and Pliny, both of whom we do not normally think of as hunters – unless as hunters of tyrannical emperors.

14

Nervous in Bithynia: Those quarrelsome little Greeks

In the years after becoming consul in 100, Pliny continued his career in public office, if intermittently. He received a priesthood in 103, but that was probably an honorary office. Then by contrast, over the period 104–6, he was given the much more mundane-sounding job of supervising Rome's river banks and sewers. Mundane, but vitally important to the life of this huge (by the standards of the time) city of perhaps a million people. The river could flood, and efficient sewers made life in the city tolerable and kept some check on the spread of disease. Doubtless this meant expenditure and control of public money, and that was why a financial expert like Pliny was deemed suitable – he was of course not a sewerage engineer.

Then in the year 110, or thereabouts, in total contrast to Rome's rivers and sewers, Pliny was sent by his emperor Trajan as the emperor's special envoy to the Roman province of Bithynia-Pontus.[1] This hybrid province, essentially Greek in character, lay sprawling along the southern coast of what is now the Black Sea, in the north of modern-day Turkey. It also included Byzantium on the European side of the great Bosphorus waterway, still a comparatively small city compared to the magnificent imperial capital that it became two centuries later under the emperor Constantine. Pliny was armed with full and overriding powers as the emperor's personal deputy and appointee to tackle the financial mess into which the public finances of many of the quarrelsome and competitive cities of this province had fallen. Money, it seems, had been misappropriated from public funds, 'borrowed' but not returned, or spent on badly planned and unfinished public works, with hints of corruption and fraud. So the emperor had been informed by his own sources, and he decided to act. His main worry may have been whether these cities might be forced to default on the tax revenues payable to the imperial treasuries. But maintaining public order, or preventing disorder, would also have been a prime concern. So he turned to Pliny, his friend and financial expert.

We have no idea how often the emperor, any emperor, had to step in to try to sort out local financial scandals. But what makes Pliny's mission remarkable is that the letters, the diplomatic cables if you like, that passed both ways between Pliny and Trajan during Pliny's time in Bithynia-Pontus have not only survived (they form most of Book Ten of Pliny's collected letters) but also give us the only detailed glimpse we have of how Roman imperial administration actually worked at ground level. These letters are therefore a unique documentary record without parallel in Roman history. The letters, over 100 of them, numbered from 10.15 to 10.121 in the letter collection, appear to offer a direct insight into the day-to-day problem-solving that preoccupied Roman governors and Roman emperors, and to show where the decision-making power lay and how it was exercised. But that insight has to be treated with some caution. Why were these letters, and no others, published for posterity to read?

In fact, it is little short of a miracle that we have these letters at all. Book Ten only comes down to us through two editions published in 1502 (incomplete) and in 1508 (complete), both in Venice, and both based on the sixth-century manuscript preserved in the Abbey of St Victor in Paris (see Chapter 2). That manuscript was then largely lost. The letters are therefore remarkable both as a unique record of classical Roman history, and as an example of the fragility of survival from the once immense literary output and administrative archives of that lost classical world.

Propaganda value

But there may be a catch. It is inconceivable that these particular letters could have been published for the world to read without the express permission of the emperor himself, whether that be Trajan or, quite possibly, Trajan's successor Hadrian. In other words, the letters were meant to show, or were thought to show, imperial power at its most benign, well-intentioned and purposeful. But how far can we generalise from Pliny's letters to Trajan and Trajan's replies to Pliny? Pliny was on a special mission, as a personal emissary of the emperor, with a special remit or set of instructions (*mandata*) from Trajan. His time in Bithynia may not be typical. Indeed, one reason for obtaining official permission to have these letters published at all (whoever did so) may be that the standard of provincial administration and judicial fairness at this time was low, and whatever one may say about Pliny's extreme caution in exercising his wide powers as Trajan's personal emissary, he does at least emerge as a conscientious and scrupulous administrator.[2] So publication of this exchange of letters between Pliny and the emperor was good PR for the regime.

Perhaps, like the rest of Pliny's letters, these 100 or so letters had and still have a propaganda value, a background political agenda that has to be teased out from the apparent first-hand evidence of these diplomatic cables. After all, Pliny had composed and delivered that famous and flattering speech in praise of Trajan, the *Panegyricus*, some 10 years previously, and there may be a closer connection between that praise-speech and the Bithynian letters than has been generally allowed. The letters portray an emperor who cared about and watched over his subjects, right down to the details of their daily lives in the public spaces of the often small cities they lived in. The composition and publication of these letters almost look like premeditated acts. This is not to imply that they are false. Only that they are not such simple evidence as may at first appear. That, of course, is true of Pliny's letters generally.

Just get on with it, Secundus

But if these letters were good for Trajan and his reputation, they have not been good for Pliny or his reputation. They may have done Trajan a favour by bearing out his claim to be 'the best of princes' – the *optimus princeps*. But they have earned contempt for Pliny as indecisive, frightened of the sweeping powers granted to him, kowtowing to the emperor at every turn, nervous, fussy, an 'unmitigated temporizer' as one author has called him.[3] Surely an emperor, preoccupied with grand affairs of state, would have neither the time nor the inclination to be bothered with such apparent trivia as Pliny inflicted on him in these diplomatic cables? The hint of irritation and even sarcasm in some of Trajan's replies to Pliny, while restrained in tone, was surely merited.

> As the man on the spot you will be the best person to consider and decide what ought to be done ... it will be enough for me to be informed of the decision you arrive at
>
> ...
>
> You should have been in no uncertainty, my dearest Secundus, about that matter on which you decided that I should be consulted [**40** and **82**].

For God's sake, Pliny, Trajan seems to be saying, just get on with it.

> It was for this purpose that I chose a man of your wisdom, that you might exercise control [117].

But Pliny was a lifelong bureaucrat and imperial civil servant. He had survived dangerous times by being ultra-careful. He was not going to change now. To be fair, as an experienced lawyer he also knew that what the emperor said had the force of law in the Roman Empire. His word literally was law. So where he knew that the problem, and the emperor's response (the so-called *rescript*), would set not just a precedent but become actual law, he was careful to consult the supreme lawmaker, and understandably. Nevertheless (as an example of Pliny's extreme caution) what was the point of asking the emperor to send out land surveyors from Rome, which he twice does, when the highly educated, Grecian east of the empire certainly had many such trained men and indeed supplied the rest of the empire with such experts? Trajan, irritably, tells Pliny so, in no uncertain terms, in language modified only by the fact that they were old friends, as far as any emperor could have friends.

Pliny's extreme nervousness towards the emperor contrasts with his often peremptory attitude towards the populace of that outer province of the empire with very Greek traditions but now in his care as governor with special powers.

> Fifteen hundred miles removed from Como and his neighbours, recalling the scale and splendour of Rome as he defined his mission among the cramped streets and strange gods of Amastris or Heraclea, small wonder if he looked down on the colonials as an inferior species. Small wonder if the governor forgot the finer points of the law and laid about him as he would among his slaves – and as he never would have thought to do among his neighbours in Como.[4]

To be fair to Pliny, the province was in a mess, urgent action was needed, he had the emperor on his back, so little wonder he laid about him. But the note of racial and cultural superiority in his letters to Trajan, and in Trajan's to him, is striking. Trajan refers to the colonials patronisingly as *Graeculi* – little Greeks – and Pliny had much the same condescending attitude [40].

Dating Pliny's appointment – and his death

Pliny was also up against time, though he may not have realised it at the beginning. He was destined not to remain in Bithynia-Pontus for very long – perhaps a year and a half. It is not even certain exactly when he went there. It could have been 109, 110 or 111, and there have been meticulous but ultimately unresolved arguments among scholars about the exact date.[5] But it matters little for the evaluation of the letters and of Pliny's governorship, and 110 seems the least worst choice. If so, Pliny's term of office would have spanned part of 110, all of 111, and part of 112. What brought his term to an end?

There is no record of his being recalled. So it is presumed that he died in office, in 112, and that is why the sequence of letters appears to come to an abrupt halt. We have no other way of dating his death. He would still have been a comparatively young man, even by Roman standards, not much over 50 years of age. But he had been ill on the journey out to Bithynia, as his letters show, and he may no longer have been a fit man. On the other hand, his comparative youth casts some doubt on 112 being his date of death. Perhaps he was forced to return to Rome by ill health – which is why the letters suddenly stop – but lived on in Rome or Como for – well, for who knows how long? His wife had also returned to Rome shortly before, due to ill health, as the letters attest, and Pliny may conceivably have followed her. He did, after all, protest his great love for her. The presumption that he died in office in Bithynia has been built into the scholarship about Pliny, but perhaps too hastily. Perhaps he lived on to edit and publish what is now Book Ten of his letters, the letters to and from Bithynia, with Trajan's permission of course. But short of new evidence, the matter must remain open.

Who else edited the letters, then?

If not issued by Pliny himself, how could these letters have been published? Again, we can't know for sure. But there is one other obvious candidate as editor of Book Ten. That is the author Suetonius. It is an interesting example of the Roman class system at work that it could be so. In the main collection, Pliny addresses several letters to Suetonius as if they were equals as well as friends, and Suetonius was one of the literary men of the day with whom Pliny liked to consort. These days, Suetonius is far better known than Pliny, thanks to his famous and notoriously gossipy book *Lives of the Caesars*, which covers all the emperors from Julius Caesar to Domitian and is the ultimate source-book for various modern novels, films and TV series.

But Suetonius was also a client, in the Roman sense, of the wealthy and senatorial Pliny. Pliny was the owner of large estates and the holder of the highest honour that Rome could bestow, the rank of consul. Suetonius was of equestrian rank, from the lower aristocracy, and about 10 years younger than Pliny. It was Pliny who, as a favour from a big man to a lesser man, obtained for Suetonius a small property to give him some financial security; who obtained for Suetonius certain tax privileges by petitioning the emperor of his behalf; and who probably took Suetonius with him to Bithynia as a member of his staff.

So Suetonius would have been familiar with the correspondence that passed between Trajan and Pliny. Maybe he even wrote it. In later years he held several high offices in the imperial court doing just such documentary work. So Suetonius could have had access over a long period to the imperial archives, and could have excerpted from them those letters to and from Bithynia. Or he might have taken them from Pliny's own personal archive. Someone also took out from the letters the addenda, the documents that Trajan said that he was appending to his replies but which are no longer there. All that is speculation. But if Pliny had died in office, it is entirely plausible that Suetonius acted as his literary executor – by kind permission of the emperor.

Are the letters authentic and complete?

The possible role of Suetonius also raises a related question, that of the apparent person-to-person tone of the letters. Who exactly composed the letters that Pliny signed as his own? It is generally assumed that Pliny drafted these letters himself. But if so, what (if anything) was Suetonius doing on his staff, and what about the often unacknowledged but skilled slaves that Pliny and his peers had to help them? Again, we don't know, and there must have been a lot of routine record-keeping to do. The letters do have a very personal tone that suggests Pliny's own hand, his own 'authentic' voice speaking to us as well as to Trajan, across the centuries. But equally, a skilful professional writer like Suetonius, or indeed a slave who knew his owner well, could have learnt how to clone his master's voice.

And what about Trajan's letters back to Pliny? Surely, some say, an emperor like Trajan had too much else to do to write, personally, his responses to Pliny's often detailed (even trivial) requests for a decision on this or agreement on that?

It may be supposed that the letters we have were drafted for Trajan by his court official in charge of imperial correspondence, specifically by that predecessor of Suetonius himself, that Titinius Capito who served as *ab epistolis* under three successive emperors, Domitian, Nerva and Trajan. This raises the intriguing idea that what we have in Book Ten of Pliny's collected letters is not Pliny talking to Trajan, but Suetonius (under supervision) talking to Capito (under supervision).

The contrary argument is that Trajan's letters read like personal responses, and that Pliny, a trained lawyer and self-proclaimed writer of literary works, was quite capable of dashing off his own letters. In both cases, the letters would have been dictated to a professional scribe or secretary, perhaps of slave or freedman status, acting as the equivalent of a word-processor. Moreover, studies have shown that responses to day-to-day administrative and legal problems were exactly what emperors spent much of their time doing, even if, like Trajan, they also planned and executed grand military offensives against Dacia and Persia. In the end, perhaps it does not matter very much. The letters certainly must convey what Pliny wanted to ask the emperor and what Trajan wanted to say in return. But it also indicates some caution before assuming that we have the 'authentic' voice of these two unusual and busy men.

There has also been a remarkably heated debate about whether the letters we have are a complete record of the exchanges between Pliny and Trajan, or only excerpts.[6] Again, we cannot be sure. Eleven of Pliny's letters do not get a response from Trajan (but that means most of them did) and there is at least one case where Pliny apparently does not respond to a request from Trajan [73]. But the sheer variety of subject matter in the letters, ranging far outside matters of corruption that were Trajan's original cause for concern, suggests that no particular category of letters was kept in or left out by the editor, whoever he was. The only obvious omissions are those supporting documents which are said to be attached to some of the letters, but which are not there now. But that is not enough to discredit the probability that the collection as we have it is virtually complete.

O Lord

What is more unsettling is the manner in which Pliny addresses Trajan. In the standard English translations of the Bithynia letters, his mode of greeting is rendered as 'Sir', which these days is an innocuous and common way of polite address. The problem is that the Latin word that Pliny actually uses is *domine*. That might better be translated 'My Lord' or even 'O Lord', a mode of address much more evocative of a vastly unequal power relationship between the two men. It might also be a sign of the friendship between the two men, that Pliny could address his overlord in the familiar form of the Latin noun – what the French would call *tutoyer*.

But the main problem is that the word *dominus* already had, by Pliny's date, a sorry and highly charged history in the Roman Empire. According to Suetonius, some previous emperors such as Augustus and Tiberius had refused the title *dominus* because it was too redolent of Greek-style absolutism and autocracy – it gave the game away – and what had stirred particular hatred towards the emperor Domitian was his insistence that he be addressed as *dominus et deus* – Lord and God. Indeed, in his panegyric to Trajan, Pliny particularly remarks on how Trajan, unlike his horrible predecessor Domitian, repudiated the title *dominus*. Pliny says that Trajan

> holds the place of *princeps* ['leading citizen', the traditional title of the emperor in the first century] in order that there shall be no place for a *dominus*.[7]

Yet here is Pliny using that very form of greeting to that very emperor. For modern historians, one of the fiercest debates has been about when, exactly, did the Roman Empire slip from being the Principate as established by Augustus with its veneer of legality and respectability, into being the Dominate, the undisguised and flaunted rule of an outright autocrat propped up by elaborate ceremonial and worshipped as a virtual god – the final degradation, as some see it, of the Roman Empire. At the very least Domitian had set a trend towards absolutism, even if it did not reach its fulfillment until much later, with the arrival of, say, Aurelian on the throne in 270.

Pliny therefore stands accused of being a hypocrite as well as a temporiser. In the year 100 he could praise Trajan for not going down that slippery slope towards 'Dominate' and politely advise him not to do so. Ten years later he addresses Trajan as *domine*. He had alternatives. Hadrian could be addressed as *optime imperator* ('best emperor'), a much less loaded term. So did Pliny need to be so obsequious in his letters? Consider that famous anecdote told by Philostratus in his *Lives of the Sophists*. The anecdote concerns the writer, philosopher and orator Dio Chrysostom, who came from the city of Prusa in Bithynia, who as we shall see was to figure rather embarrassingly in Pliny's time as governor of that province. Dio wrote high-minded essays on the art of kingship, some of which he may have delivered as speeches in front of Trajan himself, just as Pliny did his panegyric to Trajan. One day, or so the story goes, Trajan invited Dio to accompany him in his golden triumphal chariot. As they rattled along, Trajan turned to Dio and said:

> I don't really understand a word you say. But never mind. I love you as I love myself.[8]

It may be just a story. But it makes one wonder what this professional, pragmatic and approachable soldier-emperor made of all the flattery that was thrown at him, and whether Pliny, the distinguished senator and consul, really had to adopt such an apparently groveling tone towards him in his letters. In the end, it is baffling. But Pliny had after all survived and (up to a point) prospered under Domitian as well as under Trajan, and would have learnt all there was to know about court etiquette and the game of survival. If his greeting *domine* had become accepted, even routine, by 110, it marks Pliny as the man we already know him to be – the imperial civil servant who above all else plays it safe.

The problem with Bithynia-Pontus

Perhaps Pliny had good reason to play it safe. The affairs of the province that he was sent out to investigate and correct were in a sorry state, and contained at least one conundrum that probably neither Pliny nor Trajan expected. That conundrum was, how to deal with the Christians. That is such a momentous and much pored-over subject that it merits a separate chapter (see Chapter 15). Bithynia-Pontus had anyway for years been an persistent source of trouble to the imperial regime. As we have seen (Chapter 6), analysis of prosecutions brought against Roman provincial governors over the century or so up to Pliny's day on corruption or similar charges shows that Bithynia figured in the largest single number of cases, seven out of a total of 40.[9] Of the 40 cases, 28 resulted in a guilty verdict, with five more unknown.

Clearly, determined provincials who believed that they had been swindled thought they had a good chance of getting their money back through the Roman courts – Bithynians especially. The numbers suggest that they were right to feel aggrieved, and right to seek redress. They had some reason to be so litigious. There was some justice somewhere in the system, even if you had to fight hard to get it, and Pliny had played a part in that search for justice on whichever side it lay. What Pliny did not want was that the litigiousness of the Bithynians, which he helped to foster, be turned against himself, as had happened to a colleague. This may have been another reason why he appealed to Trajan as often as he did – to protect his back.

Two of the Bithynia law cases had been very recent, and Pliny himself had figured in both of them. In 103 Julius Bassus, proconsul (in other words, the Roman governor) of Bithynia-Pontus, was prosecuted by the Bithynians before the Senate on charges of theft and extortion, pleaded guilty, and was convicted but on the lesser of two charges. Pliny acted for the prosecution. Another man who acted with him for the prosecution, Rufus Varenus, was then himself appointed proconsul of Bithynia-Pontus, only to face prosecution back at Rome a mere three years later. This time Pliny acted for the defence, and the case was eventually dropped, with Trajan's consent, after the Bithynians apparently changed their minds about whether to press the prosecution. Pliny did not want the same to happen to him. Clearly the province was in a restive state. But it also meant that Pliny knew a lot about Bithynia before he set foot in the place. That is presumably why Trajan chose him as his special representative to the province.

Why was Bithynia particularly prominent in prosecutions? One can only guess. In addition to some Roman colonies, which were settlements of Roman ex-servicemen, it was made up of Greek cities that dated back centuries. These were often self-governing to some degree, with responsibilities for the admin-istration of surrounding non-urban territory. They seem to have been proud of their relative (strictly relative) powers of self-determination, and to have kept up a fierce rivalry between themselves for status and display of wealth. In fact, they were typical Greek cities to the core, if a bit more so. That same Dio Chrysostom of Prusa who rode in Trajan's chariot composed and delivered a series of speeches deploring the tendency for the cities in his native area of Bithynia to be riven by faction fighting, either internally or between cities, and appealing for what he calls 'concord'. He refers bluntly to the

> envy and rivalry and the strife that is their outcome, your plotting against one another, your gloating over the misfortunes of your neighbours.[10]

Dio warns his listeners that such quarrelsome behaviour just invites the unwanted intervention of the Roman provincial governor of the day, or even worse gives the governor an opportunity for extortion and seizure of private assets without risk of subsequent prosecution. Dio clearly knew how the game was played. So on Dio's own evidence, Trajan had plenty of reason to intervene in Bithynia, and it is ironic that Trajan's intervention using Pliny was to catch up with Dio himself, whose home city of Prusa was as faction-ridden as any other city in the province. Moreover, Dio's appeals for 'concord' seem to have fallen on deaf ears. The hostility between Prusa's near-neighbours, the cities of Nicaea and Nicomedia, kept recurring until late in the Roman Empire.

The emperor tightens his grip

Of the 12 known cities of Bithynia, seven figure in Pliny's letters. These are Apamea, an old Greek city with a colony of Roman citizens grafted onto it; Prusa (modern Bursa), home city of Dio and named after the Greek king who founded it; Nicaea, founded in 301 BCE; Nicomedia (modern Izmit), founded in 264 BCE; Juliopolis, a small place; Claudiopolis, probably founded by a Greek king; and Byzantium, again an old Greek colony. Five of the known six cities of Pontus also figure, at least one of which dated back to the sixth century BCE. In short, the area had a long history and tradition, of which its citizens were only too proud. The list also shows that, in his brief tenure of office, Pliny did at least make a conscientious effort to get around all of his bailiwick.

Bithynia-Pontus was, strictly speaking, what is called a 'public' province, one traditionally administered by ex-consuls sent out by the Roman Senate on one-year appointments – a relic of the old Republican system of governing the empire. To conform with legality, Trajan therefore had to ensure the passage of a new law, a *senatus consultum*, revoking this 'public' status of the province, to enable him to send out his own personal imperial nominee as governor, answerable to himself alone. That, perhaps, is another possible explanation for Pliny's cautious approach to his task. This was a political innovation, of which, as a senator himself, he must have been well aware but about which he may have had mixed feelings. It was yet another decrease in the authority of the Senate, an institution that he valued so highly as (in good times at least) an organ of good governance.

Trajan's action, however, marked a further and significant step by which the administration of the empire was increasingly centralised under the direct control of the emperor, who could put his own nominees into post for however long he chose, responsible to him alone. Some have seen this increasing centralisation as just consolidating the one-man tyranny by which the empire was ruled, part of the general long-term decline from the older republican principles of distributed responsibility. Others, perhaps more hard-headedly, argue that these senatorial proconsuls, sent out for only a year and chosen by lot from among potential candidates, rarely knew much about the province they were sent to govern, did not have time to learn, and frequently saw it as a chance for personal enrichment – an invitation to a calculated degree of corruption, despite the potential for prosecution and conviction.

If there was a prosecution, these senatorial governors were after all judged by their peer group, the Senate, in session as a trial court, and extortion must have been flagrant for a prosecution to succeed. There is little reason to suppose that these men governed well. Already, the collection of taxes was largely supervised by imperial 'procurators' directly answerable to the emperor. In retrospect it seems inevitable that the empire should move towards a uniform system of government, in place of the hybrid and inefficient system left over from the Augustan settlement dating back well over a century before Pliny's time. Pliny's appointment, therefore, had a wider significance than even he probably realised. After swinging to and fro following Pliny's departure, Bithynia came permanently under the control of an emperor's nominee (a 'legate') from the time of the emperor Marcus Aurelius some decades later.

Pliny would therefore have been well aware that, in taking on Bithynia-Pontus, he was entering a hornet's nest. To deal with Bithynia's problems, Pliny had conferred on him an impressive array of titles, pomp and staff. His grand Roman title was *Legatus Augusti pro praetor consulare potestate* – emperor's deputy with praetorian rank and consular power. In addition to Suetonius, he had with him a legate, that is, his own deputy, Servilius Pudens. His proconsular power entitled him to an escort of six lictors, the maximum allowed, men who acted as bodyguards, enforcers and escorts. There were no military forces of any consequence in the province, apart from a few small detachments about whose proper use Pliny fretted to the emperor. But there was no military command involved, which is another reason why the non-military Pliny may have seemed to Trajan a suitable candidate for this tricky job.

Dealing carefully with Dio

Trajan certainly gave Pliny a detailed mandate, a remit, of what he was supposed to do once he was in post. We do not have it. But Trajan had several sources of information about the problems of Bithynia – the two prosecutions of ex-governors, his own procurator Virdius Gemellinus, responsible for imperial estates and collection of taxes, and at least one other direct informant, his companion in that chariot ride, Dio of Prusa. Dio's full name was Dio (or Dion) Cocceianus, but he is known to posterity by his nickname Dio Chrysostom, meaning Dio with the Golden Mouth. Dio had been exiled from

Italy and from his home province by the emperor Domitian, and may have been lucky to get away with his life, because of his connections with an alleged conspirator against Domitian, Domitian's own cousin Flavius Sabinus, who was put to death.

Dio was recalled after Domitian's assassination in 96, became a friend of Trajan's (as did Pliny), and so had his own open line to the emperor. When Pliny arrived at Dio's home town Prusa on his tour of the province, care would be needed, and it is worth dwelling on events in that city as indicative of what Pliny was up against right across the province, and what local politics were like in that era and place. Allegations were made to him against Dio, and there was a whiff of potential treason about the case. But it involved a friend of the emperor, with his own direct access to the emperor. No wonder Pliny got nervous.

Dio's city of Prusa lay in south-western Bithynia, and Dio had already gained several favours for his city thanks to his friendship and influence with Trajan. During an embassy to the emperor's court headed by Dio, who after his recall seems to have become the city's chief spokesman, Trajan had granted Prusa the status of an assize centre, that is, a city with its own law court. That brought many visitors, litigants and witnesses to Prusa, not to mention judges and governors, all spending money. It was good business as well as a point of civic pride. Dio had also secured the right to enlarge the city's ruling council. This brought more of the city's better-off citizens into the ruling elite, with the associated prestige, and brought money to the city's treasury because the new councilors had to pay for the privilege.

But even then Dio's critics in the city complained that he had not secured enough benefits for Prusa, and could have got more. Prusa was not a 'free' or 'autonomous' city within the Roman system, as some other cities were, and some of its citizens perhaps resented this inferior status, which Dio (they may have argued) could have remedied by using his influence with the emperor. Dio was capable of fierce counter-attack against his critics, as they were against him. In one of his speeches he reports allegations made against himself, true or false, that he had conspired with the then Roman governor, unnamed, to have citizens of Prusa tortured, sent into exile, or driven to suicide. This is serious stuff. The governor in question may have been that same Rufus Varenus in whose trial at Rome Pliny was later involved.[11] Politics in Prusa could turn very nasty indeed, redoubling Pliny's nervousness.

Sprucing up Prusa

By the time Pliny was in Bithynia the main bone of contention between Dio and his critics was his ambitious new building project for Prusa. That is what brought him to Pliny's notice. In addition to letters between Pliny and Trajan on the subject, Dio himself devoted two of his speeches to his building plans and the opposition to them, so we can see the controversy from both sides. On his return from exile, Dio seems to have conceived a grand plan to brighten up his home city. On the evidence, it was in dire need of a facelift. Its bath house was squalid and old, Pliny told the emperor, and a prominent site within the city was 'unsightly with ruins' [**10, 70**]. Dio himself complains of 'low, squalid ruins'.[12] These blots on the city-scape must have been the result, not of poverty since Prusa was well-off, but of negligence and mismanagement. Dio thought he could remedy the situation, armed with the knowledge that Trajan had given his personal permission for the bath house to be rebuilt. This is, incidentally, an example of the level of detail down to which the emperor's agreement could be sought and given.

Dio himself proposed to build, partly at his own expense, a street with a colonnade which people could promenade in,[13] and by the time of Pliny's visit to Prusa he had also taken charge of a (probably separate) project for a library next to a courtyard enclosed once again by a colonnade. But Dio had been the object of controversy in Prusa ever since his younger days, when grain shortages triggered bread riots, an attack on his house with stones and firebrands, and accusations that he had hoarded grain and profited from the crisis by money-lending – all of which he of course denied.[14] But the animosity lived on, as he was to find when his ambitious building plans ran into trouble. It was, says a modern author, 'a sorry tale of jealousy, mismanagement and intrigue'.[15]

For the library complex, Dio served as *curator*, the man who on behalf of the city collected the money from subscribers and supervised the work. His request for the city authorities to formally take delivery of the new buildings and discharge him from his duty as *curator* caused the vendetta against him to flare up once more, with accusations of misuse of public funds. Pliny tells of how the charge was led by one Claudius Eumolpus, acting as representative for Flavius Archippus, also a philosopher and also from Prusa, and also the subject of a separate nasty law-suit at Prusa that went to the ears of Trajan. Eumolpus told Pliny, in Pliny's role as judge, that before the new buildings were transferred to the community Dio should be obliged to render a set of accounts, since either he or some of the other subscribers had (alleged Eumolpus) misused these funds through embezzlement or fraud.

The hint of treason

Moreover, said Eumolpus, Dio had placed in the same building complex not only a statue of Trajan but also the graves of his own wife and son. This is where the suggestion of treason came in. The law said that people should not be buried within the city walls. Not only was Dio getting above himself, thus provoking the jealousy of his rivals, but by associating dead bodies with the emperor he may – so it was hinted – have committed a treasonable act. Pliny adjourned the case to his next assize session at Nicaea and asked all the parties to submit memoranda of evidence. This Dio did, but his accusers did not. So given the tinge of treason Pliny did what was probably the wisest thing – he wrote at length to Trajan about it [81]. He confirmed that he had seen both the statue and the graves. But by the way in which he described in detail the accusers' repeated procrastinations, he dropped a heavy hint to Trajan that he thought the charges should be dismissed as frivolous. Trajan not only agreed, but ticked Pliny off for not making his own mind up without bothering the emperor. It was the occasion for his rebuke, already quoted in part, that:

> you should have been in no doubt, my dearest Secundus, about that matter on which you decided that I should be consulted, since you are very well aware of my determination not to obtain respect for my name through inspiring men with fear or terror or through charges of treason. Accordingly, that charge, which I should not allow even if it were supported by precedent, should be dropped. Rather, let the accounts of the building carried out under the super-vision of Cocceianus Dion be examined, since the interest of the city requires it and Dion does not object, nor ought he [82].

This common-sense admonition was in tune with Trajan's determination not to give space for anonymous or unsupported accusations. His dislike of *delatores*, informers, is consistent. But there is a catch. It was not accusations, but anonymous or unsupported accusations that he disliked, as will also become evident in the case of the Christians.

Pliny's letters from Bithynia make it clear that a provincial governor relied upon personal accusations and formal complaints made to him to know what and who he should investigate. That was how the system worked throughout the Roman Empire. The test was whether the accuser came forward in person and produced evidence. There was a subtle but blurred distinction between 'informer' (bad) and 'informant' (neutral or good). It tended to be the emperor of the day who defined this wobbly distinction in practice. If Pliny had a failure of nerve, it was understandable, in a case which might set a precedent about what did, or did not, constitute treason. Additionally, Dio was the emperor's friend. If in doubt, ask.

A sea of troubles

Pliny found that there were much worse cases of bad construction and financial management than at Prusa – without that hint of treason but equally liable to earn him a rebuke from the emperor. Pliny reports that the new theatre at Nicaea was still unfinished, despite having swallowed up the huge sum of 10 million sesterces, and the work may have been in vain anyway because the building was sinking, with gaping cracks appearing due to spongy soil and/ or crumbly stone. Also at Nicaea, they had begun to restore a gymnasium which had been destroyed by fire, at considerable cost but to no purpose. It was ill-planned and rambling, and the walls might not be strong enough.

At Claudiopolis, the citizens were building a large bath house, but on a low-lying site with a mountain hanging over it. Pliny feared that it was entirely the wrong site. Would Trajan please send out a trustworthy surveyor to advise on both places? No, he would not. Pliny was the best man to decide, being on the spot, and there were plenty of local architects. Once again, Pliny was told to stiffen his resolve [**39, 40**].

At Nicomedia, a costly aqueduct was begun but abandoned while still unfinished, and was then demolished. Another aqueduct was started but also abandoned. Nevertheless, the city needed a better water supply – could Trajan supply a specialist water engineer to advise? Trajan ignores this request, no doubt on the same grounds as the previous one, but reminds Pliny roundly that it is his duty to investigate diligently why so much public money had been wasted, perhaps as a result of collusion among contractors. This time, Pliny is to report back, and one may presume that he did so [**37, 38**].

On a happier note, Pliny is able to report that in several cases he had recovered moneys owed to the city treasury, and was investigating the feasibility and financing of new public works that would enhance the cities of Bithynia-Pontus. His letters give more detail. If ultra-cautious, Pliny was conscientiously carrying out his duties.

First Dio – then the Christians

Overall, Pliny's mission did not last long enough for it to be called successful, and anyway the problems were too endemic in Greek city life. Later, other imperial nominees were to be sent out by the emperor on a similar mission to the same province. But Pliny of all people knew full well the tendency of the Bithynians to take their Roman governors to court on completion of their term. He did not want to get sued like Bassus and Varenus. That dictated caution, and in the matter of Prusa he had especial reason for playing it safe. Dio had the means to retaliate.

Even more caution was needed when he ran into an unexpected problem that had nothing to do with finance or buildings, a problem quite outside his previous experience or his imperial remit. His problem, fiercely debated ever since, right down to the present day, was what to do about the followers of that new-fangled religious cult, Christianity? And entwined with the puzzle of the Christians came the insistent problem which dogged all of Pliny's professional life: how to react to *delatores*, informers or informants, people who denounced others, whether for personal gain or for the alleged public good. Where and how did you draw the line between supported and unsupported allegations, between anonymous and signed depositions, in this case against alleged Christians? It was a potent and dangerous mixture, especially when 'the line' you drew could mean the death of some, the pardon of others, and could define imperial policy towards that bothersome new religious movement.

Christians – what is the crime and what is the punishment?

Until cultural tourism made Pliny's two letters about the eruption of Mount Vesuvius familiar to thousands of visitors to Pompeii, it was his letter from Bithynia to the emperor Trajan about Christians [**10.96**] that attracted the most intense scrutiny and heated debate.[1] As governor of the region, what was he to do about these suspicious characters? This letter, and the reply to it from the emperor [**10.97**], remain to this day the most fiercely controversial of all Pliny's letters. Are they proof of early repression of the Christian religion? Or are they witness to a long period of relative tolerance? There also recurred the perennial question that dogged Pliny at all stages of his career, what to do about informers, *delatores*, in this case those who, often anonymously, levelled hostile accusations against practising Christians. The letters also show up Pliny's personal attitudes and prejudices on religious matters, probably typical of upper-class Romans and many others of that time.

These two letters are therefore of critical importance to scholars of early Christianity and to students of Judaism as well as to historians of so-called 'paganism' and of the administration of the Roman Empire.[2] It is a unique exchange of views between an all-powerful Roman emperor and a distinguished Roman senator and governor, offering an insight without parallel into how the Roman governmental machine went about dealing with that most extraordinary phenomenon of the empire, the rise and rise of Christianity from obscure sect to compulsory universal orthodoxy. There is nothing else quite like this exchange between Pliny and Trajan, and it occurred very early in the history of Christianity, within 80 years or so, almost within living memory, of the crucifixion of Jesus which is generally dated to 33 CE. So the letters provide us with very early, though not the earliest, evidence of Roman law and policy towards the followers of Jesus.

Pliny's dealings with the Christians take his autobiography into the immortality of Roman legal history.[3]

The letters have been interpreted and re-interpreted from their rediscovery in the early 1500s right down to our time. So not surprisingly, given the often heated and sometimes violent controversies that have beset the whole long history of Christianity, the debate over Pliny's letters has frequently been polarised and partisan.

To some, Pliny was a wicked persecutor and an agent of the Devil. The letters are seen as corroborative evidence of systematic Roman persecution of Christians from the word go, a view encouraged by many Christian writers of that and later eras who saw martyrdom and the courage of the suffering martyrs as a sure sign of the endurance and truth of their Christian faith. So, for them, paradoxically, persecution was almost a good thing to be welcomed. On the other hand, apologists for Rome and for its generally tolerant attitude towards religious differences, more akin to our own multi-cultural age than to the dogmatic history of the Christian Church itself, have been keen to emphasise the relative (strictly relative) degree of tolerance shown in these letters towards Christians, and Pliny's willingness to raise questions about the right policy to follow. What exactly, asks Pliny the famously adroit lawyer, have these people done wrong, and what exactly is the charge against them? He was certainly not open-minded on this question: but neither was his mind closed. Trajan's answer, carrying the force of law, set the tone for Roman policy on this tricky matter for a century and a half to come.

Pliny's time as governor of Bithynia-Pontus, and the action he took there about the unexpected problem presented to him by denunciations of Christians made by local people hostile to the new sect, must not be confused with the state-sponsored, empire-wide persecutions of the Christian religion that set in well over a century later. Those persecutions started with the emperor Decius and his attack on the Church in 250, some 140 years after Pliny's days as governor. Those later persecutions culminated with that ultimate anti-Christ figure, the emperor Diocletian and his great persecution of 303. Pliny lived and worked well before all that, at a time when Roman attitudes were still uncertain, even fluid, as Pliny's letter and Trajan's reply show clearly. In his letter to Trajan, Pliny became interested in the detail. He was anxious to establish what the charge against Christians was, and what exceptions there were, if any, to the initial presumption of guilt and consequent penalty. Pliny's own attitude became flexible the more he examined the problem. His enquiries to the emperor resulted in an official policy that offered a degree of toleration towards early Christianity (but within severe limits) for well over a century. For this the Christian Church might even feel grateful, since it gave its followers time to expand their faith to the point where later bouts of much worse persecution were almost bound to be failures.

If Pliny was at all typical of his time, then his increasing doubts, worries and willingness to seek out the facts about Christianity, rather than be swayed by conventional Roman prejudice and popular hysteria, indicate a period at which history might have taken a different turn of global significance. Might Christianity have been different, more pacific by nature and less dogmatically crusading, if it had experienced a more peaceful birth as a world religion? That is an unanswerable what-if question, but one that still bears forcefully upon today's debates about the nature of Christianity in the twenty-first century and its relationship to other faiths. What if early Christians had not been so keen to make martyrs of themselves, so that they went cheerfully to appalling deaths, whatever chance to repent governors like Pliny had given them? What if Roman emperors had been willing to make exceptions for Christians to the standard rules governing conventional Roman religious observance, just as they did for Jews? Pliny stood at some sort of early crossroads in the evolution of the pagan *versus* Christian conflict that merits close attention to what he and Trajan said and did not say, did and did not do. Pliny's letter shows him standing uncertainly and unwillingly at that momentous crossroads.

Pliny's personal attitudes

Awkwardly for Pliny's apologists, he leaves us in no doubt about his starting point when he first arrived in Bithynia-Pontus, about his personal attitude towards Christianity when he began his term as governor. It was probably the conventional attitude of his time. In his letter he calls it 'a madness' (*amentia*) and 'a depraved and gross superstition' (*superstitio prava et immodica*) and 'a contagion' (*contagio*). Pliny, Tacitus and Suetonius all use the same hostile language when referring to Christianity. Tacitus in his *Annals* says that Christianity is a superstition that is destructive (*exitiabilis*) and an evil (*malum*), associated with cruel (*atrocia*) or shameful (*pudenda*) acts.[4] Suetonius in his biography of the emperor Nero calls Christianity 'a new and dangerous superstition' (*superstitio nova ac malefica*).[5] Trajan does not seem to have disagreed with Pliny's use of this language, and we may assume that Pliny was expressing the general attitude of educated Romans of the time. There seems to have been no argument that the penalty, if and where merited, was death by some means.

Prison was not a recognised form of punishment in the Roman Empire, though it was sometimes illegally used as such.

That may help to explain why, in certain circumstances, neither Pliny nor Trajan had any hesitation in executing Christians. It is an unpleasant fact for admirers and defenders of Pliny the humane man and of Trajan the golden-age prince, that they sometimes killed Christians, and killed without compunction. Pliny tells us bluntly that he sent away for immediate execution slaves who refused to recant their Christian beliefs, and sent away to Rome for trial and probable execution anyone holding Roman citizenship who similarly refused to recant. He does not say how many, but that is irrelevant. Pliny butchered some Christians. Similarly, when Trajan was in Antioch, which he used as his headquarters for his war against Persia in 114–15, he had no hesitation in sending off the bishop of Antioch, Ignatius (soon to become St Ignatius), for barbaric execution at Rome.

On the other hand, there is no independent evidence of a general perse-cution of Christians in Pliny's and Trajan's time. So the bishop had presumably provoked a local crisis at Antioch by refusing to take part in the conventional rituals surrounding a Roman emperor, especially one embarking on a hazardous military campaign.[6] That could look like treason and betrayal, and the bishop paid the price. In other words, in Roman eyes the crime of Ignatius was not his faith, but his (dis)loyalty to the emperor. Trajan was probably concerned in Antioch not to upset the traditional gods on the eve of war. Ignatius plainly did not see it that way, and he took the opportunity of the long journey from Antioch to Rome to write a famous series of letters in which he welcomed his fate, which was to be thrown to the lions in the arena. His letters sit uneasily but illuminatingly alongside those of Pliny. But the point is, Trajan, like Pliny, in certain circumstances did not hesitate to put Christians to death. To that extent, they were persecutors. But in their defence, persecution was not typical or systematic.

> Christians fell into the category of potential subversives … there was repression certainly, sometimes savage, but it was sporadic, as for astrologers … the problem for Christians was probably lack of security … it seems quite likely that there were only a couple of hundred Christians put to death for Christianity in the 200 years or so before [the Emperor] Decius.[7]

So repression; but not mass or systematic repression. That came later. Nor was it official state policy at this time. A fair summing up of Roman policy towards Christians in this early period is that:

There is no reason to believe that Christianity as such was illegal [i.e. a crime that contravened a law] any more than the cult of Isis … The Romans treated the cults of Isis and Christ with equal indifference, and repressed them with equal brutality when it seemed expedient for public discipline. Well-behaved cults like that of Mithras were left alone: abominable ones like druidism were suppressed.[8]

Informers Anonymous

In his dealings with Pliny on this emotive issue, Trajan was also concerned about wider issues of imperial policy, most notably that deeply political and emotive issue of the role of informers, those people who denounced others to the authorities on matters ranging from potential treason to alleged financial irregularities and (in this case) suspicious non-conformist religious beliefs. Trajan had made it plain to Pliny in other cases that he disliked anonymous or unsupported allegations. But where was the dividing line between legitimate reports to the authorities on matters that might be in the public interest, and unsubstantiated or vindictive claims not backed by evidence?

Despite his earlier castigation of *delatores* in the context of Rome itself (see Chapter 8), Pliny certainly used anonymous accusations as a basis for investigating the Christians. So at first he appears to have been unaware of, or he chose to ignore, the emperor's rule against such practices, until brought up short by Trajan. As with other judicial cases heard by Pliny in Bithynia, it was almost as if informing was not OK at Rome where it concerned Pliny's elite friends and colleagues, but was OK in the provinces as a necessary and inevitable part of the rough-and-ready local justice system, such as it was. Unlike Pontius Pilate, Pliny could not simply wash his hands of the cases brought to him by informers. He was after all the governor and the emperor's special representative, and his instruction was to sort any problems that came to his notice, by whatever means.

What Pliny said to Trajan: Is it the name or the crime?

For all these reasons, reading the full text of Pliny's fascinating and complex letter to Trajan about Christians, a letter of world-historical importance, is very rewarding. With characteristic nervousness, Pliny begins with a half-apology for such a lengthy dispatch to the emperor, as well he might, since he gets a polite but firm rebuke in return. Pliny then says apologetically that he has never attended a trial of Christians in Rome and does not know what either the normal charge or the normal punishment usually is – a surprising admission for a top member of the Roman legal profession. But it does show that there had been trials of Christians at Rome which Pliny might have attended, but had not. But perhaps not many. There is no other reliable evidence of such trials at Rome since Nero's notorious persecution of Christians at Rome in 64, after the great fire of Rome.

Lawyer-like, Pliny pursues the detail. He wants to know if younger people and people who recant their Christian beliefs should be let off and not punished; and exactly what the offence was if someone confessed to being a Christian. In a question which has provoked heated argument ever since, he asks:

> is it the name of Christian itself (*nomen christianum*) or the crimes (*flagitia*) associated with the name, which are being punished?

This may sound like a typical lawyer's nit-picking question, but it is the crux of the whole letter. Popular opinion, as Christian writers themselves attest, attributed to Christians horrible crimes such as incest, sacrifice of children and cannibalism – conventional charges leveled by many orthodox faiths against their unorthodox enemies throughout the ages, but no less emotive for that. In trying to deal with these allegations, Pliny then tells Trajan what administrative procedure he has so far adopted, revealing that he was responding to actual formal prosecutions brought before him by others as well as to anonymous allegations. In other words, Christians were arousing a lot of local hostility in the province, which manifested itself in various ways. Pliny did not initiate anything: he was reacting. Pliny's procedure was that he questioned the accused three times, warned them of the likely punishment, and if they still refused to retract their beliefs, he ordered them to be 'led away' (*duci iussi*) – the standard Roman euphemism for death by beheading.

If however the accused were Roman citizens, he had no power to impose the death penalty, so he sent them to 'the city' – presumably Rome – to be dealt with 'for a similar madness' (*similis amentia*). He then makes another remark that has provoked heated argument ever since.

> I was in no doubt that their stubbornness and unyielding obstinacy ought to be punished.

Was the offence therefore not to do with religion at all, but with disobeying and defying the legitimate Roman governor? There was in Roman legal practice a well-known offence labeled *contumacia*, which might be translated 'contempt of court', but Pliny does not use that word, and as a lawyer he might be expected to do so if that is what he meant. I suspect that Pliny was just expressing his exasperation that these people would not accept the olive branch which, both metaphorically and literally, he was extending to them. He gave them three chances to save their lives. Just go through some traditional religious ceremonies, he said in effect, for appearance's sake, then go away. What's the big deal?

But then things started to get out of hand. Someone anonymously posted up a long list of alleged Christians in a public place. Pliny made the mistake (as Trajan sharply reminded him) of investigating the names despite the accusation being anonymous. He discharged those who denied being Christian after they had proved it by the ritual acts of homage to the traditional religion that Pliny prescribed. He does not say what he did with the others, but one may guess. Then an informer came forward with fresh names, some or all of whom admitted that they had been Christians but no longer were. They too went through Pliny's ritual procedure. Pliny clearly had that typical lawyer's insistence on procedure, and in this case surely rightly. But what now intrigued Pliny was the information these former Christians gave him about what, as Christians, they actually did and did not do.

What Christians did

This letter therefore provides us with a very early – but not uncontroversial – glimpse of what early Christian ceremonial was like. That is one of the many fascinations of the letter. They would meet before dawn on a fixed day, they said, sing hymns, and take oaths not to commit theft or adultery and to return money entrusted to their care when asked. Later they would meet to share food that was 'ordinary and harmless' – a rebuttal of the common belief that Christians ate human flesh. But they had given up such meetings after Pliny had, following his official remit from Trajan, banned clubs and secret societies. In some doubt whether to believe all this, Pliny then subjected two unfortunate Christian women, church officials but slaves, to torture. Under Roman practice, evidence from slaves was only admissible if obtained under torture. The women held out, and Pliny admits that he found

nothing other than a depraved and gross superstition.

In other words, while disapproving of a 'gross superstition', he found no evidence for the crimes (*flagitia*) commonly attributed by popular opinion to the Christians.

Experts on early Christianity have pointed out that Pliny's description of oath-taking and hymn-singing differs from accounts elsewhere of what Christians did in their Sunday services at that early formative period of their religion. But that is the point. Celebration of their belief may have differed from one community or area to another, and/or be adapted to Roman social circumstances. An example is the oath to return on request any money entrusted to one's care as a sort of human safety deposit box. Juvenal sneers at a man who is foolish enough to expect money entrusted to someone else's care to be returned to him.[9] So there was a point to the Christian oath, even if it might not today be regarded as a key part of Christian beliefs. There are also echoes of Jewish practice. The oaths not to commit theft or adultery echo the seventh and eighth of the Jewish Ten Commandments.

By now thoroughly confused about what he was dealing with and alarmed that prosecutions of Christians were now multiplying and mass executions might even trigger civil unrest or disobedience, Pliny called a halt to court hearings and decided to consult Trajan. He tells Trajan that this 'contagion' (*contagio*) had spread through both towns and villages and countryside, but offers the hope that if people are given a clear avenue for repentance, a way out, many can be brought back into the folds of traditional religion. There is a heavy hint here that he hopes Trajan with agree to this flexible approach. Pliny was not cut out to be a hard-liner on any issue. His letter implies that, if Trajan does accept Pliny's wish to be lenient towards those who repent of their Christianity, it will be an innovation in the detail of imperial policy that requires imperial sanction. Pliny got his way. There was method in his caution.

Pliny's relatively (one must stress again, relatively) benign attitude is in sharp contrast with what happened in Lyons in France some years later, in 177. There, according to local Christian sources, the local council, frightened by a popular outcry against Christians, banned them from public places, dragged them to the forum, then imprisoned them. The governor arrived, yielded to mob pressure, broke all the rules, used torture on Christians to extract confessions of incest and cannibalism, and many were then strangled in prison or otherwise died there. Others were tortured in the arena. This despite a reminder from the emperor of the time, Marcus Aurelius, about official policy.[10]

In Bithynia-Pontus, Pliny at least avoided such ghastly scenes.

What Trajan said and didn't say to Pliny

By the end of this letter Pliny circles back to his opening and central question – what exactly was the charge against Christians? Just the name and fact of being a Christian, or the crimes popularly attributed to them? In a sense, he had already answered his own question, which is just as well, since Trajan in his reply does not attempt to answer it. But perhaps, not being a lawyer, Trajan thought that the question was best left vague. His response concentrates on procedure. You were only following the procedure you ought to have been following, Trajan tells Pliny, because there can be no universal rule about what to do. You must use your own judgement, case by case. That is what you are there for. Pliny is by implication rebuked, ever so politely, for bothering Trajan on such procedural matters. At a policy level, Trajan was probably reluctant to limit the powers of initiative of provincial governors by laying down general rules.

But the meat of Trajan's response comes next. Once published as part of Pliny's collected letters, his statement of imperial guidance on the matter of the Christians achieved the status of official imperial policy for the next hundred years or more, despite intermittent outbreaks of violence such as that at Lyons. Where there is a formal accusation, says Trajan, that is, one brought by a named person who can be held accountable in court for his allegations, then you have to investigate and punish those Christians who refuse to recant. The point of this is that a person who brought a frivolous or malicious accusation could under Roman law be himself convicted and punished for bearing false witness (*calumnia*). This gave some protection against malicious accusation. Then, Trajan goes on, Pliny should give full opportunity to the accused to repent and rejoin traditional worship, with no further questions asked about their past. Conversely, Christians must not be deliberately sought out or hunted down. In particular, anonymous denunciations, such as the unsigned list posted up in public that Pliny describes and that Pliny followed up, must in future not be entertained.

> They set the worst precedent and are not in keeping with the spirit of our age.

Another rebuke to Pliny there. On taking office, Trajan had set his face against the plague of informers which had blighted the reign of previous emperors, and his attitude was consistent. Moreover, he accepts Pliny's heavy hint that those who repent of their 'superstition' should go free and are exonerated. What Trajan does not do is answer all of Pliny's original questions. For example, he does not say whether young people and those who recanted – the so-called apostates – should automatically be let off, presumably again on the basis that it is up to the governor to decide case-by-case. And Trajan does not respond to that over-arching question – what precisely is the charge? Just the name Christian, or a criminal act? And if criminal, under what law?

Nomen Christianum

Could it possibly have been true that just being a Christian, just owning up to the name and description as 'Christian', could have been in itself a crime that, if properly witnessed and proven, warranted the death penalty – and an often gory death at that? Pliny was clearly puzzled by this question, and it has puzzled scholars ever since, citing Pliny as the original source, the *fons et origo*, of this legal and religious controversy. Surely there must have been more to it than that, such as an actual Roman law prohibiting Christianity? But Pliny seems not to know of such a law, and as a lawyer might be expected to know and cite such a law if it existed. On the other hand, on whatever basis, persecution of Christians had set in well before Pliny's time. Nero hunted them down in order to make them scapegoats for the Great Fire that burned down a large part of the old city of Rome in the year 64. Numbers of Christians found at Rome were put to dreadful deaths in the arena, and these famous scenes of martyrdom have been the subject of numerous history paintings ever since. But Nero's pogrom, however bloody, did not amount to a law or policy, and anyway he died soon afterwards, assassinated. Nero needed a suspect group onto which to shift the blame for the Great Fire and divert popular anger, and the Christians got into his firing line.

But surely, some have argued, some subsequent emperor, taking his cue from Nero, must have passed a law banning Christianity, making it illegal to join the movement? Surely the Romans, with their passion for law and legal procedures, would not have let the matter drift and just rely on ad hoc reactions and subjective judgements? How could being Christian be a crime without a law defining it as a crime? The trouble with this otherwise sensible argument is precisely that Pliny was obviously unaware of any such law. Even if he had forgotten about it, Trajan would surely have reminded him of it – but he did not. So we may conclude that there was no law, and that Trajan was happy to leave it that way. That is why Pliny was feeling his way with such nervousness.

Perhaps, some say, Christianity was too small a phenomenon in Trajan's day for him to worry much about it, despite Pliny's anxieties on the subject. But that won't do either. Christians were numerous enough, and important enough, for full Roman citizens to be put to death for adhering to the religion, and killing a Roman citizen without substantial cause and proper procedure was a serious matter in the Roman Empire, as Pliny knew full well. So he prudently tried to pass the buck back to his emperor in Rome. But Trajan's refusal to lay down exact rules meant that, within that emperor's equivalent of an Edict of Tolerance, there remained a core ambiguity that worsened over time.

Emperor worship?

Another possible solution to the question is that faithful Christians refused to pay religious homage to the emperor, a living man, and refused to have any truck with emperor-worship and its rituals. Since the idea of worshipping a living person is also widely viewed as repulsive today, this at least (so the argument goes) shows the Christians to have been principled people in revolt against one of the more sinister aspects of the Roman Empire. It also defines an actual legal offence – disrespect to the emperor, in effect treason – for which they were, on this view, prosecuted and put to death. The trouble with this argument is that emperor-worship in its full manifestation only set in some 150 years later, well after Pliny's time.

So this argument contains a degree of anachronism. It is wrong to read backwards from the days of the emperors Decius and Diocletian to Pliny's day. Of course you had to treat an emperor like Trajan with deference. As we have seen, Pliny addresses him as *domine*, and this smells of subservience. But neither Pliny nor Trajan suggest that Christians in their day were required, as a test, to offer worship to Trajan personally as a living god. Gestures of respect towards his statue or other image would probably be enough. There was indeed a debate about how much sanctity should attach to statues of the emperor, as both Pliny and Dio Chrysostom discovered in their tricky encounter at Apamea (see Chapter 14). But Pliny does say that one of his tests for people who claimed that they had given up Christianity was that they should pay homage to images of the emperor and of the traditional gods. Conversely, the general rule seems to have been that if a statue had been properly consecrated, then disrespect to it could be seen as treasonable.[11]

But that is not the same as the later cult of the emperor. Trajan's statue was placed alongside images of traditional gods in local shrines as a mark of allegiance and respect. He was, after all, by virtue of his office also supreme pontiff and head of Roman religion. Homage to the traditional gods is the key element, and Trajan himself is not put forward as a god. So the main driver for killing Christians, when and if it happened in Pliny's day, must have been something else.

Contrast the Jews

It was not just about having a different set of beliefs and rituals to the official state religion, as the example of the Jews shows. It does remain something of a puzzle as to why the Roman authorities officially tolerated, if grudgingly, the Jewish religion, also a monotheistic religion like Christianity, but did not officially tolerate the Christian monotheists. Popular opinion could be as hostile to the Jews as it apparently was to the Christians. But the official position drew a clear distinction between Jew and Christian. The difference seems to have been that the Jewish religion was in Rome's eyes an ancestral religion in which Jews performed the rites handed down for generations – just as the Romans did. They respected that adherence to tradition, and made room for it. Tacitus says that the Jews and Jewish religion were 'defended by their antiquity' (*antiquitate defenduntur*).[12] Christianity on the other hand was in their eyes a breakaway from Judaism, peopled by men and women who denied and revoked their ancestral traditions. That made them sinister, even revolutionaries – as indeed they were, as time would tell. It is there that we may locate the main driver for distrust and dislike of the Christians.

Christians as atheists

The root of the matter is perhaps that, in Roman eyes and in the eyes of Pliny and his literary colleagues like Tacitus and Suetonius, Christianity was a form of atheism. Its adherents were atheists. To a modern reader, that statement may sound odd. Atheism today is and has been a prime enemy of Christianity. But what the Romans meant by 'atheism' was that the Christians denied the traditional gods, were 'godless' in that sense. The Jews were 'licensed atheists',[13] but the Christians were not. Refusal to worship the traditional gods could also be seen as offensive to the emperor, and so potentially treasonable. The Christians therefore threatened the established order of things, that compact between the ancestral gods of Rome and the Roman people that had brought success and a huge empire to a once small city-state in the middle of Italy. But if the gods were offended, they might in revenge take it all away again. That is why Christianity was at this time such a threat, if as yet a dimly perceived one. That is also why, at the very end of his famous letter 96, Pliny returns to the subject of the traditional temples in his area and explains how, since he arrived at Bithynia and began to take measures against Christians, the temples had begun to fill up again. That is what mattered.

Pliny's swansong?

For Christianity, however, what mattered was that the policy developed by Pliny and approved by Trajan, neither totally repressive nor totally permissive, gave time enough for *its* temples to fill up also, and for their religion to become firmly established outside the slave class in which it had at first found most adherents. Paradoxical as it may seem after his open admission of having put some Christians to death, Pliny can therefore emerge as an unsung and unwitting hero, would Christians but admit it, of the Christian Church. That is perhaps why it is not so odd after all to see a statue of Pliny placed prominently on one side of the entrance to the Christian cathedral in Como, Pliny's birthplace, with a statue of his uncle, the elder Pliny, on the other side. Of course they were both famous sons of the locality. But if Pliny did indeed die in office, in or around the year 112 and in Bithynia-Pontus, then this letter about the Christians forms a fitting epitaph to his life. It shows a cautious but politically astute man in high office, grappling with one of the fundamental issues of all western European history – the relationship between church and state, still a burning issue in many countries to this day. Pliny shows how the Roman government could, at times, apply a degree of legal and moral principle to administration, and how it struggled, as we do today, to deal with religious diversity inside any community which had traditionally seen religious unity as the key to its survival and prosperity.

Meeting Pliny

So after all that, what do we make of Pliny, or Plinius Secundus as we really ought to call him? We have no idea what Pliny looked like, and that in itself makes it difficult to feel very close to him. Modern representations of Pliny, like the thin man adorning the entrance of Como Cathedral, are laudable, but fictional. His uncle and namesake was short and fat, with breathing problems. Pliny may have been the same, but he doesn't tell us. Towards the end of his fairly short life he was not a well man. So maybe there was a family resemblance, a systemic family frailty of the lungs. He may have been one of many overweight, middle-aged men in a toga on the central streets of Rome whom you might pass by and wonder exactly who he was, until by chance you met Tacitus at the races and Tacitus pointed him out as the man who wrote *those* letters and eye-witnessed *that* volcanic eruption – and more.

Reading the letters, you get the impression of Pliny as a rather prim and slightly vain man without much sense of humour, as might be expected from a lawyer, but with a gift for telling stories when he relaxes a bit. He is anxious about his public image, keen to advertise the good things about himself, and worried about what posterity might think about him (as well he might, given the subsequent arguments about his political and private morality). He has a version of his life and career that he is anxious for us to accept, and is aware that in troubled times there can be different versions of the truth. So his letters seek to get in first with his own plausible version. Many prominent men have gone through the same exercise, knowing full well that questions will still be asked, as they have been about Pliny.

> There is something unsettling about the volume and intensity of Pliny's self-praise and his appetite for it.[1]

This insistence on self-praise to ward off darker versions of his life keeps us at arm's length from Pliny. We cannot pretend to get as close to him as to many modern authors and political figures. The evidence is just not there. What he was like to meet in the flesh is hard to grasp, as is what made him angry, depressed or lose his cool. We may know him better than almost any other Roman. But still not well. Pliny is really rehearsing his public and professional life through his letters, and it must have been his choice that he published only a few of his letters to or about his wife and his love for her. But at least they are there.

The letters as political manifesto

It is a commonplace that Tacitus wrote about the dark side of Roman politics, Pliny about the bright side. Tacitus is full of sinister tales of repression, greed and revolt. Pliny is full of praise for his contemporaries, goodwill towards most men except his rival Regulus, and cheerful hope for a new era under Trajan. He has been criticised for this blandness and geniality – is it a pose, or a lack of critical judgement on his part? But Pliny is as critical as anyone of the emperor Domitian, his retrospective insults as vicious as any other writer's – 'that terrible monster'. His references to the reign of Nero echo those of Tacitus. There is not an absolute contrast between the two writers, who were after all close friends and legal colleagues.

Rather, in the writings that have survived, Tacitus is keen to place on record what can go wrong, how a state can tear itself to pieces through internal dissent. Pliny on the other hand is interested in how you can pick up the pieces, how you can hold a state together, how to make a new beginning under a new emperor untarnished by past events. What might the rules be for a new political order, what roles should the emperor play, what rules should the Senate observe? How could they manage their working relationship, that key to the stability of the empire, and do it better in the future than in the past? Pliny was not a deep political theorist. But as an experienced lawyer and administrator he had ideas about it. He dressed these ideas up in ways we now find somewhat repugnant, like his praise-speech to Trajan, but that conformed to the social conventions of his time.

Pliny's constant praise of his friends is certainly irritating. These are not objective character references. But personal recommendation must have been the main method of securing appointments in an age before personnel departments, selection procedures, recruitment agencies or formal training schemes, at least until you got to the upper reaches of the administration where the emperor himself took a direct personal interest in who held what jobs. Even then, the emperor took note of who was recommending whom for what, so a man who could make recommendations took great care about those he recommended. It could backfire. So when Pliny was giving a character reference, it was carefully couched within the conventions of *amicitia*, the network of friendly obligations that was part of the glue of Roman upper-class society.

So the idea that Pliny was naively ignoring or masking a harsher reality, glossing over the cracks with his insistent geniality, is unfair. His letters were almost certainly genuine letters, if edited to some degree (we don't know that, but may assume so). But taken collectively as a whole, the letters and the *Panegyricus* do represent an attempt to outline how a plausible new social compact might work, under an emperor who just might make a difference compared to the troubled past. It is not just the *Panegyricus* that can be read as a political document. So can the letters. They show how a new ethos could govern the management of the state, still with an all-powerful autocrat – Pliny took that for granted, like slavery – but with an active and respected senatorial upper class to support and debate with the autocrat, free of the imperial terrorism of the previous century that Tacitus has recorded for posterity. Mutual respect was a key part of this, and that is what many of his letters express.

The reigns of the emperors Nerva and Trajan did after all usher in a long period of internal stability in the Roman Empire, that period which famous writers like Edward Gibbon regarded as the finest period of the empire, its summertime. Of course, that was not all down to Pliny. But it is plausible to argue that Pliny, not single-handedly but as a vocal contributor, helped to create that new and better ethos, which lasted through several changes of emperor for several generations after him. It is not Pliny's fault that this compact eventually broke down again. Let Pliny take credit for what contribution he did make.

The accusation against Pliny

If that is the credit side, what is the debit side? The main accusations leveled at Pliny are those of hypocrisy and double-dealing. The charge is that in his letters – written and published safely after the event – he pretends to have been in personal danger during the last, repressive years of the reign of the emperor Domitian. But in fact he enjoyed the positive favour of Domitian, was promoted by that emperor, was close to him, held high office even during the worst years of Domitian's vicious purge of alleged opponents, and so was complicit in that emperor's misdeeds and expropriations. So his letters are, it is concluded, an attempt to rewrite history, to doctor the historical record, by (at best) re-arranging the truth to look better. If the letters are a sort of autobiography, it is a heavily edited or selective autobiography that we have to re-rewrite to get back to the historical reality.

He had to cover his tracks and his conscience by flaunting in his letters his acts of assistance to those who survived Domitian, but omitting from his letters any mention of one important post he held or may have held under Domitian (that of Prefect of the Military Treasury) and conveniently telescoping his visits to the out-of-favour philosopher Artemidorus so as to fabricate the idea that even when in another high office (that of *praetor*) he was risking or even courting danger from Domitian. Those who take this hostile line are then driven to dismiss the famous dossier, supposedly found on Domitian's desk after his assassination, as just another fabrication or at best an exaggeration.

Once you set off down this road of distrusting what Pliny says, it is but a short step to see him as an imperial toady not just towards the 'bad' emperor Domitian, but also towards the 'good' emperor Trajan, the would-be *optimus princeps*, best of princes. Being an imperial sycophant became a habit for Pliny, so this second accusation reads. His tediously long and ultra-flattering speech of praise of Trajan, the *Panegyricus*, is a symptom of this endemic weakness, and so are his crawling letters to Trajan sent from Bithynia-Pontus. Both in praise-speech and in nervous references back to his boss from Bithynia, Pliny grovels and buck-passes. No backbone, say the critics, just a time-server and placeman, maybe even a liar.

Lurking just below the surface of these cumulative accusations on the charge sheet against Pliny lies a profound distrust and disdain of the absolute autocracy of the Roman imperial regime that set in from the time of the first emperor Augustus, by contrast to the noble Republic that had preceded it. This had been a political system of checks and balances in which free and open debate flourished and men were men and high principle reigned. Now, in Pliny's time, power reigned and principles succumbed. This dislike of the imperial system, built largely round the writings of Tacitus, Suetonius and Pliny himself, goes back a long way in the study, understanding and interpretation of the Roman Empire.

Pliny has become the focus of that dislike, a convenient target for the arrows of the latter-day republicans – just because he is there. Through his letters, he is by far the best known of the top imperial civil servants (to use a modern and anachronistic term) who administered the empire on behalf of the all-powerful emperors whose one-man rule, it is said, destroyed those republican freedoms and replaced them with what has aptly been called 'autocracy tempered by assassination'. So it comes about that Pliny acts as a lightning rod for the flashes of scorn heaped upon the empire, a conduit for the general condemnation of the imperial regime, one man standing for the whole. To judge Pliny is to judge the system he supported and served – and vice versa.

The alternative view

But there is an alternative view of Pliny. As we have seen, the hostile attitude towards him turns primarily on a particular reconstruction of the dates at which he held various public offices and state appointments. Were they, or were they not, under and thanks to the 'evil' emperor Domitian? Unfortunately, nowhere in the letters does he tell us those dates with any exactitude. Nor indeed in his letters does he even list or mention all of the offices he held. So both offices and dates have to be deduced with the help of inscriptions, and even then there is significant room for argument. Anyway, to the extent that Pliny held office during the earlier and better years of Domitian's reign, that need not be a reproach to Pliny.

There is as a result another way of interpreting the key dates of Pliny's career. In essence this alternative means accepting Pliny's summary statement that at first he advanced quickly up the public career ladder, then paused, then resumed. This 'pause' in his career would coincide with, and so be attributable to, the later 'bad' years of that 'bad' emperor Domitian. On this interpretation, Pliny was allowed to retire from public life during his 'pause' years, a withdrawal that in some circumstances might have been regarded as treasonable because it implied distrust of the reigning emperor. But in Pliny's case perhaps it was a sign that he was not yet a senior enough figure for Domitian to worry about. But as time went on, and as informers searched for yet more victims, that might have changed, that famous dossier submitted to Domitian might have been actual, and Pliny might have been in real danger as a silent collaborator of Domitian's enemies.

As for not mentioning in his letters his job at the military treasury, that need not be suspicious. He held several other public offices which he does not mention in his letters, but which we know about from the inscriptions. His letters are not meant to be an exhaustive autobiography – more like notes for an autobiography. It is quite plausible to reconstruct the sequence of dates in Pliny's career so as to show that 'pause' in Pliny's career in public office, a six-year gap during which in effect he retired from the danger zone. In short, the broad outline of Pliny's own account in his letters could be correct. He would emerge, not as a hero, not as a brave man, but as a prudent survivor who knew he could not change the world he lived in, but only make the best of it. Which of the two versions of Pliny you accept depends, in the last analysis, not on evidence that proves or disproves, but on what you think of Pliny the man. Do we for other reasons like or dislike Pliny? Do we find him admirable and worthy of belief – or not?

Pliny as professional lawyer

By the professional standards of his time, Pliny was clearly an effective and successful lawyer/advocate/barrister – whatever modern term you care to use. He was repeatedly asked to take on the prosecution case or the case for the defence, most notably in high-profile corruption cases that could not be entrusted to just anyone, and that were heard in the highest court of the land, the Senate in its capacity as Supreme Court. Moreover, while acting with a colleague in each case, he seems to have been the lead prosecutor or defence lawyer. And he won his cases, if not on all counts. His professional reputation must have been high, and no-one except the satirist Juvenal has seriously challenged his legal track record. Pliny might argue, if he got the chance, that it was difficult enough getting even a formal conviction and some financial penalty in the context of the self-defensive members' club that was the Roman Senate. Pliny anyway had a far longer and wider track record in pursuing corruption among the senior officials of the empire – an activity that did not make him popular – than the one case sneered at by Juvenal.

It is striking that both emperors and provincial authorities turned to Pliny as often as they did to secure some degree of justice in the administration, or at least some degree of retrospective redress where criminality could be established. It is this overall track record, rather than one particular case, that should impress us. Of course, we have no one to compare Pliny with at this period. But whether he was typical or exceptional makes no difference to the credit that Pliny deserves from us and that he clearly enjoyed from his contemporaries. Otherwise, he would not have received so much 'repeat business'.

Pliny as finance man

Pliny's expertise with money and financial matters also seems well established, both through his years in the inheritance court, the Court of One Hundred

Men, and by his acting as assessor for the Prefect of Rome and for the emperor himself. It is hard to believe that the emperor of the day would have entrusted the military treasury and then the state treasury to someone who could not be trusted with money and could not do his numbers. The corruption cases he handled were essentially about money. So his financial track record also looks solid.

Similarly, whatever the political significance of the timing, the office of *praetor* was a pivotal one for the operation of the Roman legal system, while at the other extreme you could not put just anyone in charge of the rivers and sewers of the capital city of the Roman Empire; and it was vital that some competent official ensured that there was the money in the bank to pay the soldiers – the most basic thing that an emperor had to do if he was to stay in office, even stay alive. Pliny's career in public office was not just a series of sinecures. As a professional man, therefore, Pliny emerges as a distinguished figure in the hot-house of Roman public life.

Pliny as patron

Another point in Pliny's favour is that he was without doubt a generous patron, especially towards his home town of Comum but also towards individuals he supported and towards the towns that lay near to his estates. This is clear from his letters and is backed up by the inscriptions. You can argue that to be a patron was part of the social obligations of a rich and successful man, especially towards his native area. But Pliny also seems to have been financially generous towards people he was related to, and to have done more than be needed to for his home town. His recommendations of his friends for jobs and privileges were certainly part of the fabric of Roman society, the patron–client relationship that underpinned so much of Roman upper-class life. But how he did it became a model for others.

His treatment of slaves

We may instinctively fault Pliny for taking slavery for granted as an institution, and for owning hundreds of slaves with scarcely a mention of their existence except when they were part of his immediate and trusted entourage. But Pliny himself must be judged by the standards of his day. Slavery was just part and parcel of life and society at the time, rarely if ever questioned. He was evidently a better slave-master than many of his fellow slave-owners. The slaves on his country estates were not kept in chains, unlike (we may infer) the agricultural slaves on many other estates. He did take steps to grant freedom to a number of his slave-servants, and to ensure that they were adequately provided for financially in their later years.

Against that, he had no hesitation in torturing slaves when governor of Bithynia-Pontus, in order to extract evidence from them about Christian beliefs and rituals. But that again was (however horrifyingly) normal Roman practice. Evidence from slaves which was not extracted under torture was not held to be valid, and Pliny does admit that the torture he applied – we don't know what it was – evinced nothing. Being by Roman standards a good Roman towards slaves may deserve only the faintest praise, but some praise nevertheless. For him, slavery was part of normality, a continuing institution whose periodic reaffirmation helped to stabilise a society prone to being rent by civil war and assassination.

Pliny as governor

Pliny's short period as a provincial governor shows him acting in a rather high-handed manner towards the people under his rule, adopting a lordly and imperious attitude towards them, verging on contempt for their petty dealings and squabbles. We may suppose that this was normal among the upper classes of Rome in a top-down society. Pliny was under heavy pressure as the emperor's personal representative with extensive special powers to get results, and get them quickly. There were long-lasting and deep-seated problems in the province, which the emperor was anxious to see sorted. Pliny dare not fail, and laid about him in imperious manner – except when he felt it prudent to refer back to the emperor. He did try to do the rounds of his allotted province, and did burrow diligently into its financial peccadillos. He was a conscientious if careful administrator, well aware of the hazards his job presented in a fractious area of the Greek east.

Christians: not exactly tolerance, but …

In contrast to his high-handed manner on matters of finance, it is surely striking that, once Pliny began to investigate the cult of the Christians in Bithynia-Pontus, he became uneasy and began to raise questions about what exactly the crime of these Christians was. What had they done wrong? Having looked into it, he came up with the answer – not much, if anything. But he was up against the deep-seated objections of the imperial regime against any form of association between groups of its citizens, even to the extent of disallowing such an obviously desirable organisation as a local fire brigade. True, Pliny had executed some Christians before he sought – and got – a new and more relaxed ruling from the emperor on what to do about them. The executions leave a sour taste, even if Pliny was reflecting both local and official prejudices. But after his second thoughts he may have secured a ruling from the emperor that was relatively favourable to Christians compared to what it might have been and compared to what, a century or so later, became the imperial policy of active and savage repression. Living as we do in an age in which most people in Western societies believe in religious freedom (which the Romans did not), we must surely give muted praise to Pliny for securing even a limited and uncertain degree of religious tolerance for Christians.

Wife and (no) children

Pliny expresses deep regret that he had no children. Enough Romans were childless for people to wonder whether there were deeper social and financial advantages in favour of childlessness, so that Pliny's regrets are perhaps crocodile tears, token statements in order to get from the emperor the privileges legally attached to those with several children. If you believe that hypocrisy is Pliny's most notable trademark, then you can read it into this as well. But the privileges that he sought and got from the emperor were honorific as much as financial, and his lack of children did not appear to impede his career, as the law might imply. In the status-conscious world of Rome, his expressions of regret could be both genuine and status-seeking, both at the same time. Surely we must accept his protestations at their face value, not least in the light of his evident affection for his second wife (I have argued for two marriages, not three).

Pliny's so-called 'love letters' to Calpurnia are moving, if rather literary. But we might expect that from a man so steeped in the literature of his age and so devoted to poetry and literary composition. He was neither the first nor the last man to reach for literary styles and echoes to express himself. Again, if you suspect Pliny and his motives, you may also suspect the genuineness of these letters. However derivative in style, they have the ring of truth – and of affection. Why deny to Pliny a normal human emotion? So we see Pliny as a man capable of love, deeply attached to his wife, mourning the lack of children, and being, well, just like most of the rest of us.

The literary hobbyist

Pliny has been mocked for the so-called 'pantomime letter' in which he asks a friend anxiously whether he should mouth the words and wave his hands and arms about while a servant actually reads out the words of one of his literary compositions. His verses, of which he gives us a taste, have been judged to be pretty bad, perhaps too readily. Most of what was recited at the literary evenings that Pliny attended so assiduously was probably just as bad and just as derivative. These events were social as much as critical, sprung from the intense study of fashionable authors that formed the bedrock of the Roman educational system available only to those who could afford it. Pliny's letters give us a unique insight into how authors of the time went about composing their works, good or bad, how they sought to find an audience and readership for their efforts, and how their works survived the passage of time and changes in cultural fashions, or not. We should be grateful for that.

Pliny's anxiety reflects the intensely theatrical character of these evening events, where an author, however amateur, put on a show and performed for his listeners, who expected entertainment as well as instruction. Artificial these events may have been. But Pliny cared about literature and about the techniques of composition, and that is another thing to his credit.

Summing up Pliny

So, taking one thing with another, is there enough to Pliny's credit to justify us in concluding that his own account of his career can and should be believed, and the hostile account rejected? I suggest that there is. Any career such as his, like so many other careers in high office then and now, involves compromise and may not survive strict moral scrutiny. Nor can we feel emotionally close to Pliny. Except when writing to Calpurnia, there is not much passion in his letters, and much artifice that keeps us at some distance. But Pliny did believe in standards in public life, and who are we to throw stones? There were plenty of Romans far worse than Pliny. Having cleared away the problem of dates, there is no serious obstacle to accepting Pliny as a man who did not pretend to be a hero, a rebel or an innovator, but who did his best, when circumstances allowed, to maintain or re-establish some semblance of justice in the Roman administrative system, to restore some influence and self-confidence to the Senate, and to establish some new ground-rules about how centralised political power should operate, learning the lessons from the (pretty horrendous) past that he and his uncle had lived through.

His letters personalise the values and dilemmas of the huge empire he served. They are his vehicle for a unique (among Romans) act of studied self-revelation. He enjoyed high office and its trappings – and the sound of his own voice. He enjoyed 'society' but enjoyed reading privately or being read to. He enjoyed hunting but even more he enjoyed literary discussions. He liked to show off his wealth, but part of that was giving some of it away. He was probably a good friend to those who belonged to his social circle, and he was more considerate than most towards his slaves – faint praise perhaps.

We may infer that he was an honest man who took his responsibilities seriously, but saw his job as being to make the best of the system he was born in rather than step outside and offer a radical critique of it – a dangerous road to take, as he well knew. He was anxious to be liked – too anxious, perhaps. Similarly, he tries too hard to be nice to and about those around him. It is as if his insistent geniality – except about Regulus – acts as another irritating smoke screen between us and the inner Pliny. But if as a result it is hard to feel close enough to Pliny to actually like him, there is plenty about his life that commands respect. Above all, his letters if read carefully offer insight into myriad aspects of life at Rome in the grand days of empire. They are a much-quarried goldmine of chunky nuggets of social and political information about Rome. They make a good read. Pliny himself would be frightfully pleased to know that we still noticed him. He longed for some sort of immortality, and by his letters – and by the emperor's permission to publish them – he got it.

Notes

Chapter 1

1 Jona Lendering, 'Pliny the Younger', available online at http://www.livius.org (accessed 16 May 2013).
2 R. Syme, *Tacitus* (Clarendon Press, 1958), p. 77.
3 Betty Radice, *The Letters of the Younger Pliny* (Penguin, 1963), pp. 12–16
4 C. L. Whitton, 'Pliny Epistle 8.14: Senate, Slavery and the Agricola', *Journal of Roman Studies* 100 (2010).

Chapter 2

1 This inscription and other relevant inscriptions can be found at CIL 5.5262, CIL 5.5263, CIL 5.5667, and probably CIL 11.5272 – CIL being short for *Corpus Inscriptionum Latinarum*, the Corpus of Latin Inscriptions.
2 C. Newlands, 'The Eruption of Vesuvius', in A. J. Woodman (ed.), *Latin Historiography and Poetry in the Early Empire* (Brill, 2010), p. 121.
3 R. K. Gibson and R. Morello, *Reading the Letters of Pliny the Younger: an Introduction* (Cambridge University Press, 2012), pp. 1 and 10–15 for excellent discussion of these similes.
4 J. Henderson, *Pliny's Statue* (2002), quoted in Gibson and Morello, *Reading the Letters of Pliny the Younger*.
5 S. Hoffer, *The Anxieties of Pliny the Younger* (Scholar's Press, 1999), pp. 9–10.
6 J. Henderson, 'Portrait of the Artist as a Figure of Style', *Arethusa* 36 (2003).
7 R. Morello, 'Pliny and the Art of Saying Nothing', *Arethusa* 36 (2003).
8 A. N. Sherwin-White, *The Letters of Pliny: an Historical and Social Commentary* (Oxford University Press, 1966), pp. 11–12.
9 R. K. Gibson, 'Pliny and the Art of (In)offensive Self-praise', *Arethusa* 36 (2003).
10 Jacqueline Carlon, *Pliny's Women* (Cambridge University Press, 2009), pp. 6, 215.
11 R. Syme, 'Pliny's Early Career', in A. Birley (ed.), *Roman Papers*, vol. 7 (Oxford University Press, 1991), p. 561.
12 Pierre de la Ruffinière, *The Villas of Pliny* (University of Chicago Press, 1994), p. 40.
13 L. D. Reynolds, *Texts and Transmission* (Clarendon Press, 1983), pp. 321–2 (both quotations) in an invaluable survey of the recovery of Pliny and his text.

Chapter 3

1   Martial 4.4 and Statius, *Silvae* 3.5 and 4.4. See C. Newlands, 'The Eruption of Vesuvius' in Woodman (ed.), *Latin Historiography and Poetry in the Early Empire*.

2   E. D. Carolis and G. Patricelli, *Vesuvius A.D. 79: The Destruction of Pompeii and Herculeneum* (Getty, 2003), p. 5.

Chapter 4

1   In this chapter I am particularly indebted to J. M. Kelly's *Studies in the Civil Judicature of the Roman Republic* (Clarendon Press, 1976), which is far from confined to the Republic, and to his book *Roman Litigation* (Clarendon Press, 1966).

2   Cicero, *About the Orator* 1.173.

3   Festus, however, says that the Hundred Men actually numbered 105 (as quoted by Paulus, 54). Varro singles out the Hundred Men as a specific example of how not to take Roman numbers too literally (*Res Rusticae* 2.1).

4   Martial 7.63.

5   Martial 10.19 and Letters 3.21.

6   Statius, *Silvae* 4.4.

7   Seneca, *Controversiae* 9, preface.

8   Quintilian 12.6.

9   Macrobius, *Saturnalia* 3.16.

10 The name of Pliny's friend may not be exact.

11 See D. Roebuck and B. Fumichon, *Roman Arbitration* (Holo Books, 2004).

12 Roebuck and Fumichon, *Roman Arbitration*, p.64.

13 Cicero, *About the Orator* 1.180.

14 Statius, *Silvae* 1.4.

15 Cicero, *About the Orator* 1.173. Loeb translation, adapted.

16 Suetonius, *Augustus* 36 and Dio 54.26.

17 Kelly, *Studies in the Civil Judicature of the Roman Republic*, pp. 68–9 and Aulus Gellius, *Attic Nights* 13.12.

18 See especially two inscriptions detailing Pliny's offices held, CIL 5.5262 and CIL 5.5667.

19 Suetonius, *Vespasian* 10.

20 Suetonius, *Domitian* 8.

21 Cicero, *Pro Caecina* 71.

22 See A. Borkowski, *Textbook on Roman Law* (Oxford University Press, 1994/2005), especially p. 208.

23 Kelly, *Studies in the Civil Judicature of the Roman Republic*, pp. 71–92.

24 S. Rutledge, *Imperial Inquisitions* (Routledge, 2001), p. 80.

25 Dio 60.6, 60.17 and 64.6.

26 Suetonius, *Domitian* 9 and 12.

27 Rutledge, *Imperial Inquisitions*, p. 81.

28 Suetonius, *Domitian* 12.

29 Pliny, *Panegyric* 43.

Chapter 5

1 Pliny, *Panegyric* 34.

2 Rutledge, *Imperial Inquisitions*, Appendix.

3 Pliny, *Panegyric* 36

4 R. Syme, *The Roman Revolution* (Oxford University Press, 1939/1960), p. 505.

5 Tacitus, *Histories* 4.42.

6 Tacitus, *Dialogue* 12.

7 Hoffer, *The Anxieties of Pliny the Younger*, pp. 55–6.

8 Hoffer, *The Anxieties of Pliny the Younger*, pp. 58–9.

9 Martial 11.66 and 11.77.

10 Martial 6.64 and 10.19, plus mainly 1.12, 1.111, 2.74 and 4.16.

11 Martial 10.19.

12 O. Figes, *The Whisperers* (Allen Lane, 2007), p. 261.

13 Rutledge, *Imperial Inquisitions*, p. 181

14 Tacitus, *Annals* 4.40-44.

15 Dio 60.13, 66.19, 67.1, 68.1.

Chapter 6

1 M. C. Alexander, *Trials in the Late Roman Republic* (University of Toronto Press, 1990).

2 Peter Brunt, 'Charges of Provincial Maladministration under the Early Principate', *Historia* 10 (1961).

3 Jill Harries, *Law and Crime in the Roman World* (Cambridge University Press, 2007), p. 65. I am much indebted to this excellent analysis.

4 Tacitus, *Annals* 1.2.

5 Tacitus, *Annals* 1.75.

6 Rutledge, *Imperial Inquisitions*, p. 67.

7 Rutledge, *Imperial Inquisitions*, p. 71.

8 See Brunt, 'Charges of Provincial Maladministration under the Early Principate'.

9 For the law in detail, see O. F. Robinson, *Penal Practice and Penal Policy in Ancient Rome* (Routledge, 2007), a work to which I am also much indebted for this chapter.

10 Oxford Classical Dictionary, under 'Corruption'.

11 In Justinian's *Digest of Roman Law* 1.16.6.3.

12 Oxford Classical Dictionary, under 'Corruption'.

13 See discussion in Rutledge, *Imperial Inquisitions*, p. 131.

14 It is probably this speech that Pliny refers to in **2.19**.

15 Pliny, *Panegyric* 76.

16 Juvenal, *Satires* 1.49–50.

17 Harries, *Law and Crime in the Roman World*, pp. 66, 68

18 Robinson, *Penal Practice and Penal Policy in Ancient Rome*, p. 78.

Chapter 7

1 Pliny, *Panegyric* 90.

2 Tacitus, *Agricola* 45.

3 Syme, 'Pliny's Early Career', pp. 564 onward.

4 See B. W. Jones, *The Emperor Domitian* (Routledge, 1992) and Suetonius, *Domitian*.

5 Miriam Griffin, 'Domitian', in *Cambridge Ancient History*, vol. 2 (Cambridge University Press, 2000).

6 Tacitus, *Agricola* 45.

7 That is, those inscriptions identified as CIL 5.5262, CIL 5.5263, CIL 5.5667 and CIL 11.5272.

8 I am here following the argument and timetable put forward by A. R. Birley, *Onomasticon to the Younger Pliny* (K. G. Saur, 2000), pp. 1–17.

9 Pliny, *Panegyric* 48.

10 Birley, *Onomasticon to the Younger Pliny*, p. 14.

11 Syme, 'Pliny's Early Career', pp. 564 onward.

12 Shadi Bartsch, *Actors in the Audience* (Harvard University Press, 1994), pp. 168–9, but also quoting from Ronald Syme and Adalberto Giovannini.

13 Pliny, *Panegyric* 95.

14 See here R. H. Harte, 'The Praetorship of the Younger Pliny', *Journal of Roman Studies* 25 (1935).

15 Suetonius, *Domitian* 10.

16 Aulus Gellius, *Attic Nights* 15.

17 For fuller discussion, see again Birley, *Onomasticon to the Younger Pliny*, pp. 11–13.

18 Dio 67.13.

19 See Dio 68.3.

Chapter 8

1 The Loeb translation of the so-called *Panegyricus* is used throughout, for consistency. I have found no other English translation of it. Reference numbers are to sections of the *Panegyricus* unless otherwise indicated.

2 P. Roche (ed.), *Pliny's Praise* (Cambridge University Press, 2011), pp. 14–15.

3 Tobias Gregory, review of Ariosto's *Orlando Furioso*, *London Review of Books* (9 September 2010).

4 C. F. Norena, 'Self-fashioning in the *Panegyicus*', in Roche (ed.), *Pliny's Praise*, pp. 29, 43.

5 R. Syme, *Tacitus* (Clarendon Press, 1958), 1.94.

6 F. R. D. Goodyear, 'Pliny the Younger', in *Cambridge History of Classical Literature*, vol. 2, part 4 (Cambridge University Press, 1982), p. 164.

7 Syme, *Tacitus* 1.94.

8 S. Dill, *Roman Society from Nero to Marcus Aurelius* (Macmillan, 1904).

9 Syme, *Tacitus* 1.95.

10 Joy Connolly, 'Fear and Freedom: a New Interpretation of Pliny's *Panegyricus*', conference paper (2008), available online at https://sites.google.com/a/nyu.edu/jconnolly/home/recent-work/Connolly-Pliny.pdf?attredirects=0&d=1 (accessed 16 May 2013), pp. 260–1.

11 Bartsch, *Actors in the Audience*, pp. 186–7; Connolly, 'Fear and Freedom', pp. 273–4.

12 Dio 68.

Chapter 9

1 Carlon, *Pliny's Women*, p. 105. In this chapter, I am particularly indebted to this illuminating and thoughtful book. I was not able to take proper account of J. O. Shelton's more recent book *The Women of Pliny's Letters* (Routledge, 2012).

2 Tacitus, *Annals* 16.8.

3 Carlon, *Pliny's Women*, p. 16.

4 Sherwin-White, *The Letters of Pliny*, p. 407.

5 Carlon, *Pliny's Women*, p. 169.

6 Carlon, *Pliny's Women*, p. 169.

Chapter 10

1 Sherwin-White, *The Letters of Pliny*, pp. 71, 149–50.

2 R. Duncan-Jones, *The Economy of the Roman Empire* (Cambridge University Press, 1974/1982), pp. 18–20.

3 Tacitus, *Dialogus* 8.1.

4 Duncan-Jones, *The Economy of the Roman Empire*, p. 4.

5 Sherwin-White, *The Letters of Pliny*, p. 149.

6 Dio 79.22 says that a century later, in 217, a certain Aufidius Fronto would have got a salary if he had taken up an important governor's job, so we may perhaps assume that the salary applied in Pliny's day. The Loeb translation of Dio says the salary for Fronto would have been a million sesterces, but I read the Greek as saying 250,000 – either way, a substantial rate for the job.

7 For this calculation, and the argument about it, see Duncan-Jones, *The Economy of the Roman Empire*, pp. 25–6.

8 See CIL 5262 = ILS 2927.

9 Duncan-Jones, *The Economy of the Roman Empire*, pp. 31–2.

Chapter 11

1 This and following quotation: de la Ruffinière du Prey, *The Villas of Pliny*, pp. 8–9.

2 Varro, *On Agriculture (De Re Rustica)* Bk. 2. Intro.

3 Gibson and Morello, *Reading the Letters of Pliny the Younger*, p. 169.

4 This and previous quotation: de la Ruffinière du Prey, *The Villas of Pliny*, pp. 8–9.

5 This and previous quotation: A. Wallace-Hadrill, *Houses and Society in Pompeii and Herculaneum* (Princeton University Press, 1994), p. 47.

6 De la Ruffinière du Prey, *The Villas of Pliny*, p. 26.

7 H. Tanzer, *The Villas of Pliny the Younger* (Columbia University Press, 1924), p. 47.

8 A. Riggsby, 'Pliny in Space (and Time)', *Arethusa* 36 (2003).

9 De la Ruffinière du Prey, *The Villas of Pliny*, p. 5.

10 De la Ruffinière du Prey, *The Villas of Pliny*, p. 6.

11 Gibson and Morello, *Reading the Letters of Pliny the Younger*, p. 211.

12 De la Ruffinière du Prey, *The Villas of Pliny*, p. 14.

13 Gibson and Morello, *Reading the Letters of Pliny the Younger*, p. 233.

14 Wallace-Hadrill, *Houses and Society in Pompeii and Herculaneum*, p. 44 (both quotations).

15 Gibson and Morello, *Reading the Letters of Pliny the Younger*, pp. 228–30.

16 Riggsby ('Pliny in Space (and Time)') calculates 38 and 28 rooms respectively.

17 De la Ruffinière du Prey, *The Villas of Pliny*, p. 13.

Chapter 12

1 Gibson and Morello, *Reading the Letters of Pliny the Younger*, pp. 170–1, quoting Cicero, *Tusc.* 5.105 and Seneca Ep.82.3.

2 For a fuller treatment see this author's *The Roman Book* (Duckworth, 2009).

3 Plutarch, *De Audiendo* 45.

4 Juvenal 1.1–18.

5 Suetonius, *Claudius* 41.

6 See Tacitus, *Dialogus* 9.3, where Tacitus describes a poetry recital by Bassus, and the costs.

7 Persius, *Satire* 1.1.15–23.

8 Suetonius, *Virgil* 29.

Chapter 13

1 Statius, *Silvae* 4.7.

2 Martial 12.18.

3 Juvenal, *Satires* 12.11 and 6.74.

4 Juvenal, *Satires* 1.49–50.

5 G. Highet, *Juvenal the Satirist* (Oxford University Press, 1962), p. 292.

6 For these alleged barbs, see Juvenal 7.178-9, 3.133, 1.40 and 3.203, with Highet, *Juvenal the Satirist*, pp. 292–3.

7 Martial 10.19.

8 C. L. Whitton, '"Let Us Tread Our Path Together": Tacitus and the Younger Pliny', in *A Companion to Tacitus* (Wiley-Blackwell, 2011), p. 345.

9 Whitton, '"Let Us Tread Our Path Together"', p. 346. The quote is a famous phrase of Thucydides.

10 M. T. Griffin, 'Pliny and Tacitus', *Scripta Classica Israelica* 18 (1999), pp. 139–58, quoted in Whitton, '"Let Us Tread Our Path Together"'.

Chapter 14

1 For this chapter, I rely gratefully on W. Williams's *Pliny the Younger: Correspondence with Trajan from Bithynia* (Aris and Philips, 1990), for both translation and commentary, and on C. P. Jones's *The Roman World of Dio Chrysostom* (Harvard University Press, 1978). All references to Pliny's letters in this chapter are to Book 10, the Bithynia letters.

2 See Harries, *Law and Crime in the Roman World*, especially p. 38.

3 J. Bennett, *Trajan: Optimus Princeps* (Routledge, 2001), p. 117.

4 R. MacMullen, *Corruption and the Decline of Rome* (Yale University Press, 1998), p. 139.

5 For the fine detail see Sherwin-White (*The Letters of Pliny*) and Williams (*Pliny the Younger*) in their respective commentaries on Pliny's letters.

6 Well summarised by Williams in his Introduction to *Pliny the Younger*.

7 Pliny, *Panegyric* 55.7

8 Philostratus, *Lives of the Sophists* 1.488.

9 P. A. Brunt, 'Charges of Provincial Maladministration under the Early Principate', *Historia* 10 (1961).

10 Dio, Speeches (Orations) 38, 39 and 40.

11 Speech 43.

12 Speech 47.

13 Speech 47.

14 Speech 46.

15 Jones, *The Roman World of Dio Chrysostom*, p. 52.

Chapter 15

1 This chapter relies gratefully not only on the Pliny commentary by W. Williams (*Pliny the Younger*) referred to elsewhere, but in particular to the wonderful exchange of views contained in M. I. Finley (ed.), *Studies in Ancient Society* (Routledge, 1974) between two great scholars, G. E. M. de Ste Croix and A. N. Sherwin-White. This waspish exchange is a wonderful example of academic infighting, but en route lays out better than anywhere else the arguments about why exactly the Romans had it in for Christians (sometimes).

2 The letters are numbered 10.96 and 97 and datable to late 111 or early 112 CE, written from Pontus, either the city of Amisus or from Amastris.

3 J. Henderson, 'Portrait of the Artist as a Figure of Style', *Arethusa* 36 (2003).

4 Tacitus, *Annals* 15.44.

5 Suetonius, *Nero* 16.

6 The story of St Ignatius is told from the Christian point of view in the *Martyrium Ignatii*, possibly written or partly written by two men who accompanied him on his journey to Rome. This document alleges a general persecution. Some date the condemnation of Ignatius to 108 CE, but Trajan was not, as far as I can discover, in Antioch at that time, and if he was, Pliny in 111 CE would surely have known about it.

7 Robinson, *Penal Practice and Penal Policy in Ancient Rome*, pp. 102–3.

8 O. F. Robinson, *The Criminal Law of Ancient Rome* (Duckworth, 1995), p. 96.

9 Juvenal, *Satire* 13.11

10 The story is told in Eusebius's *Church History* 5.1. One must allow for possible exaggeration by a Church source.

11 See Harries, *Law and Crime in the Roman World*, p. 79.

12 Tacitus, *Histories* 5.5.

13 The phrase is from G. E. M. de Ste Croix.

Chapter 16

1 Gibson, 'Pliny and the Art of (In)offensive Self-Praise'.

Bibliography

Alexander, M. C., *Trials in the Late Roman Republic* (University of Toronto Press, 1990).

Bartsch, S., *Actors in the Audience* (Harvard University Press, 1994).

Bennett, J., *Trajan: Optimus Princeps* (Routledge, 2001).

Birley, A. R., *Onomasticon to the Younger Pliny* (K. G. Saur, 2000).

Borkowski, J. A., *Textbook on Roman Law* (Oxford University Press, 1994/2005).

Brunt, P., 'Charges of Provincial Maladministration under the Early Principate', *Historia* 10 (1961).

Carlon, J. M., *Pliny's Women* (Cambridge University Press, 2009).

Carolis, E. D. and G. Patricelli, *Vesuvius A.D. 79: The Destruction of Pompeii and Herculaneum* (Getty, 2003).

Connolly, J., 'Fear and Freedom: a New Interpretation of Pliny's *Panegyricus*', conference paper (2008), available online at https://sites.google.com/a/nyu.edu/jconnolly/home/recent-work/Connolly-Pliny.pdf?attredirects=0&d=1 (accessed 16 May 2013).

De la Ruffinière du Prey, P., *The Villas of Pliny* (University of Chicago Press, 1994).

De Ste Croix, G. E. M., 'Greek and Roman Accounting', academic paper (1956).

Dill, S., *Roman Society from Nero to Marcus Aurelius* (Macmillan, 1904).

Duncan-Jones, R., *The Economy of the Roman Empire* (Cambridge University Press, 1974/1982).

Figes, O., *The Whisperers* (Allen Lane, 2007).

Finley, M. I. (ed.), *Studies in Ancient Society* (Routledge, 1974).

Gibson, R. K., 'Pliny and the Art of (in)offensive Self-Praise', *Arethusa* 36 (2003).

Gibson, R. K. and R. Morello, *Reading the Letters of Pliny the Younger: an Introduction* (Cambridge University Press, 2012).

Gilman, B. and B. Moser, *Ashen Sky* (Getty, 2007).

Goodyear, F. R. D., 'Pliny the Younger', in *Cambridge History of Classical Literature*, vol. 2, part 4 (Cambridge University Press, 1982).

Gregory, T., review of Ariosto's *Orlando Furioso*, *London Review of Books* (9 September 2010).

Griffin, M., 'Domitian', in *Cambridge Ancient History*, vol. 2 (Cambridge University Press, 2000).

Harries, J., *Law and Crime in the Roman World* (Cambridge University Press, 2007).

Harte, R. H., 'The Praetorship of the Younger Pliny', *Journal of Roman Studies* 25 (1935).

Henderson, J., 'Portrait of the Artist as a Figure of Style', *Arethusa* 36 (2003).

Highet, G., *Juvenal the Satirist* (Oxford University Press, 1962).

Hoffer, S. E., *The Anxieties of Pliny the Younger* (Scholar's Press, 1999).

Jones, B. W., *The Emperor Domitian* (Routledge, 1992).

Jones, C. P., *The Roman World of Dio Chrysostom* (Harvard University Press, 1978).

Kelly, J. M., *Roman Litigation* (Clarendon Press, 1966).

—*Studies in the Civil Judicature of the Roman Republic* (Clarendon Press, 1976).

Lendering, J., 'Pliny the Younger', available online at http://www.livius.org (accessed 16 May 2013).

MacMullen, R., *Corruption and the Decline of Rome* (Yale University Press, 1988).

Marchesi, I., *The Art of Pliny's Letters* (Cambridge University Press, 2008).

Morello, R., 'Pliny and the Art of Saying Nothing', *Arethusa* 36 (2003).

Morello, R. and R. K. Gibson (eds), 'Re-imagining Pliny the Younger', special issue of *Arethusa* 36 (2003).

Pagán, V. E. (ed.), *A Companion to Tacitus* (Wiley-Blackwell, 2012).

Radice, B., *The Letters of the Younger Pliny* (Penguin, 1963).

Reynolds, L. D. (ed.), *Texts and Transmission* (Clarendon Press, 1983).

Riggsby, A. M., 'Pliny in Space (and Time)', *Arethusa* 36 (2003).

Robinson, O. F., *Penal Practice and Penal Policy in Ancient Rome* (Routledge, 2007).

—*The Criminal Law of Ancient Rome* (Duckworth, 1995).

Roche, P. (ed.), *Pliny's Praise* (Cambridge University Press, 2011).

Roebuck, D. and B. Fumichon, *Roman Arbitration* (Holo Books, 2004).

Rutledge, S., *Imperial Inquisitions* (Routledge, 2001).

Sherwin-White, A. N., *The Letters of Pliny: an Historical and Social Commentary* (Oxford University Press, 1966).

Syme, R., *The Roman Revolution* (Oxford University Press, 1939/1960).

—*Tacitus* (Clarendon Press, 1958).

—'Pliny's Early Career', in A. Birley (ed.), *Roman Papers*, vol. 7 (Oxford University Press, 1991).

Tanzer, H. H., *The Villas of Pliny the Younger* (Columbia University Press, 1924).

Tellegent, J. W., *The Roman Law of Succession in the Letters of Pliny the Younger* (Zutphen, 1982).

Wallace-Hadrill, A., *Houses and Society in Pompeii and Herculaneum* (Princeton University Press, 1994).

Whitton, C. L., 'Pliny Epistle 8.14: Senate, Slavery and the Agricola', *Journal of Roman Studies* 100 (2010).

—'"Let Us Tread Our Path Together": Tacitus and the Younger Pliny', in *A Companion to Tacitus* (Wiley-Blackwell, 2011).

Williams, W., *Pliny the Younger: Correspondence with Trajan from Bithynia* (Aris and Phillips, 1990).

Winsbury, R., *The Roman Book* (Duckworth, 2009).

Woodman, A. J. (ed.), *Latin Historiography and Poetry in the Early Empire* (Brill, 2010).

Index of Names

Aelianus, Casperius 121
Agricola 95
Albinus, Lucceius 83–6, 89
Antoninus, Arrius 173–4
Artemidorus 103–18
Asinius, Rufus 129
Atticinus, Montanius 89
Augurinus, Sentius 168, 174
Aurelian (emperor) 192

Bassus, Julius 85–7, 194, 201
Bruttianus, Lustricus 89

Calvina 143, 177
Capito, Titinius 165, 174, 181, 191
Caracalla (emperor) 78, 86
Carus, Mettius 93, 106, 179
Casta (wife of Classicus) 84
Certus, Publicius 69, 106–7, 112
Classica (daughter of Classicus) 84–5
Classicus, Caecilius 82–4
Constantine (emperor) 185
Crispus, Vibius 136

Decius (emperor) 204, 206, 213
Diocletian (emperor) 204, 213
Domitian (emperor)
    assassination of 68, 71, 106–7, 111
    'bad' emperor 3–4, 6–7, 12, 66, 81, 91, 218
    Dominus 192–3
    dossier on Pliny 92–3
    informers and 53–4, 72
    Jews, tax on 54
    law courts and 48–9, 52
    patron of Pliny 12, 27, 78, 80, 94–5,
        98–102, 219, 221
    philosophers and 104, 117
    purge by 12, 33, 78, 94, 99, 103–4, 111,
        115, 174
    Regulus and 62–5, 68
    Senate and 95
    wills and 53

Encolpius 140
Eumolpus, Claudius 198–9
Euphrates (philosopher) 97

Fabatus, Calpurnius 19, 127–30
Fannia 93, 104, 107
Firminus, Hostilius 81
Fuscus, Claudius 83

Gillo 177

Hadrian (emperor) 18, 123, 174, 181, 186,
    192
Helvidius 95, 104, 106–7
Hispanus, Fabius 83,
Hispulla, Calpurnia 129–31, 176–7
Honoratus, Vitellius 80–1

Ignatius (bishop) 206

Lentulus, Cornelius 136
Liberalis, Salvius 84
Licinianus, Norbanus 84

Marcianus, Flavius 80–1
Massa, Baebius 78–80, 92–3, 102, 182
Mercellus, Eprius 136
Musonius, Rufus 104
Mustius 148–9

Narcissus (freedman) 137
Nero (emperor)
    Christians and 208, 212
    Fabatus and 29
    informers and 71–2, 93, 130, 136, 170,
        179
    Regulus and 60–9
    sets up Treasury 112
    in Tacitus 218
Nerva (emperor)
    executes Domitian's assassins 107,
        121–3

informers and 72
letter to Pliny 79
Nicetes and 27
Regulus and 63, 66
stop-gap emperor 97, 102

Ovid (poet) 132

Paullus, Passennius 174
Persius 166
Philostratus 27, 192
Pliny (elder)
  adoption of Pliny 24
  books by 7, 151, 169
  career of 8, 25
  death of 29–30, 182
  inheritance from 51, 139, 154–5
Plutarch 165
Priscus, Marius 80–2, 86, 106, 177, 182
Priscus, Stilonius 83
Probus, Baebius 83

Regulus
  bites Piso's head 62
  career of 60–1
  character of 6–7, 55, 59–60
  death of 20
  in defence of 69–70
  Domitian and 62–3
  informers and 57–9, 70, 93
  Martial and 67, 168
  Nerva and 63
  nervous with Pliny 68, 174
  not prosecuted 90, 106
  as orator 65–6
  seeks legacies 59, 63–4
  trap for Pliny 64–5
  wealth of 136
Romanus, Vergilius 175

Sabinus, Flavius 197
Saturninus, Pompeius 170
Seneca (elder) 42, 160
Senecio, Herennius 78–9, 93, 95, 102, 104
Septimius Severus 78, 86
Silius Italicus 170, 179
Spurinna, Vestricius 169, 174

Suetonius
  as author 171, 179
  career of 181
  edits Pliny's letters 189–90
  on emperors 48, 53–4, 91, 94–5, 104, 165, 192, 205, 220
  friend of Pliny 9, 15, 19, 128, 175, 180
  patron, Pliny as 181, 190

Tacitus
  Christianity and 205, 214
  colleague to Pliny 80, 82, 106, 112, 143, 177
  friend of Pliny 1, 9, 171, 182
  on governance 74, 78, 89, 95
  as historian 4, 9, 29, 107, 164, 171, 183, 218–20
  hunting 183
  informers and 75, 130
  on law courts 45, 53, 58
  letters to, by Pliny 19, 182
  at races 159, 217
  Regulus and 60, 62, 64, 66, 69–70, 72
Tertullus, Cornutus 92
Trajan (emperor)
  Bithynia and 88, 185–6, 193–6
  Christians and 203–7, 211–13
  Dio's friend 197–9
  as *Dominus* 191–3
  friend of Pliny 25 and passim
  as 'good' emperor 4, 6, 219
  informers and 57–8, 72, 207, 209, 211
  law courts and 80, 82, 88, 107
  Pliny's letters to 11, 15, 189–91, 220
  Pliny's marriages and 127
  Panegyricus and 109–23, 162, 167, 230
  rebukes Pliny 187, 199
  rise to power 121–2
  security of wills 54–5, 59

Ulpian 78

Varenus, Rufus 20, 87–8, 194, 197, 201
Varro 148
Verres 73, 75
Vitellius (emperor) 53
Vitruvius 147–8

Index of Place Names

Amastris 188
Antioch 206
Apamea 195, 213
Ashmolean Museum 152

Basilica Julia 39, 41
Bellagio 151
Bithynia-Pontus
    Bassus and 85–7
    Calpurnia and 131–2
    Christians in 203–10, 224
    dates Pliny there 11, 215
    Dio and 192, 196–200
    letters from 185–7, 190
    Pliny's death in 189
    Pliny's salary 142
    problems of 73, 76, 193–6
    Varenus and 87–88
British Museum 135
Byzantium 185, 195

Città di Castello 154
Claudiopolis 195
Comum 15, 19, 21, 23–6, 51, 129–30,
    141–4, 223

Dacia 191

Heraclea 188
Herculaneum 7, 29–31
Hippo Regius 179

Juliopolis 195

Leptis 80
Lyons, France 210–11

Misenum 29–30, 33

Naples 7, 23, 25, 28–32
Nicaea 195, 200
Nicomedia 195, 213

Ostia 151–2

Persia 191
Pierpoint Library 21
Pompeii 7, 29–30, 183, 203
Prusa 192, 194–201

St Victor, Abbey of 21, 186

Torno 151
Tuscany 154

Vesuvius 1, 7, 18, 28–34

Index of Latin Terms

A bibliothecis 181
A studiis 181
Ab epistolis 174, 181, 191
Aerarium militare 100–1, 121
Aerarium Saturni 112
Album 39, 44, 96
Amanuensis 140
Amator exclusus 132
Amentia 205, 208
Anagnostes 140

Basilicani 39, 52

Calumnia/calumnator 67, 79, 211
Causidici 38
Centumviri 39
Ceres 148
Clepsydra 81
Codicilli 165
Comes 89
Consilium (emperor's) 88
Contagio 205, 210
Curator 198

Decemviri stlitibus
    iudicandis 48, 96
Delator 52–5, 57, 67, 69–71, 75, 85, 87,
    136, 199, 201, 203, 207
Dominus/domine 94, 191–2
Duci 208

Epistolae 16
Equites 8

Fenero 142
Fiscus 53
Flagitia 208, 210
Fraudator 67

Graeculi 188

Impietas 79
Inquisitio 79, 88
Iuridici 38
Ius trium liberorum 127–8, 181

Lector 140, 166
Lex Julia Repetundarum 77
Libellus/libelli 92, 165
Libertas 110–11, 115, 117–23
Librarius 140, 169

Maiestas 75
Mandata 186

Notarius 140

Orbitas 128
Otium 148–9, 160

Patroni 38
Praetor 11–12, 51, 69, 97–100, 102–5,
    220, 223

Quaestor 5, 47, 69, 79, 97–99, 102

Recitatio 163–5, 167–8
Recuperatores 77
Relegatio 74
Repetundae 74–5
Rescripta 188

Senatus consultum 195
Sevir 97
Superstitio 205

Togati 38, 52

Unus iudex 40, 44, 47, 49

Vicesima hereditatum 54, 120

Index of Subject Matter

absence letters 131
accountability
  of provincial governors 74–5
  of emperor 118, 211
accusations against Pliny 2, 4–9, 91, 95, 99,
    107, 110, 219–20 *see also* questions

Basilica Julia 39, 41
birth of P. 11
Board of Ten 48
books *see* literature

character of Pliny
  cautious 16, 88, 125, 170, 195, 200, 215
  generous 90, 143–5, 156, 223
  hard-working 90, 178
  honest 5, 227
  humour 164, 217
  nervous 93, 169, 171, 185, 187–8, 197,
    207, 212, 220
  prim 17, 60, 125, 177, 217
  survivor 12, 31, 183, 222
  truthful? 12, 16–7, 42, 90–1, 99, 102,
    105, 107, 115, 156, 217, 220, 225
  vain 47, 90, 217
children 1, 11, 34, 126–9, 181, 225
Christians
  as atheists 214
  crimes of 207–8, 211
  early history of 4, 203
  imperial policy on 211–15, 224–5
  in Bithynia 193, 199, 201, 203–15
  informers and 207, 209
  law and 212
  martyrs 204
  name of, as crime 208, 212
  Pliny's view of 205, 208, 224
  persecution of 204–6, 210, 212
class, social
  boundaries of 116, 165
  emperor and 94, 101, 116, 118, 121,
    138, 219

freedom and 111–2, 117, 123
  knights 8, 25, 44, 83, 97
  literature and 173–9, 189
  senatorial 2–6, 20, 26, 44, 137, 219
  wills and 54
composition, literary *see* literature
consul, Pliny as 1, 23–5, 69, 91, 97, 106,
    111–2, 190
corruption
  defining 77–8
  financial 28, 73, 177, 185, 193, 223
  government and 75–6, 82, 118, 222
  in courts 52
Court of One Hundred Men
  as judge and jury 43
  scope of 46
  why 100? 49

danger
  history writing as 16, 163–4
  in law courts 37, 52, 64–5, 73, 79–80
  to Pliny 4, 6, 8, 25, 92–5, 99–104, 118,
    219–22
  Vesuvius 30, 33
dates
  of publication of letters 20–1
  problem of Pliny's 10–12, 95, 97–102,
    105, 221
dossier on Pliny 92–4, 220–1

education of P. 26–8, 38, 171, 226
emperor
  choice of 6, 8, 24
  Christianity and 203–6, 225
  confers honours 97, 127–9
  decisions of, as law 50, 188, 190–1
  as friend 1, 8, 25, 37, 197
  on gifts 78, 86
  helps poor senators 137
  informers and 58, 62, 67, 71–2, 93,
    116, 200, 207, 211
  law and 47–8, 52, 74–5, 82, 88, 118–20

provinces and 85, 185–7, 195–6
role of 70, 116, 122, 218–9, 223
wills and 53–4, 120
worship of 213–4
extortion 49, 73–80, 84–8, 194, 196
eyesight, Pliny's 157

father, Pliny's 1, 23–6
freedom, concepts of 2–5, 45, 110–1,
　　118–23, 162, 220, 225
French Revolution 62, 69, 172

Gestapo 70

history
　　dangers of writing 164
　　letters as 16, 18, 69, 105, 182, 186,
　　　　220
　　of Pliny's letters 22, 24
hunting 155, 159, 168, 183, 227

income, Pliny's 135, 141–3, 153–7
informers
　　Christians and 199, 201–3, 207
　　in law courts 52–3, 120
　　in politics 57, 61, 68, 93
　　Nero and 130, 136
　　punishment of 57, 72, 119–20
　　slaves as 116
　　state security and 71, 86
　　Trajan and 211
　　types of 70–1, 75, 199
inheritance
　　court 4, 37–40, 46–9
　　informers and 54–5
　　law 38–9
　　penalties of 49
　　politics and 52–5
　　tax 120–1
　　wills and 59, 120
Isis 207

Jews 54, 205, 214
justice
　　emperor and 48, 75, 94, 106–7
　　informers and 70, 75
　　for provinces 71, 75, 81–2, 85, 89, 120,
　　　　193, 207
　　standards of 44, 52, 89–90, 222, 226

KGB 70

law courts
　　Basilica Julia 39, 41
　　bribery in 48–9, 52, 74
　　Court of One Hundred Men 37, 43, 64
　　informers in 54
　　legal fees 51–2, 141–2
　　Pliny's training for 28, 38
　　quiet in July 164
　　single judge 40, 44–5, 47
legacy hunting 52, 59–69, 128
legal qualifications of Pliny 27–8, 38
letters of Pliny
　　arrangement of 18
　　as collection 15–16
　　dates of 20
　　panto letter 160
　　as propaganda 186–7
　　recipients 19–20
　　relation to truth 16–18
　　survival of 21–2, 186
liberty *see* freedom
literature
　　book launch 163
　　composition of 19, 28, 114, 140,
　　　　155–71
　　as hobby 3–4, 9, 160, 175
　　organisation of 9–10, 159–69, 226
　　Pliny's circle 173, 178–80, 189
　　Pliny's talent 1, 10, 130, 226
　　right to rule and 10
　　role of slaves 140
　　as salon/club 159–60, 162, 164, 175
litigation, statistics of 50

marriages *see* wives
mediator, Pliny as 44
Mithras 207
name, Pliny's 1, 24–5

panegyric(us)
　　flattery in 110
　　language of 110, 117
　　length of 113–4
　　political message of 110, 118, 219
　　survival of 114
Panegyrici Latini 114
patron, Pliny as

of Comum etc. 141–4, 223
in law courts 38, 77–80, 82
of Martial 9, 67, 178
of Suetonius 180–1
patronage 8, 94, 100, 137–8, 178
Plinian eruption 29, 32
political system
   advancement in 8, 48, 55, 58, 96
   agenda of Pliny's letters 187, 218
   as bargain with emperor 3, 111, 123,
      172, 218–20
   freedom 'from' or 'to' 5, 28, 110
   new moral order 104, 117–19, 122,
      187, 218, 226
   Republican 5, 75, 220
   stages of 6, 23, 59, 99
political power 1, 3, 5, 49, 52, 75, 111–12,
   192
politics
   career in 37, 46, 48, 90, 96, 99, 215
   dangers of 33, 37, 64, 78, 93–4, 121
   denunciations 6, 55, 59, 137
   language of 65, 109–10, 117
   money and 137
praetor
   job of 51, 223
   when was Pliny? 11–12, 97–105, 220
praise speech 4, 65, 109–17, 122–3, 168,
   187
prosecutions
   informers and 71, 75
   by Pliny 71–3, 76–8, 82, 85–6, 194, 208
   by Regulus 61–3
   no state service 59, 70–1, 77
   numbers of 58, 76, 193
purge, Domitian's 12, 78–9, 93–105, 174,
   219

quality of Pliny's writing 10, 171
questions about Pliny *see also* accusations
   about his career 78–80, 91, 95, 98–9, 105
   his income 157
   his self-praise 217
   survey of 4–9

races (horse) 159, 176, 217
rich-list, Roman 8, 135–6
rule
   of law 116, 118

one-man 3, 5, 111, 117–18, 123, 165,
   220
right to 10, 89, 162, 218

Senate
   expulsion from 62, 81
   freedom and 28, 45, 110, 119
   (im)partiality of 76, 80, 82, 84, 89, 196,
      222
   power of 2, 8, 95, 195, 218, 226
   as supreme court 28, 39, 49, 73–7
show-trials 1, 58, 100
slaves
   as assets 8–9, 139–40
   bequests for 144
   Christian 206, 209, 215, 224
   as informers 116
   literate 140, 161–2, 166, 168–9
   numbers of 139
   proper place of 116
   in Pliny's villas 153–5
   rural 9, 139
   taken for granted 139, 223
Stazi 70
stoic opposition 95, 104–5

treason
   Dio and 197–200
   Domitian and 115–16
   emperor-worship and 213–4
   Ignatius and 206–7
   informers and 75, 120, 207
   public life and 105, 221
   wills and 53
Treasury of Saturn 73, 106, 112
treasury, military 12, 73, 100–2, 121,
   220–3
Tribune of the People 97–9, 102
tribune, military 96, 104

villas
   Comedy 150
   income from 141, 153, 156–7
   leisure in 148–9, 153, 155
   at Ostia 151–2
   rooms in 149–50, 152–3, 156
   slaves in 153
   tour of Pliny's 147ff
   Tragedy 150

in Tuscany 139, 154–6
  wife and 154
Vesuvius 1, 7, 23, 25, 28–31, 92, 182

water-clock 81
wealth, Pliny's 3, 8, 23, 26, 135–7
wife, first 34, 126
wife, second 125–32

wills
  Christians and 139
  gifts in 143, 182
  informers and 53–5, 59, 120
  Pliny as expert in 24, 38
  statistics of 50

youth, Pliny's 3–35

Lightning Source UK Ltd.
Milton Keynes UK
UKOW06f0438150515